SPECTRUM®

Reading

Grade 6

Spectrum®
An imprint of Carson-Dellosa Publishing LLC
P.O. Box 35665
Greensboro, NC 27425 USA

ISBN 978-0-7696-3866-9

11-063137811

Index of Skills

Reading Grade 6

Numerals indicate the exercise pages on which these skills appear.

Vocabulary Skills

Abbreviations 5, 11, 15, 27, 39, 59, 61, 69, 79, 81, 111

Affixes 3, 9, 21, 29, 35, 51, 59, 65, 71, 77, 89, 95, 109, 111, 117, 123, 125

Antonyms 13, 31, 45, 53, 61, 67, 83, 91, 105, 135, 141

Classification 5, 21, 41, 55, 125, 137, 151

Compound Words 7, 15, 19, 23, 25, 45, 51, 71, 75, 79, 83, 95, 99, 127, 133, 139, 145

Frequently Used Foreign Words 87, 103, 131, 149

Homographs/Multiple Meaning 19, 23, 37, 47, 49, 85, 107, 113, 115, 139, 143

Homophones 11, 19, 31, 43, 47, 57, 75, 87, 99, 107, 117, 123, 133

Idiomatic and Figurative Language 3, 11, 13, 25, 37, 63, 71, 85, 89, 93, 97, 123, 129, 137, 147

Latin and Greek Roots 81, 91, 93, 101, 115, 135, 141, 145, 151

Multisyllabic Words 13, 23, 35, 41, 57, 67, 83, 105, 137

Possessives 17, 27, 43, 49, 55, 63, 73, 93, 119, 131, 143

Sight Vocabulary *all activity pages*

Synonyms 17, 29, 33, 45, 53, 63, 67, 73, 91, 97, 113, 141

Word Meaning from Context *all activity pages*

Reading Skills

Author's Purpose 5, 15, 23, 33, 43, 51, 63, 73, 81, 87, 95, 105, 113, 121, 149

Cause and Effect 3, 5, 17, 19, 21, 23, 27, 29, 35, 39, 41, 43, 45, 49, 51, 53, 55, 59, 61, 63, 67, 69, 73, 75, 79, 81, 85, 87, 89, 91, 93, 97, 99, 107, 109, 111, 117, 119, 123, 125, 131, 137, 143, 145, 147, 149, 151

Character Analysis 11, 29, 37, 47, 61, 79, 83, 103, 115, 119, 141, 151

Comparing and Contrasting 3, 7, 9, 21, 23, 33, 45, 57, 65, 67, 69, 73, 83, 85, 91, 97, 101, 107, 109, 115, 125, 127, 129, 137, 139, 141, 145

Context Clues 3, 9, 17, 27, 35, 43, 45, 65, 69, 85, 99, 105, 125, 129, 149

Drawing Conclusions 3, 7, 17, 23, 25, 29, 31, 33, 41, 43, 47, 51, 61, 65, 75, 79, 87, 89, 93, 95, 97, 99, 101, 103, 107, 109, 113, 117, 121, 123, 127, 133, 135, 139, 143, 151

Fact and Opinion 7, 31, 45, 53, 71, 83, 99, 115

Facts and Details *all activity pages*

Fantasy and Reality 39, 57, 125, 143

Formulates Ideas and Opinions 103, 107, 131, 143, 149, 151

Identifying the Theme 85, 141,

Main Idea 5, 11, 27, 39, 47, 53, 61, 91, 101, 113, 131

Mood and Tone 19, 25, 71, 101

Persuasive Text 45, 73, 87

Predicting Outcomes 3, 11, 19, 25, 35, 41, 43, 49, 57, 71, 77, 79, 89, 101, 107, 117, 127, 147, 151

Prior Knowledge 15, 17, 45, 61, 107,

Purpose for Reading 9, 67, 87, 103, 111, 119, 123, 133, 139

Recognizes Story's Problem 13, 19, 25, 55, 63, 85, 127

Recognizes Features of Familiar Genres 7, 15, 27, 37, 47, 55, 57, 61, 69, 79, 91, 97, 117, 119, 141, 151

Sequence 5, 15, 19, 27, 39, 51, 59, 75, 77, 89, 93, 127, 137

Shows Comprehension by Identifying Answers in Text *all activity pages*

Summarizing 21, 37, 59, 65, 87, 99, 111, 121, 135

Understand and Identify Simple Literary Terms 13, 25, 31, 41, 43, 49, 71, 75, 83, 85, 93, 97, 109, 115, 117, 123, 127, 133, 143

Study Skills

Charts, Graphs, and Maps 5, 75, 101, 147

Dictionary Use 7, 9, 25, 39, 59, 69, 77, 83, 89, 109, 125, 145

Following Directions *all activity pages*

Life-Skills Materials 33, 103, 113, 121, 137

Parts of a Book 15, 87, 129

Reference Materials 41, 55, 65, 95, 127

Table of Contents

JBall

Have you ever been to a baseball game in another country or watched one on television?

1   Alex and Emily Godfrey had been in Japan with their parents for nearly a week. They were there to visit their mother's old college roommate, who had moved to Japan after college to teach English. She had planned to come home after a few years, but she had fallen in love with the country and with the man who would eventually be her husband.

2   "What's our plan for the afternoon?" asked Alex after lunch one day.

3   "Well," said Mr. Ito, "we have tickets for a 4:00 baseball game. How does that sound?"

4   "I had no idea baseball was popular in Japan," replied Alex.

5   "Dad takes us to professional games a few times a year at home," said Emily. "Alex and I keep a list of cities we've visited where we have had a chance to go to a game. I had no idea that Tokyo would ever be on our list!"

6   The Itos and the Godfreys prepared for the afternoon's events. Just a few hours later, they found themselves standing inside the stadium among a crowd of excited fans.

7   "What are the names of the teams that are playing today?" asked Alex, looking around curiously.

8   "The home team is the Yakult Swallows. They will be playing the Hiroshima Toyo Carp," said Mrs. Ito. "Baseball isn't my cup of tea, but this promises to be a good game."

9   The two families found their seats in the bleachers. Alex and Emily grinned as they listened to all the noisemakers around them. Some people were hitting together plastic bats, and others were yelling through megaphones that looked as though they had been hinged together.

10   "Are those cheerleaders?" asked Emily. She was referring to a group of men on the ball field who led the crowd in chants and cheers.

11   Mrs. Ito nodded, "I forget that Americans don't have cheerleaders for baseball games. It also probably seems unusual that they're all men. That's just one of the differences between American and Japanese baseball culture."

12   Once the game began, Emily and Alex became quickly engrossed. The game itself didn't seem much different at all from the American baseball games they had attended. They were surprised, though, to see people waving American flags from time to time.

13   Mr. Ito explained, "Japanese teams are each allowed to have three foreign players. When American players come up to bat, their fans show support by waving your country's flag."

14   In between innings, Mrs. Ito bought Alex and Emily a snack. Some vendors sold pretzels, popcorn, and hot dogs, but Alex and Emily decided to try one of the Japanese alternatives. With Mrs. Ito's help, they selected *yakisoba*, noodles flavored with ginger and soy sauce.

15   At the end of the game, the Godfreys and the Itos piled back into the car to head home. Alex and Emily were tired, but their minds were racing with all they had seen that day.

16   "Did you have a good day, kids?" asked Mrs. Godfrey, turning to Alex and Emily.

17   They nodded. "I wish we could go to JBall games at home, too," said Emily. "After today, I have a feeling that American baseball may never be quite as interesting again."

Vocabulary Skills

Write the words from the story that have the meanings below.

1. happening after some time

   ~~eee ven chuly~~ *(eventually)* ⟵ eventually
   _{Par. 1}

2. cone-shaped devices used for projecting sounds

   ✓ mics
   _{Par. 9}

3. directing attention

   ~~refering~~ referring
   _{Par. 10}

4. completely absorbed or occupied

   en grossed ⟵ messy
   _{Par. 12}

5. options; choices

   alternatives
   _{Par. 14}

An **idiom** is a group of words that has a special meaning. For example, the idiom *hit the hay* means *to go to bed*. Write the idiom from paragraph 8 on the line next to its meaning.

6. something of interest; something a person enjoys ___cup of tea___

A **prefix** is a group of letters added to the beginning of a word to change its meaning. The prefix **un-** means *not*. For example, *uninterested* means *not interested*. Add **un** to each word below. Then, write the meaning of the new word.

7. _un_ aware _not aware_ _____

8. _un_ fortunate _not fortunate_

9. _un_ healthy _not healthy_ _____

10. _un_ even _not even_

Reading Skills

1. Why were the Godfreys in Japan?

   to vist a collage room mate

2. What do you think Emily meant when she said, "American baseball may never be quite as interesting again"?

   because they played in japan & japanese baseball seems more exciting & interesting.

3. What is one way American and Japanese baseball are similar? What is one way they are different?

   same spor t - snacks
   difert lanvage- made cheer-leaders

4. Do you think that Alex and Emily will go to another JBall game if they have a chance? Why or why not?

   They will because they enjored it

Circle the word that best completes each sentence.

5. Alex and Emily decide to try food that they would not be _____ to find at an American game.

   allowed   (likely)   impressed

6. The Godfreys are _____ to learn how American and Japanese baseball are different.

   (curious)   refusing   apprehensive

7. Noisemakers are a popular _____ at Japanese baseball games.

   explanation   resource   (custom)

Yakyu

Who is Sadahara Oh, and why is he so famous in the world of baseball?

1   What could be more American than baseball? It was one of the earliest sports played in America, created during the mid-1800s. But the Japanese have been playing for nearly as long. In fact, baseball's popularity in Japan rivals its popularity here in the United States.

2   In the early 1870s, Horace Wilson, an American professor living in Tokyo, introduced baseball to his students. They loved it, calling the game *yakyu*, which means *field ball*. It quickly caught on with students all over the country. Japanese leaders also embraced baseball because they thought that it contained elements that were already part of Japanese culture. For instance, baseball's focus on the mental competition between pitcher and hitter was similar to the one-on-one competitions of martial arts.

3   By the early 1900s, amateur baseball leagues had been established in secondary schools and colleges throughout Japan. To this day, the enthusiasm for college baseball in Japan is equivalent to the excitement people have for college football or college basketball's March Madness in the United States.

4   To make baseball even more popular, American teams regularly toured Japan in the early 1900s and played exhibition games against the local amateurs. Top American baseball stars like Babe Ruth and Lou Gehrig came to Japan in the 1930s and played against the top Japanese college teams. The Americans won all 17 games they played, but baseball fever swept the whole country. A professional Japanese baseball league was formed in 1936. The Great Tokyo baseball club—known today as the Yomiuri Giants— was the first team, but it was soon joined by six others.

5   Like so many other things around the world, World War II interrupted Japanese baseball when almost all of the players became soldiers. After the war, the United States occupied Japan.

The military commanders who were in charge recognized that baseball was an important part of Japanese culture, so they encouraged the professional teams to reform and continue playing. By 1955, with the help of television, professional baseball in Japan became bigger than ever.

6   The Yomiuri Giants are not just the oldest pro team in Japan; they may also be the greatest. From 1965 through 1973, the Giants won nine consecutive national championships, partly because of the legendary player Sadahara Oh. The surname *Oh* means *king*, and he certainly was the king of baseball in Japan. Among his many incredible statistics, Oh holds the world record for career home runs—868! That is more than Hank Aaron, Babe Ruth, Mark McGuire, and Sammy Sosa.

7   Japanese professional players have also come to the United States and played in Major League Baseball, setting records here as well. Current players include the New York Yankees' Hideki Matsui and the Seattle Mariners' Ichiro Suzuki. In 2004, Suzuki broke a baseball record for hitting that had stood for more than 80 years! Kazuhiro Sasaki, who also played for the Mariners, was named the American League Rookie of the Year in 2000, and Hideo Nomo of the Los Angeles Dodgers was MLB's 1995 Rookie of the Year.

Vocabulary Skills

Write the words from the passage that have the meanings below.

1. the process of growing and caring for something

   _____
   Par. 1

2. to trim away the unwanted parts of a tree or bush

   _____
   Par. 2

3. copied; made again

   _____
   Par. 4

The prefix **mis-** means *badly* or *wrongly*. For example, *misunderstand* means *to understand wrongly*. Write a word to match each definition below. Then, write a sentence using each word.

4. to behave badly _____

   _____

5. to spell wrongly _____

   _____

6. to match badly _____

   _____

Reading Skills

Write **T** before the sentences that are true. Write **F** before the sentences that are false.

1. _____ The tradition of raising bonsais was begun in Europe.

2. _____ Japanese bonsais are usually grown in containers outdoors.

3. _____ The owner of a bonsai must spend some time caring for the plant.

4. _____ There are three basic styles of bonsai.

5. What do you think the phrase *time-honored tradition* means?

   _____

   _____

6. What are the three elements needed to create a successful bonsai?

   _____

7. How are the cascade and semi-cascade styles of bonsai similar?

   _____

8. What purpose would a reader have for reading this selection?

   _____ for pleasure or entertainment

   _____ for information

   _____ to form an opinion about bonsais

Study Skills

Read the dictionary entry below, and answer the questions that follow.

patient (pā′ shənt) *adj.* able to put up with things that are annoying without complaining
n. someone who is receiving medical treatment

1. What part of speech is *patient* when it is used to mean *able to put up with things that are annoying without complaining*?

   _____

2. What is the definition of *patient* when it is used as a noun?

   _____

   _____

3. Which syllable is stressed in *patient*?

   _____

A Schoolyard Garden

What are your favorite fruits and vegetables?

1   Have you ever eaten something that you grew in your own garden? Many people have not had the pleasure of this experience. Alice Waters, the owner of Chez Panisse Restaurant, set out to change all that for a special group of students at Martin Luther King Junior Middle School in Berkeley, California.

2   Waters worked with the school's principal, Neil Smith, to create a cooking and gardening program at the school. Waters believes in the importance of people knowing where their food comes from. She also believes that there is a strong relationship between food, health, and the environment. Her goal at the middle school was to show children the pleasure in gardening and in preparing the foods that they cultivated. She wanted to teach them that a healthy body and a healthy environment go hand in hand.

3   The project that Waters began took a lot of time and patience. She relied on the help of teachers, students, and community volunteers to turn an asphalt parking lot into a garden. At the same time, renovation was begun to turn an old, unused cafeteria into a kitchen where students could prepare foods and share meals with their teachers.

4   In the 1995–1996 school year, the first usable crops were planted. They included greens such as arugula and mustard, as well as lettuce, kale, bok choy, carrots, turnips, beets, and potatoes. The following year brought the addition of plants such as citrus trees, apples, plums, black currants, hazelnuts, figs, raspberries, runner beans, and hibiscus. Every year since then, new crops are added and old crops are evaluated to make sure that they are best suited for the environment and the needs of the school.

5   Students have found that they look forward to the time they spend in the garden each week. They have learned how to weed, prune, and harvest. They have learned about the life cycles of various plants. They also know how to enrich the soil through composting, a process in which leftover scraps of fruits and vegetables are used as fertilizer. Many have discovered that they like fruits and vegetables that they had never before been willing to try.

6   Alice Waters dreams that one day there will be a garden in every school in the United States. She hopes that school lunches can be prepared using the produce from the gardens and other locally-grown organic produce. If you are interested in learning more about Martin Luther King Junior Middle School's Edible Schoolyard, seeing pictures of the students and their garden, and finding out about how to start a garden at your school, visit www.edibleschoolyard.org.

Vocabulary Skills

Write the words from the passage that have the meanings below.

1. the renewal and repair of a building

   _____
   Par. 3

2. determined the worth or condition of

   _____
   Par. 4

3. viewed as appropriate for

   _____
   Par. 4

4. to make richer or improve the quality of

   _____
   Par. 5

5. grown without the use of chemicals and pesticides

   _____
   Par. 6

Read each word below. Then, write the letter of its abbreviation in the space beside it.

6. _____ California   **a.** Jr.

7. _____ United States   **b.** CA

8. _____ Junior   **c.** yr.

9. _____ year   **d.** U.S.

Write the idiom from paragraph 2 on the line next to its meaning.

10. goes together _____

A word that sounds the same as another word but has a different spelling and meaning is a **homophone**. Circle the homophone that correctly completes each sentence below.

11. Neil Smith is a middle school _____. (principle, principal)

12. I added a cup of chopped _____ to the vegetable soup. (beets, beats)

Reading Skills

1. What is *composting*?

   _____

   _____

2. Name four fruits or vegetables that are grown in the Edible Schoolyard.

   _____

   _____

3. Do you think that other schools will create gardens based on Alice Waters's ideas?

   _____

   _____

4. Check the sentence that best states the **main idea** of the selection, or tells what the passage is mostly about.

   _____ Alice Waters owns Chez Panisse Restaurant in California.

   _____ Students look forward to the time they spend gardening each week.

   _____ Alice Waters founded the Edible Schoolyard, a program in which students learn to grow and prepare their own foods.

5. Check the words that describe Alice Waters.

   _____ generous

   _____ unfriendly

   _____ talented

   _____ ambitious

   _____ stingy

A Growing Plan

Does your school have a garden?

1 Drew, Emilio, and Michi sat at a picnic table in the park on a beautiful, crisp fall afternoon. The air around them was filled with the sounds of children playing, dogs barking, and people laughing or calling to one another. But Drew, Emilio, and Michi ignored the sounds around them and focused on the task they had set out to complete.

2 They wanted to start a school garden at Jefferson Middle School. Initially, it had been Drew's idea. He had first seen a school garden when he went to visit his cousin P.J. in Washington. He was amazed at the variety of fruits and vegetables the students at P.J.'s school grew. "It's a lot of work," P.J. had warned. "But it's also my favorite part of the week. I love putting on my boots, getting outside, and seeing all the new things that have happened since I was last out there."

3 When Drew returned from his trip to Washington, he told Emilio and Michi all about what he had seen. Now the three of them were determined to come up with a plan to bring a school garden to Jefferson.

4 Drew opened his notebook and prepared to record any ideas they had for convincing Ms. Milano, the school principal, that the garden was a good idea.

5 "We're going to need an adult to supervise the whole operation," said Drew thoughtfully. "I know that Mr. Hasselbach gardens at home. Just last week he brought in a whole basket of tomatoes and zucchini from his garden. He might be willing to help." Drew jotted down Mr. Hasselbach's name in his notebook.

6 "We might need donations to get this project up and running," added Michi. "We could tell Ms. Milano that we would be willing to organize a bake sale or yard sale to raise funds."

7 "That's a great idea," said Emilio. "I think we need to be able to present her with a realistic plan. My aunt is the co-owner of a nursery. She could help us design the garden, select plants, and create a budget. That way, Ms. Milano wouldn't feel as though she were committing to something unknown."

8 Drew nodded and made some more notes. "P.J. mentioned that the students at his school cook meals with the produce from their garden. If we do something like that too, think of all the lessons we'd learn. We'd have to measure and weigh things and follow a recipe. Combine that with the science lessons we'd get from working in the garden, and there's no way Ms. Milano could turn us down!"

9 Michi and Emilio grinned. "If everything goes as planned, we'll be digging in the dirt in no time at all!"

Vocabulary Skills

Write the words from the story that have the meanings below.

1. at first; originally

_____
Par. 2

2. decided; fixed on an idea

_____
Par. 3

3. money that is contributed to a good cause

_____
Par. 6

4. money raised for a specific purpose

_____
Par. 6

5. pledging or devoting oneself to an activity

_____
Par. 7

An **antonym** is a word that means the opposite of another word. Find an antonym in the story for each of the words below.

6. departed _____
Par. 3

7. impossible _____
Par. 7

8. destroy _____
Par. 7

9. separate _____
Par. 8

Write the idiom from paragraph 6 on the line next to its meaning.

10. to start something _____

Words that have two middle consonants are divided into syllables between the consonants. For example, *pic/ture*. Divide the words below into syllables using a slash *(/)*.

11. g a r d e n

12. b a s k e t

13. p i c n i c

Reading Skills

The **point of view** tells the reader whose view of the story he or she is reading. In **first-person point of view**, the reader knows the thoughts and feelings of the person telling the story. In **third-person point of view**, the reader only knows what an outsider knows about a character. Mark each phrase below **F** for first-person and **T** for third-person.

1. _____ My cousin P.J. lives in Washington.

2. _____ Emilio's aunt is the co-owner of a nursery.

3. _____ Mr. Hasselbach has a vegetable garden.

4. _____ I hope Ms. Milano likes our idea.

5. What problem do Drew, Emilio, and Michi have at the beginning of the story?

_____

_____

6. Where did Drew get the idea to start a school garden at his middle school?

_____

_____

7. How do Drew, Emilio, and Michi know that Mr. Hasselbach has a garden at home?

_____

_____

8. Name two ideas that the students have that they think will make Ms. Milano more likely to approve their plan.

_____

_____

_____

_____

What's Cooking?

What are some other meals you could make using the fresh vegetables from your garden or from a farmer's market?

Before you begin:

- Never use the stove or a knife without an adult's supervision.

- Always remember to keep the handle of the skillet turned in so you cannot accidentally bump into it.

Garden Lasagna

1 16-ounce package lasagna noodles

2 teaspoons olive oil

$1\frac{1}{2}$ cups diced red bell pepper

1 cup diced green bell pepper

1 small yellow onion, diced

2 cups diced tomatoes

1 large zucchini, thinly sliced

1 6-ounce can tomato sauce

$\frac{1}{2}$ cup grated Parmesan cheese

1 15-ounce container part-skim ricotta cheese

1 8-ounce package part-skim shredded mozzarella cheese

2 eggs

$\frac{1}{4}$ teaspoon black pepper

$\frac{1}{4}$ teaspoon dried oregano

1. Here are some other things you will need: a measuring cup, a teaspoon, a cutting knife, a colander, a wooden spoon, wax paper, a large pot, a bowl, aluminum foil, a saucepan, a spatula, and a 9-inch by 13-inch baking dish.

2. Bring a large pot of lightly salted water to a boil. Cook the noodles in boiling water for 8 to 10 minutes, stirring occasionally. Have an adult pour the noodles into a colander in the sink. Rinse the noodles with cold water and place them in a single layer on wax paper to cool.

3. Cook the diced bell peppers and onion in olive oil in a large saucepan until the onions are translucent. Stir in the tomatoes, zucchini, and tomato sauce. Simmer for 10 minutes.

4. Preheat the oven to 375°F. In a medium bowl, combine $\frac{1}{4}$ cup of the Parmesan cheese with the ricotta cheese, mozzarella cheese, eggs, black pepper, and oregano. Remember to wash your hands after handling the eggs.

5. Reserve $\frac{1}{2}$ cup of the mixture. Then, place a small amount of the vegetable mixture in the bottom of the baking dish. Place three lasagna noodles lengthwise in the dish. Layer some of the cheese mixture and the vegetable sauce on top of the noodles. Continue to layer the remaining ingredients, ending with noodles.

6. Spread the reserved cheese mixture on top of the noodles. Sprinkle with the remaining half of the Parmesan cheese.

7. Cover the dish with foil, and bake for 20 minutes. Remove the foil, and bake for 10 more minutes so the cheese can brown.

8. Allow the lasagna to cool for about 10 minutes before serving. Then, invite your friends and family to the table to sample this tasty dish. It serves 8, so there is a good chance that you won't finish it all. Just freeze the leftovers, and enjoy them on another day.

Vocabulary Skills

Write the words from the recipe that have the meanings below.

1. once in a while

   _____
   Step. 2

2. letting some light through; somewhat clear

   _____
   Step 3

3. chopped into small pieces

   _____
   Step 3

4. to set aside for later use

   _____
   Step 5

5. parallel to the longest side

   _____
   Step 5

Read each word below. Then, write the letter of its abbreviation on the line beside the word.

6. _____ teaspoon   **a.** oz.

7. _____ ounce   **b.** tsp.

8. _____ inch   **c.** F

9. _____ Fahrenheit   **d.** in.

Underline the compound word in each sentence. Then, write the two words that make up each compound.

10. Simmer the vegetables and tomato sauce in a large saucepan.

    _____   _____

11. Freeze leftovers to enjoy on another day.

    _____   _____

Reading Skills

1. Check the line beside the word or words that best describe what type of nonfiction passage this is.

   _____ how-to

   _____ biography

   _____ persuasive text

2. Number the tasks below to show the order in which they should be done.

   _____ Combine the cheeses, eggs, and spices.

   _____ Ask an adult to drain the lasagna noodles.

   _____ Boil a pot of water.

   _____ Simmer the vegetable mixture.

   _____ Allow the lasagna to cool.

3. Why do you think you should wash your hands after handling the eggs?

   _____

4. For how long should you boil the lasagna noodles?

   _____

5. What is the total amount of time the lasagna will bake?

   _____

6. What five vegetables are used in this recipe?

   _____

7. Check the phrase that best describes the author's purpose.

   _____ to tell a story about a family who makes a lasagna

   _____ to explain how to make lasagna

   _____ to persuade the reader to make lasagna for dinner

Garden Gourmet

Have you ever helped to prepare a meal for a large group of people?

1   Emilio and Michi spread the colorful tablecloth on the table. They made room for Drew, who was carrying a covered casserole dish with potholders. Small beads of water had condensed on the inside of the lid. "Watch out," Drew warned. "This is pretty hot."

2   A moment later, Kent and Alyssa added another steaming dish to the table. "That smells so good!" exclaimed Michi. "Are most of the parents here yet? I'm famished."

3   Kent peeked through the doors that led into the hallway. "I think Ms. Milano and Mr. Hasselbach just finished giving them the garden tour. They should be heading into the cafeteria next."

4   The students of Jefferson Middle School had spent all afternoon preparing for the evening meal. They did their best to transform the lunchroom into an elegant and beautiful dining area for their families. The gray metal tables were hidden beneath brightly-colored cotton tablecloths. Each table held a small glass vase with fresh flowers from the school's garden.

5   Only about half of the overhead lights were on. The rest of the lighting was provided by the small white lights that Michi and Alyssa had carefully wrapped around the columns that were scattered throughout the cafeteria. They thought that candles would do an excellent job of creating an elegant mood, but Ms. Milano would not be swayed from her conviction that candles were too risky to use in a school.

6   As the families found their seats, Ms. Milano motioned to Drew, Emilio, and Michi to join her at the front of the room. "Could I have everyone's attention?" asked Ms. Milano. "I know you can smell all the wonderful foods our students prepared, so I won't keep you from your dinners for long. I just wanted to take a moment to congratulate Drew, Emilio, and Michi for their wonderful idea."

7   Mrs. Milano continued, "A year ago, they first came to me with the plan for starting a garden at Jefferson. I was a bit skeptical at first, but they had thought through everything. Anytime I had a question about how we would make this work, they had an answer prepared. As you can see, they were absolutely correct. About three-quarters of the food you'll be enjoying tonight came from the school garden. The students prepared the entire meal themselves, with some guidance from Mr. Hasselbach."

8   Ms. Milano handed Drew, Michi, and Emilio each a tissue-wrapped package. They unwrapped their packages as Ms. Milano addressed the room. "As a thank-you to these students for their creative idea, hard work, and perseverance, they have each received a stepping stone for the garden. Their names and the date are engraved on the stones."

9   She turned to them. "Students for years to come will be enjoying the garden that you helped create," she said. "We thought it would be appropriate for them to have a reminder of our garden's ambitious founders."

10   Drew, Emilio, and Michi held up their stepping stones and grinned as the crowd clapped. "And now," said Ms. Milano, "please help yourselves to some of the mouthwatering food our young chefs have prepared. Dinner is served!"

Vocabulary Skills

Write the words from the story that have the meanings below.

1. changed from a gas into a liquid form

   _____
   Par. 1

2. very hungry

   _____
   Par. 2

3. to change in a dramatic way

   _____
   Par. 4

4. a strongly held belief

   _____
   Par. 5

5. questioning; not convinced

   _____
   Par. 7

6. continuing to do something even when it gets difficult

   _____
   Par. 8

A **synonym** is a word that has the same meaning as another word. Read each word below. Then, write the letter of its synonym on the line beside the word.

7. _____ warned   **a.** imaginative

8. _____ creative   **b.** under

9. _____ absolutely   **c.** cautioned

10. _____ beneath   **d.** totally

Fill in the blanks below with the possessive form of the word in parentheses.

11. _____ casserole was very hot. (Drew)

12. The stepping stones symbolized the _____ appreciation. (school)

13. _____ speech was brief. (Ms. Milano)

Reading Skills

Circle the word that best completes each sentence below.

1. The students put a great deal of _____ into the preparation of the meal.

   effort   guidance   transformation

2. Ms. Milano _____ Drew, Emilio, and Michi's contributions.

   regrets   appreciates   plans

3. The stepping stones are _____ with their names and the date.

   requested   remembered   engraved

4. Name two things the students did to transform the lunchroom.

   _____

   _____

5. Why did Ms. Milano give Drew, Michi, and Emilio stepping stones?

   _____

   _____

6. Why do you think Ms. Milano was skeptical when the students first presented her with the idea of starting a school garden?

   _____

   _____

7. About how much of the food the students served did they grow themselves?

   _____

   _____

A Shriek in the Night

Have you ever been frightened by a sound in the night?

1   Savannah read under her covers with a flashlight until her eyes were closing. She switched off the flashlight and let her book drop to the rug beside her bed. She turned over and snuggled deeper into the soft flannel sheets.

2   It felt as though Savannah had been sleeping for only a few minutes when she awoke with a start to a terrible, bloodcurdling scream. She lay stiffly and silently in her bed waiting to see what would happen. Her clenched muscles had just begun to relax when she heard another scream coming from outside her bedroom window. This scream was followed by a series of wails and shrieks.

3   Savannah slipped from her bed and ran as quickly as she could to her parents' bedroom. "Mom," she whispered urgently. "Did you hear that screaming?"

4   Savannah's mom was already awake, sitting up and hunting for her slippers. Savannah's dad continued to snore. Neither Savannah nor her mother was surprised. Savannah's dad was notorious for being able to sleep through anything. When he lived alone before he got married, he had to set three alarm clocks every night. He positioned them in various places around his bedroom to make sure that he would get up in time for work.

5   Savannah's mom finally found her slippers and motioned Savannah toward the bedroom door. She shut the door behind them. "What do you think it is, Mom?" asked Savannah.

6   Before Mom could answer, she and Savannah heard the terrible shrieks again. They waited until it was over to speak. "I'm pretty sure it's an animal," said Mom. "Let's see if we can spot anything through the kitchen window."

7   Savannah and her mom scanned the dark backyard but couldn't see anything. They were getting ready to head back to bed when the noises began again. This time they both looked up into the large old oak trees that towered over the backyard. They could see two small eyes gleaming in the moonlight from one of the highest branches.

8   "I think it's an owl," said Mom, craning her neck to get a better look. "All I can see are its eyes, though."

9   "I feel so much better," said Savannah with relief in her voice. "Maybe we can look online in the morning and see if we can figure out what kind of owl it is," she suggested. "My teacher showed us a great Web site for wild animal identification."

10   Savannah and her mom both returned to bed. They heard the owl's cries one more time before they drifted back to sleep, but it didn't sound nearly as frightening anymore.

11   In the morning, Savannah and her mom were able to identify the owl from the night before as a barn owl. They used the Web site that Ms. Petrovic had recommended to listen to sound bytes of different types of animals.

12   As they were listening, Savannah's dad came downstairs for breakfast. "What's all that racket?" he asked cheerfully, pouring himself a glass of orange juice.

13   "Doesn't that sound at all familiar, Dad?" asked Savannah, replaying the barn owl's call.

14   "Nope," said Dad. "Should it?"

15   Savannah and her mom just laughed.

Vocabulary Skills

Write the words from the story that have the meanings below.

1. causing fear

   _____
   Par. 2

2. held tightly together

   _____
   Par. 2

3. needing immediate attention

   _____
   Par. 3

4. well known for something unpleasant or unfavorable

   _____
   Par. 4

5. stretching the neck to see better

   _____
   Par. 8

Circle the homophone that correctly completes each sentence below.

6. Lucy had three mosquito _____ on her arm. (bytes, bites)

7. The owl's _____ woke Savannah and her mom. (wails, whales)

8. Check the sentence in which *racket* has the same meaning as it does in paragraph 12.

   _____ Hasaan borrowed my tennis racket on Monday.

   _____ There was a great deal of racket when Mattie dropped the box of toys down the stairs.

Find the compound words from the selection that contain the words below.

9. light _____
   Par. 1

10. moon _____
    Par. 7

11. stairs _____
    Par. 12

Reading Skills

1. Number the events below to show the order in which they happened.

   _____ Savannah switched off her flashlight.

   _____ Savannah and her mom saw the owl's eyes gleaming in the moonlight.

   _____ Savannah's dad poured himself a glass of orange juice.

   _____ Savannah ran into her parents' bedroom.

   _____ Savannah's mom looked for her slippers.

2. Find one sentence that shows Savannah was frightened by the screaming she heard.

   _____

   _____

3. If Savannah hears a barn owl again someday, do you think she will be frightened? Why or why not?

   _____

   _____

4. What problem did Savannah have in the story?

   _____

   _____

5. Why weren't Savannah and her mom surprised when the owl's cries didn't wake up Savannah's dad?

   _____

   _____

6. How were Savannah and her mom able to identify the owl's call?

   _____

   _____

Night Flyers

What other creatures are associated with the night?

1   Have you ever heard a hooting or screeching sound in the night and wondered if you were hearing an owl? It's more likely that you have heard an owl in the wild rather than seen one. Owls are nocturnal, which means that they are active mostly at night. Owls feed on live prey, and the darkness makes it harder for them to be seen by the small animals they hunt.

2   There are more than 175 species of owls, but they are generally divided into two categories—common owls and barn owls. Barn owls have a light-colored, heart-shaped face. Common owls are a diverse group with many different patterns and colorings, but all have a round face. The largest owls are as big as eagles. The smallest is the elf owl, which lives in Mexico and the southwestern United States. It measures only five inches and makes its home in the holes woodpeckers create in large cacti.

3   One attribute that is common to all owls is their sharp sense of hearing. Because they hunt at night, hearing is especially important to their survival. Owls have the ability to hear a rodent's movements from hundreds of feet away. In many species, the ear openings are positioned asymmetrically, or unevenly, on the owl's head. This is important to the owl's keen sense of hearing because it allows the owl to more accurately locate the source of the sounds.

4   Owls are farsighted, meaning they cannot see well at close distances. However, they can see well in dim light, which enhances their hunting skills. Unlike most animals, an owl's eyes do not move. Instead the owl must turn its entire head to see anything that is not directly in front of it. For this reason, the owl has an extremely flexible neck. It is able to turn its head about 270 degrees. That is three quarters of a circle!

5   Another common attribute to all owls is their nearly silent flight. This keeps the owl's prey from hearing it approach, but it also permits the owl to use its hearing to locate the exact position of the animal. Owls' wings are a very soft, downy type of feather that muffles the sound in flight. A fringe of feathers along the edges of the wings is also thought to quiet the flapping sound of the owls' wings.

6   Owls are found in the myths, folklore, and legends of many cultures. In France, archaeologists discovered cave paintings between 15,000 and 20,000 years old that contain images of owls. Mummified owls have also been found in Egyptian tombs, which indicates they were respected in ancient Egyptian culture.

7   Owls symbolize wisdom in some cultures. In others, they are feared and thought to bring bad luck. It is likely that the negative associations with owls came about because they are nocturnal creatures. Things associated with night and darkness have often been feared throughout history.

8   The next time you are out at night, listen quietly for the sounds of an owl. You may be lucky enough to catch a glimpse of an owl's gleaming eyes or watch an owl soar across a field in nearly silent flight.

Vocabulary Skills

Write the words from the passage that have the meanings below.

1. different; unlike others

   _____
   Par. 2

2. a quality or characteristic

   _____
   Par. 3

3. sharp; sensitive

   _____
   Par. 3

4. makes better or stronger

   _____
   Par. 4

5. dulls the sound

   _____
   Par. 5

6. connections made between things

   _____
   Par. 7

In each row, circle the word that does not belong.

7. precise   ability   exact   accurate

8. approach   nocturnal   darkness   night

9. diverse   different   symbolize   varying

The suffix **-ly** means *in a certain way*. For example, *gently* means *in a gentle way*. Write a word to match each definition below. Then, write a sentence using each word.

10. in a smooth way _____

    _____

11. in a certain way _____

    _____

12. in a sudden way _____

    _____

Reading Skills

1. How are barn owls different from common owls?

   _____

   _____

2. Why is the owl's sense of hearing important to its survival?

   _____

   _____

3. How do archaeologists know that ancient Egyptians respected owls?

   _____

   _____

4. What is unusual about the owl's neck and eyes?

   _____

   _____

5. In what part of the world does the smallest owl live?

   _____

6. What is one reason that owls have been feared in some cultures?

   _____

   _____

7. A **summary** is a short sentence that tells the most important facts about a topic. Check the sentence below that is the best summary for paragraph 3.

   _____ Owls hunt at night.

   _____ Owls have a sharp sense of hearing, which helps them to be strong hunters.

   _____ Some owls' ear openings are positioned asymmetrically.

A Beacon of Light

Have you ever had the opportunity to visit a lighthouse?

1   Lighthouses can symbolize many different things. For tourists, they can be an interesting place to visit, explore, and photograph. For historians, they are a window to the past and a reminder of a different way of life. For sailors and ship captains, they are a sign of safety.

2   Lighthouses are structures located along the shorelines of large bodies of water. They project a strong beam of light that alerts sailors of their location. They can protect a boat from running aground at night or other times when visibility is poor because of fog or a storm. Lighthouses alert sailors that land is near and warn them of potential dangers, such as reefs or rocky harbors.

3   Originally, lighthouses were constructed with living quarters for the lighthouse keeper. It was the job of the keeper to maintain the lighthouse and make sure that it was always working properly. Although it could be lonely at times, it was an important job. Today, almost all lighthouses are automated, which means that there is no longer a need for lighthouse keepers.

4   No one is certain when lighthouses first came into existence. We do know that the concept of lighthouses is more than 3,000 years old. An epic Greek poem titled *The Iliad* was written by a man named Homer around 1200 B.C. In the poem, Homer refers to a lighthouse, giving modern scholars an idea of how long lighthouses have been a part of human life.

5   Early versions of lighthouses were quite different from today's lighthouses. They were usually made of iron baskets that were suspended from long poles. The baskets contained burning coal or wood. In the 1700s, these baskets were replaced with oil or gas lanterns. When electricity was invented, the lanterns were replaced with electric beacons.

6   In 1822, a French physicist named Augustin Fresnel invented a lens that would prove to be very important in lighthouse technology. The Fresnel lens uses glass prisms to concentrate light and send it through a very powerful magnifying lens. With the invention of the Fresnel lens, it became possible to project a beam of light as far as 28 miles from shore!

7   Lighthouse beams can be used in a variety of ways to help sailors identify the lighthouse and their own location. Different patterns and lengths of flashes are unique to a specific lighthouse. Sailors can observe a sequence and then look it up in a reference book that will tell them which lighthouse they have spotted.

8   During the day, sailors can identify lighthouses simply by their appearance. Some are short and fat, while others are tall and thin. They can be constructed of many different materials, such as wood, stone, brick, steel, and aluminum. The patterns also differ greatly. Some lighthouses are painted with stripes or a series of diamond shapes that distinguish them. Others are distinguished by their shape—round, square, rectangular, or conical (shaped like a cone).

9   Many lighthouses along America's coastlines are no longer functioning. Historical societies, concerned community members, and even the National Park Service have preserved them. They are sometimes converted into museums, inns, educational centers, or even private homes. If you ever have a chance to visit one, getting a glimpse of history is worth the trip.

Vocabulary Skills

Write the words from the passage that have the meanings below.

1. to stand for or represent

   _____
   Par. 1

2. the quality or condition of being able to be seen

   _____
   Par. 2

3. attached in midair; hanging

   _____
   Par. 5

4. to bring together in order to make more powerful

   _____
   Par. 6

Check the meaning of the underlined word in each sentence.

5. Uncle Jasper gave two <u>quarters</u> to each of his nephews.

   _____ currency worth 25 cents

   _____ an area in which one sleeps or lives

6. The <u>beam</u> of the flashlight illuminated the hallway.

   _____ a ray of light

   _____ a big, happy smile

Compound words are divided into syllables between the two words that make the compound. For example, *eye/sight*. Divide the words below into syllables using a slash (/).

7. l i g h t h o u s e

8. s h o r e l i n e

9. c o a s t l i n e

Reading Skills

1. How do we know that lighthouses have existed for at least 3,000 years?

   _____

   _____

2. How far can the Fresnel lens project light?

   _____

3. Why aren't lighthouse keepers necessary for today's lighthouses?

   _____

4. What are two ways in which lighthouses may be different from one another?

   _____

   _____

5. Why do you think that historians think it is important to preserve lighthouses?

   _____

   _____

6. What did early versions of lighthouses look like?

   _____

7. Check the phrase that best describes the author's purpose.

   _____ to share the history of lighthouses

   _____ to persuade the reader to visit a lighthouse

   _____ to explain how lighthouses were built

Lighthouse Life

Where will Paloma's imagination take her?

1   Paloma sat at a computer in the school library. She stared at the blank screen and the blinking cursor. She rummaged around in her backpack for a rubber band, and then she pulled her hair into a thick ponytail. Paloma looked at the computer screen. It was still blank. Paloma sighed and flipped through her notebook to reread Mr. Molina's assignment. It was due in just two days, and Paloma knew that she couldn't procrastinate any longer.

2   *Write a creative short story using an experience that you have had recently,* Paloma read. *Your story should include two examples of figurative language. The finished story should be three to four pages long. Your first draft is due on Friday. Be prepared to share your story with the class and make notes for a revision, which you will have an additional week to complete.*

3   Paloma and her family had taken a trip to North Carolina's Outer Banks just before school began. They had visited four different lighthouses, and Paloma had wondered what it would be like to live in a lighthouse. She knew that before lighthouses were automated, they were run and maintained by a lighthouse keeper who lived on the premises. Paloma thought that would have been an interesting job to have, but she wanted to actually live in a lighthouse. Without thinking about it any longer, Paloma began to write the story.

4   I sat with Sadie curled on my lap and looked out the window at the crashing waves. The heavy rain beat against my lighthouse like a thousand footsteps racing up and down the walls. I held Sadie closer, and she let out a small meow of displeasure. I knew that the coming storm could not be too dangerous if Sadie was still acting normally. I have read that animals can sense changes in weather and will seek shelter from a tornado or hurricane. I was relying on Sadie's calmness to get me through my first hurricane on the island.

5   I knew that my lighthouse was sturdily built. It had survived more than one hundred years' worth of hurricanes and tropical storms. There was no reason to believe that the bricks and wood could not survive another. I looked up at the staircase that spiraled above me and shuddered as I felt the tower sway slightly in a gust of wind.

6   Paloma stopped and reread what she had just written. She smiled to herself, saved her story, and then settled into her chair to continue writing. She wasn't sure what was going to happen next, but she knew that if she just kept going, the story would continue to tell itself. Paloma couldn't wait to find out where it would take her.

Vocabulary Skills

Write the words from the story that have the meaning below.

1. to put something off for a later time

   _____
   Par. 1

2. a new and improved version of something

   _____
   Par. 2

3. shook or trembled with fear

   _____
   Par. 5

Underline the compound word in each sentence. Then, write the two words that make up each compound.

4. Paloma looked for a rubber band in her backpack.

   _____   _____

5. Paloma wore her hair in a ponytail.

   _____   _____

6. The notebook contained Mr. Molina's assignment.

   _____   _____

7. The heavy rain sounded like footsteps.

   _____   _____

A **simile** compares two things using the words *like* or *as*. Find the simile in paragraph 4 and write it on the line below.

8. _____

Reading Skills

1. What kind of animal is Sadie? How can you tell?

   _____

2. What problem does Paloma have at the beginning of the story?

   _____

   _____

3. Find an example of a sentence or phrase Paloma uses to create tension in her story.

   _____

4. The next time she has to write a story for school, do you think Paloma will put it off again? Why or why not?

   _____

   _____

5. Where does Paloma get her story idea?

   _____

Mark each sentence below **F** if it is in first-person point of view and **T** if it is in third-person point of view.

6. _____ I was relying on Sadie's calmness to get me through the hurricane.

7. _____ Paloma reread Mr. Molina's assignment.

8. _____ I looked up at the staircase and shuddered.

Study Skills

Use a dictionary to help you divide these words into syllables.

1. p r o c r a s t i n a t e

2. f i g u r a t i v e

3. d a n g e r o u s

4. h u r r i c a n e

5. t o r n a d o

Lighthouse on the Move

How would you move a building that is 193 feet tall?

1 There are certain things that people just don't expect to see move. We expect structures like houses, schools, and office buildings to be stationary objects. That is why many people were surprised to learn that the tallest lighthouse in the United States, the Cape Hatteras Lighthouse in Buxton, North Carolina, was going to be moved in June of 1999.

2 Why would anyone want to move a lighthouse? The 193-foot-tall lighthouse was built between 1868 and 1870. It weathered countless storms, as well as many hurricanes. It guided sailors away from the Diamond Shoals, a dangerous, shallow area about 14 miles off the coast of Cape Hatteras.

3 The coastline around the Outer Banks is known as the Graveyard of the Atlantic. It is estimated that more than 230 ships sank there between 1866 and 1945. The Cape Hatteras Lighthouse faithfully did its duty in protecting sailors from harm. This is exactly why it was determined that the lighthouse would have to be preserved. Experts were worried that continued erosion by the pounding waves of the ocean would destroy the lighthouse. They wanted to move it before it collapsed and was swept out to sea.

4 Moving the 4,800-ton lighthouse was no small project. Many people protested the move. They believed that the lighthouse was not strong enough to withstand it. They felt that it should be allowed to remain in the place it had always been. Others thought that moving the lighthouse was not important enough to justify spending the 9.8 million dollars the move would cost. After much debate, it was decided that the project could proceed as planned.

5 The new location for the lighthouse was chosen. It would move a total of about 2,900 feet. In the new location, the Cape Hatteras Lighthouse would stand 1,600 feet from the ocean that threatened to destroy it. The planners

estimated that it would take between four and six weeks to move the lighthouse. In reality, it took only about three weeks to complete the job.

6 The lighthouse was moved using the power of seven hydraulic jacks. It sat on pads of rollers that rested on a set of rails, similar to train tracks. After the lighthouse had moved from one set of tracks to the next, the first set of tracks was moved in front of the lighthouse so that it could pass over them again. The process was extremely slow. Many people came to watch what they figured would be a dramatic moment in North Carolina history. But the lighthouse only moved an average of about two inches per minute, which wasn't all that exciting to watch.

7 The Cape Hatteras Lighthouse survived the move and has settled into its new home. Some people still look at the vacant spot on the beach where it stood for so many years and feel a sense of sadness. Others are just relieved that the lighthouse was saved so that future generations could appreciate its bold, spiral stripes and proud history.

Vocabulary Skills

Write the words from the passage that have the meanings below.

1. unmoving

_____
Par. 1

2. survived

_____
Par. 2

3. the process of being worn away over time by natural forces

_____
Par. 3

4. to show to be reasonable

_____
Par. 4

5. empty

_____
Par. 7

Write the words from the story that match the abbreviations below.

6. NC _____
Par. 1

7. wks. _____
Par. 5

8. ft. _____
Par. 5

9. min. _____
Par. 6

Rewrite each phrase using a possessive. If the noun is plural and ends in **s**, add the apostrophe (') after the **s** to show possession. For example, *bags of the girls* would be written as the *girls' bags*.

10. the history of the lighthouse

_____

11. the opinion of the protesters

_____

12. the estimate of the planners

_____

Reading Skills

1. Number the events below to show the order in which they happened.

_____ People were worried that the lighthouse would collapse.

_____ The relocation was a success.

_____ The Cape Hatteras Lighthouse was completed in 1870.

_____ The lighthouse was removed from its existing foundation.

_____ Onlookers watched the slow progress of the lighthouse's move.

2. Check the line beside the word or words that best describe what type of passage this is.

_____ biography

_____ historical nonfiction

_____ fiction

3. Check the sentence that best states the main idea of the passage.

_____ The Cape Hatteras Lighthouse in Buxton, North Carolina, is the tallest lighthouse in the United States.

_____ The process used to move the Cape Hatteras Lighthouse was very slow.

_____ In 1999, the Cape Hatteras Lighthouse was moved further inland to prevent its destruction due to erosion.

4. What are the Diamond Shoals?

_____

5. What is one reason that some people protested moving the lighthouse?

_____

_____

Keeping the Light

What would it be like to live in a lighthouse?

1   Imagine living in an isolated place where bad weather was not uncommon and people's lives depended on you doing your job. This was the life of a lighthouse keeper before lighthouses became automated. Lights that had mirrors and lenses had to be cleaned and polished regularly. The keepers had to be watchful at night to make sure that the lamps stayed lit and there was enough fuel to last the night. When ships wrecked in nearby areas, lighthouse keepers were expected to help with the rescue effort.

2   Because the work was physically demanding and women rarely worked outside the home, the job of lighthouse keeper was most often given to men. However, the job often fell to the daughters or wives of lighthouse keepers when the men were called to war, became ill, or died. Women proved themselves to be equally capable of holding this difficult job that was as much a way of life as it was a career.

3   One of the most famous female lighthouse keepers was Ida Lewis of Newport, Rhode Island. Her father was the keeper of Lime Rock Lighthouse, but after only a few months at the job he had a stroke. Because Hosea Lewis was no longer able to perform his duties as keeper, 15-year-old Ida and her mother took over in 1853. Captain Lewis lived about 20 years longer, but Ida and her mother performed all the required duties of a keeper.

4   Ida was known as the best swimmer in Newport. She was also skilled at handling a rowboat, something that was not seen as particularly appropriate for a woman of that time. However, during her 39 years keeping the light at Lime Rock, Ida rescued between 18 and 25 people. That certainly made it seem less important whether or not Ida's behaviors were appropriate!

5   People were intrigued by this woman who appeared to make her own rules for living. Thousands of visitors came to Lime Rock in hope of seeing Ida Lewis in person. Ida was used to the quiet solitude of a lighthouse keeper's life, and she was uncomfortable with all the attention. Even so, she couldn't help being honored by the awards she received for her service. President Ulysses S. Grant made a trip to Rhode Island to visit Ida and to commend her on her heroism.

6   In 1924, Lime Rock was renamed Ida Lewis Rock in honor of the keeper who had died in 1911. The lighthouse service of Rhode Island also renamed Lime Rock Lighthouse the Ida Lewis Lighthouse. It is the only lighthouse to be named for its keeper.

Vocabulary Skills

Write the words from the passage that have the meanings below.

1. remote; set apart

   _____
   Par. 1

2. accepted; suitable or proper

   _____
   Par. 4

3. curious about; interested in

   _____
   Par. 5

4. the state or quality of being alone or far away from things

   _____
   Par. 5

5. to praise

   _____
   Par. 5

Write a synonym from the story for each of the words below.

6. unusual _____
   Par. 1

7. seldom _____
   Par. 2

8. responsibilities _____
   Par. 3

9. talented _____
   Par. 4

Check the meaning of the underlined word.

10. The lenses had to be polished <u>regularly</u>.

    _____ in a regular way

    _____ capable of being regular

    _____ not regular

11. Captain Lewis was <u>unable</u> to perform his duties as lighthouse keeper.

    _____ extra able

    _____ not able

    _____ the act of being able

Reading Skills

1. Check the words that best describe Ida Lewis.

   _____ hardworking

   _____ determined

   _____ nosy

   _____ strong-willed

   _____ unpredictable

Write **T** before the sentences that are true. Write **F** before the sentences that are false.

2. _____ It was more common for women than for men to be lighthouse keepers.

3. _____ After his stroke, Captain Lewis was able to resume his job as lighthouse keeper.

4. _____ Ida kept the light at Lime Rock for 39 years.

5. _____ President Ulysses S. Grant visited Ida in Rhode Island.

6. _____ Today, Lime Rock Lighthouse is called Ida Lewis Lighthouse.

7. Why did all the attention make Ida uncomfortable?

   _____

8. Why do you think that we don't know for sure how many people Ida rescued?

   _____

9. How old was Ida when she began tending the lighthouse?

   _____

10. What were two jobs of lighthouse keepers before lighthouses became automated?

    _____

    _____

A Picture Perfect Day

Have you ever taken any photographs?

1   "Hold that pose!" said Dante, snapping a photo of his mother.

2   Dante's mom looked up in surprise and spilled some of the orange juice she was pouring. "Dante, what are you doing?" she asked, setting the carton of juice on the counter.

3   "It's a project I'm doing for school," Dante explained, sitting down at the table. "For the next two days, I'm going to keep a photo diary of my life." He paused and took a bite of steaming oatmeal from his bowl.

4   Mrs. Carter smiled at her son. "It sounds interesting," she said. "I'm just not sure that a picture of me in my pajamas pouring orange juice at 7 o'clock in the morning is the most interesting part of your day."

5   "I'm not supposed to leave anything out," replied Dante. "It doesn't really matter if it's interesting. This diary should be a realistic narrative of my day. You and breakfast are both a part of my day, so I wanted to make sure they were captured on film."

6   Mrs. Carter nodded and bit into a slice of toast. "What will you do with your photographs when you're done? Do you have to present them to your class?"

7   "I'm going to mount the photos on a piece of posterboard in chronological order," Dante said. "Then, the class will try to write a brief summary of my day based on the pictures I took."

8   "Do your dad and brother know about your photo diary project?" asked Mrs. Carter. "You might want to give them a bit of advance warning if they're going to be part of it."

9   Just then, Wesley came pounding down the stairs into the kitchen. He was carrying a basketball under one arm and grabbed a piece of toast as he sat down at the table.

10   "Wesley," said Dante, peering through the camera lens at his brother, "I'm doing a photo diary for school."

11   Wesley grinned directly at the camera as Dante snapped the photo. Mrs. Carter laughed. "I forgot who I was talking about here," she said, giving Wesley a quick squeeze on the shoulder. "I guess no explanation is necessary for your brother, Dante," she said.

12   "I don't blame him for wanting to get a picture of me," said Wesley. "When I make it into the NBA, those pictures will probably be pretty valuable," he joked.

13   Dante laughed as he got up from the breakfast table. "There are some things you just can't capture in pictures," he said, shaking his head. He took his dishes to the sink and then managed to get a picture of his dad adjusting his tie as he walked into the kitchen with the newspaper tucked under his arm.

14   "Am I famous?" asked Mr. Carter.

15   "Not yet," said Dante. "But as a part of my photo diary, you will be with the members of Ms. Rutherford's class."

16   Mr. Carter nodded. He grabbed Mrs. Carter around the waist as she got up to get another cup of coffee. He waltzed her across the kitchen and then dipped her deeply as she laughed. "Isn't this going to make it into your diary?" he asked Dante.

17   Dante grinned. "I'm just not sure that my class would be able to work it into the narrative of my day. Like I said, there are some things you just can't capture in pictures."

Vocabulary Skills

Write the words from the story that have the meanings below.

1. a specific body position

_____
Par. 1

2. resembling things that are real or actual

_____
Par. 5

3. a story or description

_____
Par. 5

4. to put on display

_____
Par. 7

5. the order in which events happened

_____
Par. 7

Circle the homophone that correctly completes each sentence below.

6. The pants were too large and sat well below Meghan's _____. (waist, waste)

7. There is a small scratch on the right _____ of my sunglasses. (lens, lends)

8. Did you _____ the turkey yet? (based, baste)

Find an antonym in the story for each of the words below.

9. boring _____
Par. 4

10. worthless _____
Par. 12

11. unknown _____
Par. 14

Reading Skills

Write **F** before the sentences that are facts. Write **O** before the sentences that are opinions.

1. _____ Keeping a photo diary is a difficult assignment.

2. _____ Dante's brother's name is Wesley.

3. _____ Dante's classmates will find it easy to create a narrative from his photos.

4. _____ Mrs. Carter spilled some orange juice.

5. _____ Mr. Carter has a good sense of humor.

6. The **protagonist** is the main character in a story, or the person the story is mostly about. Who is the protagonist in this story?

_____

_____

7. Why doesn't Dante want to leave out any details of his day?

_____

_____

8. Why does Wesley joke that photos of him will be valuable one day?

_____

_____

9. During what time of day does the story take place? How can you tell?

_____

_____

Point and Click

Do you know how a camera works?

1   Cameras might seem almost unbelievable if you do not know how they work. Point a camera at something, push a button, and you end up with a realistic image of what you saw. How does that happen? The camera's ability to reproduce what you see is not actually all that complicated once you understand a few basic elements. In fact, the camera itself is just a box that controls how much light reaches the film inside. The original Latin term *camera obscura* means *dark chamber*, and it is a perfect description.

2   Traditional film is a plastic strip that has been coated with light-sensitive chemicals. Like the rods and cones in our eyes, these chemicals change according to how much light enters the camera. The image that enters through the camera's lens creates a unique pattern in the chemicals that will be used when the photograph is developed in a lab. Instead of chemical film, a digital camera contains a light-sensitive electrical device that records the image.

3   Having just the right amount of light reach the film is crucial to taking a good picture. The two main devices that control light are the shutter and the aperture. The shutter is a small door inside the camera that opens and closes when you take a picture. It affects how long the film is exposed to light.

4   On a typical sunny day, the shutter speed might be as fast as 1/125 of a second to keep too much light from getting in. A quick shutter speed is also needed when you want to capture something that is moving. If the film is exposed too long, the moving object will be a blur in the developed photo.

5   Sometimes slow shutter speeds are needed. For example, if you want to take a picture at night or in low light, you need to leave the shutter open longer so that enough light can reach the film and create an image. To take photographs of stars or the moon you would need to have the shutter open for a very long time.

6   The aperture is a circular opening behind the lens that can be adjusted to let in more or less light, similar to the iris in an eye. The aperture also determines the depth of field, or how much of the photo will appear to be in focus. When the aperture is open widely, the focus will only be on a narrow range of objects, but when the aperture is small, things both near and faraway will look sharp.

7   The aperture and shutter speed work together to get just the right amount of light to the film. For instance, if you want to photograph a fast moving object you need a fast shutter speed, but that may not let in enough light. To compensate, you need to open the aperture wider so that the proper amount of light reaches the film. Of course, a camera with an automatic setting will do all of the adjustments for you, so all you have to do is just "point and click."

Vocabulary Skills

Write the words from the passage that have the meanings below.

1. make a copy of

   _____
   Par. 1

2. a piece of equipment used for a specific purpose

   _____
   Par. 2

3. allowed to be reached by light

   _____
   Par. 3

4. to make up for something

   _____
   Par. 7

Read each word below. Then, write the letter of its synonym on the line beside the word.

5. _____ complicated   **a.** common

6. _____ typical   **b.** round

7. _____ circular   **c.** create

8. _____ produce   **d.** complex

Reading Skills

1. How is a camera's aperture similar to the iris in a human eye?

   _____

2. What is one example of a time you might want to use a slow shutter speed?

   _____

3. What does the Latin term *camera obscura* mean?

   _____

4. How are digital cameras different from traditional cameras?

   _____

5. What are the two main devices that control light in a camera?

   _____

6. Why do you think it is easier to use an automatic camera than a manual camera?

   _____

7. Check the phrase that best describes the author's purpose.

   _____ to persuade

   _____ to entertain

   _____ to inform

Study Skills

Fill out the registration form for a photography class. Then, answer the questions about the form.

1.		
last name	first name	middle initial
2.		
street address		
3.		
city	state	zip code
4.		
phone number	e-mail address (optional)	
5.		
age	grade	

What experience, if any, have you had with photography? (Use the reverse side of the form if you need additional space.)_____

1. What is the one piece of information that is optional?

   _____

2. If you need more space to answer the question, what should you do?

   _____

3. On which line should you write your age and grade in school?

   _____

Spectrum Reading Grade 6

33

Talking Photos

What will Dante learn in his interview with Mr. Salinas?

1 "Thanks for taking the time to meet with me, Mr. Salinas," said Dante, reaching out to shake the photographer's hand.

2 "I'm happy to do it," replied Mr. Salinas. "I love to talk about my work, and as patient as my family is, I'm sure they still get a little tired of hearing about it all of the time."

3 "I brought a tape recorder with me," said Dante, holding up the small black box. "Would it be all right with you if I recorded our conversation?" he asked. "That way, I won't be distracted by taking notes, and I can transcribe it later."

4 "That sounds good to me," said Mr. Salinas. He settled into his chair and took a sip of bottled water. "I'm ready when you are," he said.

5 *Dante Carter:* When did you first know that you wanted to be a photographer?

6 *Edward Salinas:* It wasn't until I had already graduated from college. I was teaching high school English, and I decided to take a photography class just for fun. The class was at a community arts center in downtown Seattle, Washington. It completely changed my life. I went back to school a year later to begin working on a degree in photography.

7 *DC:* Who has been your greatest influence?

8 *ES:* Well, I have been lucky to have had several wonderful mentors who encouraged and inspired me. After I completed my photography degree, I had a year-long internship with a very talented photographer named Elizabeth Chu. For the most part, she documented people's lives through photography. She had an amazing ability to capture so much character and personality in a single image.

9 *DC:* What other photographers do you admire?

10 *ES:* There are so many, I'm not even sure where to begin. The work of Walker Evans is extraordinary. He is probably best known for his photographs showing the poverty of life in the South during the 1930s. There is a very timeless and human aspect to his work. Alfred Stieglitz was influential in promoting the work of photographers as artists. His images of New York during the first part of the 20th century are stunning.

11 *DC:* What do you find most rewarding about your job?

12 *ES:* I suppose I'm most grateful that it doesn't feel like a job to me, even though it can often be hard work. There are plenty of frustrations when photos don't turn out the way I had anticipated. But documenting life and nature and beauty is very gratifying. I can't imagine anything else I'd rather do.

13 *DC:* Mr. Salinas, this has been really helpful. Thank you for meeting with me and sharing so much about your experiences. I'd like to be a photographer one day myself. Your comments were inspiring.

14 *ES:* I wish you the best of luck, Dante. From what I've seen, you have the motivation and ability to succeed at just about anything you put your mind to.

Vocabulary Skills

Write the words from the story that have the meanings below.

1. having attention drawn away

   _____
   Par. 3

2. to make a written copy of

   _____
   Par. 3

3. people who act as guides or teachers

   _____
   Par. 8

4. having the power to change or effect

   _____
   Par. 10

5. making a record of

   _____
   Par. 12

Words that have two middle consonants are divided into syllables between the consonants. For example, *pic/ture*. Divide the words below into syllables using a slash.

6. c a p t u r e

7. c e n t e r

8. a d m i r e

The suffix **-able** means *capable of* or *tending to*. For example, *reasonable* means *capable of reason*. Write a word to match each definition below. Then, write a sentence using each word.

9. tending to honor _____

   _____

10. capable of being washed _____

    _____

11. capable of breaking _____

    _____

Reading Skills

1. Why does Dante want to record his interview with Mr. Salinas?

   _____
   _____

2. What job did Mr. Salinas have before he became a photographer?

   _____
   _____

3. Name two people who have influenced Mr. Salinas's work.

   _____
   _____

4. What does Mr. Salinas like about his job?

   _____
   _____

Circle the word that best completes each sentence below.

5. Mr. Salinas was _____ with the work of Alfred Stieglitz and Walker Evans.

   uninterested   impressed   disappointed

6. Dante's questions for Mr. Salinas were _____.

   irritating   encouraging   thoughtful

7. Mr. Salinas _____ that his work can be frustrating at times.

   mentioned   aspired   demanded

8. After his interview with Mr. Salinas, do you think that Dante will still want to become a photographer? Explain your answer.

   _____
   _____

The World of Ansel Adams

How did Ansel Adams become one of the most well-known nature photographers?

1   The name Ansel Adams may not ring a bell with you, but there is a good chance that you would recognize his photographs. Adams's work includes some of the most beautiful and famous black-and-white nature photographs ever taken.

2   Ansel Adams was born in 1902 near San Francisco, California. Adams's interest in photography began on a trip to Yosemite National Park when he was 14 years old. His parents had given him a camera as a gift. Adams found that he was mesmerized by the scenery at Yosemite and fascinated by his ability to capture it on film.

3   Although Adams had already shown much promise as a pianist, photography became a hobby that was just as fulfilling for him. It turned out that his talent for photography was perhaps even greater than that for music.

4   The photographs for which Adams is best known are those that depict the beauty of wild areas. Many of his photos were taken in Yosemite National Park, the site of his first experience with a camera. Others captured images of wild places in the American West, as well as the California coast, near the area where Adams was raised.

5   One of the things that makes Adams's work so distinctive is the contrast that is present in so many of his photographs. Although Adams worked in black and white, there is an amazing amount of variety in tone. The darker shades are deep and rich, while the whites are crisp and bright.

6   Adams was able to achieve this through a system he developed called *zone exposure*. He divided the light in an image into ten different zones. This allowed him to accurately predict what the different shades of gray would look like in a photograph.

7   Through his photographs and the time that he spent in nature, Adams became an avid environmentalist. He became involved with the Sierra Club, a conservation group. The photography he did for them brought publicity to many issues they believed were important. His photographs serve as a record of wild areas of the American West—such as Sequoia, Mount Rainier, and Glacier National Parks—before humans had done much to disturb them.

8   Although his prints were often sold to collectors for large sums of money, Adams wanted to make sure that his photographs were available to everyone. Posters were created of several of his best-loved images. They are still available today, in addition to many books on Adams's work and even calendars that feature his photography. Ansel Adams died in 1984, but his photographs will continue to bring the joy and wonder of the natural world to people for many years to come.

Vocabulary Skills

Write the words from the passage that have the meanings below.

1. looked at with wonder; captivated

   _____
   Par. 2

2. potential; a reason for expecting future excellence

   _____
   Par. 3

3. satisfying

   _____
   Par. 3

4. represent

   _____
   Par. 4

5. unique; uncommon

   _____
   Par. 5

6. eager and enthusiastic

   _____
   Par. 7

7. Check the sentence in which *trip* has the same meaning as it does in paragraph 2.

   _____ Don't trip over that cord!

   _____ Kelly and Amy are planning a trip to Paris in the fall.

8. Check the sentence in which *tone* has the same meaning as it does in paragraph 5.

   _____ Maria was able to tone her muscles through frequent swimming.

   _____ I could see a yellowish tone in the stormy sky.

Write the idiom from paragraph 1 on the line next to its meaning.

9. to sound familiar _____

Reading Skills

1. Check the line beside the word or words that best describe what type of passage this is.

   _____ historical fiction

   _____ biography

   _____ persuasive

2. Check the sentence below that is the best summary for paragraph 7.

   _____ Adams was an environmentalist who was able to help the cause he believed in through his photographs of natural places.

   _____ Adams visited Sequoia, Mount Rainier, and Glacier National Parks.

   _____ The Sierra Club is a conservation group.

3. Check the words that best describe Ansel Adams.

   _____ talented

   _____ anxious

   _____ enthusiastic

   _____ creative

   _____ suspicious

Write **T** before the sentences that are true. Write **F** before the sentences that are false.

4. _____ Adams was born on the East Coast.

5. _____ Adams received his first camera from a teacher.

6. _____ Adams was also a talented musician.

7. _____ The majority of Adams's photographs are black and white.

8. _____ Adams is still alive and lives California today.

Photographing History

Who was Margaret Bourke-White, and why is her work still so respected today?

1   What do the following people and places have in common—the Indian leader Gandhi, the survivors of the World War II concentration camps, the Great Depression, the steel mills of Cleveland, Ohio, and the Arctic Circle? Margaret Bourke-White photographed them all during her career as a photojournalist. She was present for many monumental events of the 20th century, and she recorded them with courage and sensitivity.

2   Margaret Bourke-White was born in New York in 1904. In college, she studied biology and planned to be a herpetologist, a scientist who studies reptiles and amphibians. Then, she took a class in photography and discovered a new passion.

3   After graduating from college, Bourke-White headed to Cleveland where she photographed the steel mills that were so prevalent in that city. In the 1920s, American industry was booming and the country was growing. Bourke-White documented much of this growth and the factories where it was taking place. Although the material she was covering was cold and industrial, Bourke-White managed to make the photographs of machinery and factories both artistic and beautiful.

4   A publisher named Henry Luce was very impressed with Bourke-White's photographs of American industry and hired her to work at his magazine, *Fortune*. When he began a new magazine called *LIFE* in 1936, Bourke-White was one of Luce's first four photographers. In fact, her picture of a Montana dam was featured on the cover of the magazine's first issue.

5   Bourke-White's work with *LIFE* magazine led her on adventures all across the globe. She was the first foreign photographer to be allowed to take pictures in the Soviet Union in 1930. She took photos of the German siege on Moscow in 1941. As the first female war correspondent of World War II, Bourke-White faced danger on a

regular basis. This was at a time when it was still customary for women to work mostly in the home, taking care of a family and a household.

6   One of Bourke-White's closest brushes with danger occurred when she was assigned to cover the U.S. armed forces at the start of the war. On her way to North Africa, the ship she was traveling in was struck by a torpedo and sank. Bourke-White survived the attack and went on to follow and photograph the action of the war. When the concentration camps were liberated several years later at the end of World War II, Bourke-White was there with her camera to capture some of the most disturbing and moving images ever recorded.

7   As stressful and difficult as her work must have been, Margaret Bourke-White loved what she did. She was the eyes and ears of the world in places most Americans had never visited and never would. Although Bourke-White died at the relatively early age of 67, she had traveled the world and photographed much of what she saw. Her pictures are a permanent record of both her life and the world during the 20th century.

Vocabulary Skills

Write the words from the passage that have the meanings below.

1. very important

   _____
   Par. 1

2. widespread

   _____
   Par. 3

3. common; usual

   _____
   Par. 5

4. freed

   _____
   Par. 6

Write the words from the selection that match the abbreviations below.

5. WWII _____
   Par. 1

6. OH _____
   Par. 1

7. MT _____
   Par. 4

8. cent. _____
   Par. 7

Reading Skills

1. Check the sentence that best states the main idea of the selection.

   _____ Margaret Bourke-White photographed Cleveland's steel mills in the 1920s.

   _____ Margaret Bourke-White was a talented photojournalist who traveled the world and broke new ground for women.

   _____ Margaret Bourke-White was one of *LIFE* magazine's first four photographers.

2. Is this selection a fantasy, or does it take place in reality? How can you tell?

   _____

   _____

3. Why was Bourke-White's job unusual for a woman?

   _____

4. What did Bourke-White plan to be before she discovered photography?

   _____

5. What was unusual about Bourke-White's industrial pictures?

   _____

6. Number the events below to show the order in which they happened.

   _____ Bourke-White photographed the liberation of the concentration camps.

   _____ Bourke-White began working for *LIFE* magazine.

   _____ Henry Luce hired Bourke-White to work at *Fortune*.

   _____ Bourke-White graduated from college.

Study Skills

A pronunciation key is a list of sound symbols and key words. They show how to pronounce words. Use the pronunciation key on the inside back cover of this book to write the words that match these pronunciations.

1. /sir vī′ ver/ _____

2. /mə shē′ ner ē/ _____

3. /fāst/ _____

4. /grōth/ _____

Reality Check

What will Ari and his mom find out about owning an exotic pet?

1   Through the kitchen's glass doors, Ari could see his mom sitting on the back deck. The pale green baby blanket she was knitting was pooled at her side, and she held it up every once in a while to check on her progress.

2   Ari slid open the door and pulled up a chair across from his mom. "Well, hi there," said Mrs. Stein, smiling at Ari. "What have you been up to this afternoon?"

3   Ari took a sip of his mom's iced tea. "I was watching this amazing animal show," he said. "It was about people who have all kinds of exotic pets. Did you know that you can buy Bengal tiger cubs and raise them yourself?" asked Ari excitedly.

4   "I'm not sure that's such a good idea," said Mrs. Stein, her knitting needles clicking along busily. "Tigers are beautiful, wild creatures," she added. "I hate to see people trying to domesticate animals that are meant to live in the wild."

5   Ari nodded. "A tiger would be a lot of responsibility. It would be almost impossible to give it the space it would need to feel free.

6   "There are other exotic animals that wouldn't be so dangerous or need a lot of space, though," said Ari. "I wrote down a few Web addresses where we could find some more information. Could we go look at them?" Ari looked hopefully at his mother.

7   Mrs. Stein sighed and grinned at Ari. "Let me finish this row, and I'll come inside and take a look at the sites with you. I'm not promising anything, though."

8   A few minutes later, Ari and his mom sat side by side in the glow of the computer screen. They saw pictures of miniature foxes with enormous ears, bristly hedgehogs, and boa constrictors. They read advertisements for lion cubs, piranhas, and warthogs.

9   Then, they found a Web site that discussed some of the problems with importing exotic pets. "They didn't talk about any of this on the show I watched," said Ari, looking confused. "I had no idea that there were so many abandoned or mistreated exotic pets in this country."

10   Ari's mom shook her head. "I didn't know either," she said. "It sounds like the show you saw only presented one side of the story. That's too bad, isn't it? I'm sure lots of people see advertisements or shows like the one you saw and don't really know what they are getting into."

11   Ari looked thoughtful, "Mom, do you think I could write a letter to the show I watched? Now that we've done some more research, I've changed my mind about owning an exotic pet. They should have explained both sides of the story."

12   Mrs. Stein patted Ari on the shoulder. "That's a wonderful idea," she said. "You've made a really mature decision. Someone that responsible could probably handle taking care of a dog or a cat. Do you want to check out a few of the local animal shelters while we're online?"

13   Ari couldn't think of what to say. He hugged his mom hard and turned back to the computer to begin searching for a cat or a dog that needed a good home.

Vocabulary Skills

Write the words from the story that have the meanings below.

1. young animals such as bears, foxes, or tigers

   _____
   Par. 3

2. to tame or train something wild for human use

   _____
   Par. 4

3. bringing something into a country from another country

   _____
   Par. 9

4. responsible; like an adult

   _____
   Par. 12

Words that end in **le** are usually divided into syllables before the consonant that precedes it. For example, *ta/ble*. Divide the words below into syllables using a slash *(/)*.

5. h a n d l e

6. p e o p l e

7. g e n t l e

8. d i m p l e

In each row, circle the word that does not belong.

9. small   miniature   enormous   tiny

10. mature   innocent   trustworthy   responsible

11. argue   research   inquire   question

12. hedgehog   exotic   tiger   dog

Reading Skills

1. What kinds of exotic animals did Ari and his mom see when they were online?

   _____

2. Why did Ari decide to write a letter to the television show he watched?

   _____

   _____

3. Why did Mrs. Stein say that Ari was mature and responsible?

   _____

4. Do you think that Ari will be a good pet owner? Why or why not?

   _____

   _____

Mark each sentence below **F** if it is in first-person point of view and **T** if it is in third-person point of view.

5. _____ I can't believe we're going to get a dog or cat!

6. _____ Mrs. Stein put down her knitting.

7. _____ Ari turned on the computer.

8. _____ I think that writing a letter is an excellent idea.

Study Skills

A library's reference system can help you find a book. Use the information below to answer the questions that follow.

Call No:	441.86 WO
Author:	Wolfowitz, Eliza
Title:	Everything You Need to Know About Adopting a Pet
Publisher:	Leesburg Lane Publishing, 2004

1. What is the author's last name?

   _____

2. Who is the book's publisher?

   _____

An Exotic Dilemma

Learn how exotic pets are turning up in unexpected places in Florida.

1   Would you know what to do if you saw a python slithering across your backyard? What about an anteater looking for dinner in your bushes or a seven-foot long African monitor lizard running across your patio? People who live in most areas of the United States do not have encounters like these. But if you happen to live in southern Florida, there is a chance that you could run into a number of nonnative species that have settled in your hometown.

2   Exotic pets have become more and more popular in recent years. People often purchase an animal as a baby without realizing how difficult it may be to care for that animal when it is fully-grown.

3   For example, Burmese pythons are easy to buy at exotic pet stores or online. When the snake is young, it does not require much more work than any other pet reptile. But Burmese pythons can grow to be more than 20 feet long and can weigh about 250 pounds. There is not much space in the average American home or yard to care for such a creature! When the snake outgrows its cage and its owner tires of caring for and feeding such a large animal, the snake may be abandoned in a wild area.

4   In other parts of the country, it is likely that many of these exotic creatures would not be able to survive long in the wild. But the climate in southern Florida is wet and warm—not unlike the tropical areas where many of the animals are naturally found. Not only can many exotic pets adjust to living in Florida's natural areas, but if enough of them are released, they can start breeding.

5   The problem with invasive species is that scientists don't always know in advance which ones will alter the environment or harm native populations. In the last few years, people visiting Florida's Everglades National Park have watched fights between alligators and pythons.

6   It is not hard to imagine the impact of aggressive creatures. But even animals like vervet monkeys or Cuban tree frogs, which seem harmless, can change the delicate balance of the environment. They may compete with other animals that eat the same plants or insects. If their presence or behavior causes a change in the habits of other animals, the overall changes could be far-reaching.

7   Think about a set of dominos lined up next to one another. None of them may be touching, but as soon as you tip one over, the whole row will tumble. This is not unlike the way plants and animals in the environment react to one another. One small change can set off a whole series of changes that not even scientists can predict.

Vocabulary Skills

Write the words from the passage that have the meanings below.

1. meetings

   _____
   Par. 1

2. unusual; from another part of the world

   _____
   Par. 2

3. left or deserted

   _____
   Par. 3

4. quick to attack; forceful

   _____
   Par. 6

5. as a whole; in general

   _____
   Par. 6

Circle the homophone that correctly completes each sentence below.

6. Can you _____ this dress for me by Friday? (alter, altar)

7. Raj's _____ at the performance gave me confidence. (presents, presence)

8. How much does that bag _____? (weigh, way)

Write **S** if the possessive word is singular. Write **P** if it is plural.

9. _____ the python's cage

10. _____ the creatures' habitats

11. _____ Florida's natural areas

12. _____ the animals' environment

Reading Skills

1. Check the phrase that best describes the author's purpose.

   _____ to entertain

   _____ to inform

   _____ to instruct

2. An **analogy** is a comparison between two things that may seem to be unalike but that have at least one similarity. An analogy is used to compare two things in paragraph 7. What are they?

   _____

3. Name two animals that are nonnative species in southern Florida.

   _____

4. Why is it hard to care for a full-grown Burmese python?

   _____

   _____

5. Why are exotic pets more likely to survive in the wild in a state like Florida than they are in a state like Ohio or Montana?

   _____

   _____

6. Do you think that abandoned exotic animals will continue to be a problem in Florida? Explain your answer.

   _____

   _____

7. How would you define the term *invasive species*?

   _____

   _____

The Everlasting Beauty of the Everglades

Why is the Everglades considered to be such a unique area of the country?

1   The Florida Everglades is one of the most diverse areas of the country. Within the Everglades you can find swamps, marshes, grasslands, and dense forests. Hundreds of species of plants and animals make their homes in the Everglades. Some are found in few other places in the world. About 1.5 million acres of the Everglades are National Park land. Within the park there are more than 350 species of birds, 40 species of mammals, and 50 species of reptiles!

2   Scientists believe that the Everglades formed about eight to ten thousand years ago at the end of the last ice age. When the glaciers began to melt, they caused the sea level to rise and turned the low-lying area of the Everglades into swampland. When nearby Lake Okeechobee floods after heavy rains, the water level in the Everglades rises as well.

3   The weather is characterized by hot, wet summers and warm but dry winters. The temperature in the Everglades rarely drops below 60 degrees, and the average rainfall is often more than 50 inches per year. This wet, mild weather is the primary reason that plant and animal life is so abundant there.

4   As prevalent as living creatures appear to be in this lush landscape, the ecosystem of the Everglades must maintain its delicate balance. During the 20th century, canals were built which lowered the level of Lake Okeechobee. The lake overflowed much less frequently, which affected the water levels in the Everglades.

5   People also began looking for ways to farm the land surrounding the Everglades. This required using much of the Everglades' water supply. In addition, the pollution from fertilizers and pesticides used in farming began to run off into the water.

6   New types of flora were introduced, which also affected the balance of the ecosystem. The tiny seeds of the melaleuca tree were sprinkled from salt shakers into the Everglades from low-flying airplanes because melaleuca trees consume a great deal of water. People hoped that the trees would dry up the land and make the Everglades suitable for development. They also planned to use the trees for timber. The wood turned out to be difficult to harvest, so the trees just continued to grow, crowding out other species that are indigenous to the Everglades.

7   The Everglades National Park was founded in 1947 in an attempt to preserve the land and the plant and animal life. The area was not large enough to make a significant impact, so in 1989, the government expanded the park. In 1996, an act was passed allowing the government to purchase farmland, which could then be returned to natural swampy marshland.

8   These efforts are important because there are so many species to protect within the Everglades. It is the only place in the world where crocodiles and alligators coexist. It is also the home of the endangered Florida panther, as well as many other endangered species. Black bears, otters, pelicans, turtles, bats, deer, and manatees all make their home in the Everglades. Without a doubt, the Everglades are worth saving and preserving. Where else in the world can you find such lush diversity?

Vocabulary Skills

Write the words from the passage that have the meanings below.

1. described by

   _____
   Par. 3

2. more than enough; plentiful

   _____
   Par. 3

3. covered with thick, green plant growth

   _____
   Par. 4

4. the plants and animals that make up an environment and affect one another

   _____
   Par. 4

5. to eat, drink, or use up

   _____
   Par. 6

6. native

   _____
   Par. 6

Find the compound words from the selection that contain the words below.

7. grass _____
   Par. 1

8. fall _____
   Par. 3

9. planes _____
   Par. 6

10. farm _____
    Par. 7

Read each pair of words listed below. If the words are synonyms, write **S** on the line. If the words are antonyms, write **A** on the line.

11. _____ expanded   shrank

12. _____ suitable   appropriate

13. _____ influence   affect

14. _____ lowered   raised

Reading Skills

Write **F** before the sentences that are facts. Write **O** before the sentences that are opinions.

1. _____ The Everglades National Park covers about 1.5 million acres.

2. _____ Melaleuca trees consume a great deal of water.

3. _____ Everyone should visit the Everglades at least once.

4. _____ The Everglades are most beautiful in the summer.

5. _____ The Everglades are the only place in the world where crocodiles and alligators coexist.

6. What is the author trying to persuade the reader of in this passage?

   _____

7. Think about what you know about rain forests. Name two ways in which rain forests and the Everglades are similar.

   _____

   _____

8. About how many species of birds are there in Everglades National Park?

   _____

9. Why were melaleuca trees planted in the Everglades?

   _____

Circle the word that best completes each sentence.

10. Many people believe it is important to _____ our nation's wild places.

    destroy   investigate   preserve

11. It can be difficult to _____ the balance of an ecosystem.

    explain   maintain   cancel

It's a Bird's Life

What kinds of birds can you identify in your own neighborhood?

1   Have you ever heard of the National Audubon Society? It is probably the most well-known environmental organization for the protection and conservation of birds and their habitats. It was founded in honor of John James Audubon, who was a naturalist, ornithologist, and painter.

2   Audubon was born in the Caribbean country of Haiti in 1785. When he was 18 years old, he was sent to live in the United States at a family farm near Philadelphia, Pennsylvania. He showed a great deal of interest in natural history and conducted the first bird-banding experiment in the country. He captured eastern phoebes and tied small pieces of yarn to their legs. By marking the birds in this way, Audubon was able to conclude that the birds nested in the same places every year.

3   Over the years, Audubon spent more and more time creating realistic drawings and paintings of birds. He began to catalog the birds he drew, venturing farther and farther to locate new species. Although today's conservation groups would not approve of his methods, Audubon used the only technique he knew to create his paintings. He shot and stuffed birds to use as models for his artwork. He posed the birds in their natural habitats so that he would have the appropriate settings for his paintings.

4   Some of Audubon's explorations led him on bird-watching excursions down the Mississippi River. He became a talented outdoorsman as he followed his subjects through the South. By the late 1820s, Audubon began looking for a publisher for his catalog of American birds, but American publishers were not interested. Instead, Audubon found an audience in England and Scotland where people were fascinated by the concept of the American wilderness.

5   There, *Birds of America* was finally printed with great success. It contained 435 hand-colored plates that showed 1,065 life-sized birds.

Nothing so detailed had ever been created to document the variety of birds in America. Today, a complete set of the original prints is very valuable. There are thought to be fewer than 200 copies in existence in the world!

6   The Audubon Society was founded in 1886, several decades after John James Audubon's death. It honored a man whose lifework had been to study birds and to begin to educate the public about the importance of protecting them and their environment. The National Audubon Society still exists and continues to grow today. If you are interested in learning more about it or how you can become a junior member, visit www.audubon.org.

Vocabulary Skills

Write the words from the passage that have the meanings below.

1. the places where plants and animals live

   _____
   Par. 1

2. a scientist who studies birds

   _____
   Par. 1

3. to reach a decision

   _____
   Par. 2

4. to list and describe items of a particular type

   _____
   Par. 3

5. proceeding, even in dangerous circumstances

   _____
   Par. 3

6. short trips or journeys

   _____
   Par. 4

Circle the homophone that correctly completes each sentence below.

7. Audubon _____ a piece of yarn to the legs of the birds. (tied, tide)

8. Have you ever _____ the call of a chickadee? (heard, herd)

Check the meaning of the underlined word in each sentence.

9. Audubon conducted the first bird-banding experiments in the United States.

   _____ behaved in a certain way

   _____ directed

10. Birds were usually the subject of Audubon's paintings.

    _____ things being studied

    _____ the word or group of words in a sentence that performs the action

Reading Skills

1. Check the line beside the word or words that best describe what type of passage this is.

   _____ biography

   _____ myth

   _____ historical fiction

2. Check the sentence that best states the main idea of the selection.

   _____ Audubon was born in Haiti but moved to the United States as a teenager.

   _____ The National Audubon Society was founded to honor John James Audubon.

   _____ Audubon was a painter and ornithologist who created one of the most comprehensive catalogs of birds in America.

3. Check the words that best describe John James Audubon.

   _____ intelligent

   _____ cheerful

   _____ unfriendly

   _____ artistic

   _____ adventurous

4. Explain how Audubon's bird-banding experiment worked.

   _____

   _____

5. Why do you think that today's conservation groups would not approve of Audubon's methods?

   _____

   _____

A Bird Excursion

What birds can you identify by sight?

1   "Are you ready to go, girls?" asked Mr. Vasquez. He stood near the front door wearing a backpack.

2   "Ready, Dad," said Olivia. "Should I grab some bug spray?"

3   "Good thinking," said Mr. Vasquez. "We don't want to be eaten alive out there." Olivia grabbed the bug spray from the closet. Then, Jaya, Olivia, and Olivia's dad set out on their first joint bird watching expedition.

4   "How long have you been birding, Mr. Vasquez?" asked Jaya. She adjusted her backpack so that it sat more comfortably on her shoulders.

5   "I've only been doing it for about a year, Jaya," replied Mr. Vasquez. "Olivia's mom gave me a backyard birdfeeder for my birthday a couple of years ago. I found out that I really enjoyed watching the birds and identifying them with the field guide I bought. A friend of mine from work has been birding for years, and she helped me get started."

6   Jaya, Olivia, and Mr. Vasquez crossed the street to the park's entrance. They picked up a map of the trails. "We should look for a trail that isn't too wooded," said Mr. Vasquez. "If we can find a trail that has an open area, like a field or meadow, and some water, we'll probably have the best chance of making a number of sightings."

7   After careful deliberation, the group agreed on a trail and set off. As the sun rose higher in the sky, they grew warm and took off the long-sleeved shirts they wore over their T-shirts. Within the first half-hour, they were able to identify a blue jay, cardinal, chickadee, house sparrow, northern flicker, house finch, northern oriole, and red-winged blackbird.

8   "This is great!" exclaimed Jaya. "Do you usually spot so many birds this quickly?"

9   Mr. Vasquez grinned. "It seems like we're having an especially good day today."

10   "We haven't really seen any birds yet that are difficult to identify," said Olivia thoughtfully. "They can move so quickly, how can you identify them if you need to check the field guide?" she asked.

11   "Well," began Mr. Vasquez, "the bird's size is usually a good place to start. Is it bigger or smaller than a sparrow? What about a robin? Color is not always a reliable identifier because it can change in different types of light. Also, male and female birds frequently have different coloring, which can change by season."

12   "What about a bird's shape?" asked Jaya. "It seems like that would remain constant."

13   "You're right, Jaya," said Mr. Vasquez. "The shape of a bird's body, its tail, its wings, and its bill can all be excellent clues. Bird calls can also be helpful. Field guides often describe what a typical bird call sounds like. You can even go online and listen to a sample of most common calls."

14   "That's where your birding notebook can come in handy, Olivia," continued Mr. Vasquez. "If the bird flies away before you can identify it, your notes can help you do more research later."

15   "Look!" said Olivia, pointing to a pond that was visible in the distance. Several Canada geese took flight, their powerful wings lifting them quickly into the clear blue sky. Jaya, Olivia, and Mr. Vasquez stood quietly watching the geese soar overhead in a perfect *V* formation. No one reached for a birding notebook. They knew they wouldn't forget the image of the geese in the clear sky anytime soon.

Vocabulary Skills

Write the words from the story that have the meanings below.

1. careful thought or discussion

   _____
   Par. 7

2. dependable

   _____
   Par. 11

3. unchanging

   _____
   Par. 12

4. arrangement or place

   _____
   Par. 15

5. Check the sentence in which *rose* has the same meaning as it does in paragraph 7.

   _____ Annabelle chose a beautiful red rose for the bouquet.

   _____ The plane rose higher and higher into the air.

6. Check the sentence in which *check* has the same meaning as it does in paragraph 10.

   _____ David wrote a check to pay for the groceries.

   _____ Did you check the oil level in the car this morning?

7. Check the sentence in which *bill* has the same meaning as it does in paragraph 13.

   _____ The woodpecker's bill is long and thin.

   _____ Please ask the waiter for our bill.

Fill in the blanks below with the possessive form of the word in parentheses.

8. _____ mom gave her dad a birdfeeder for his birthday. (Olivia)

9. _____ colorings are not always a reliable way to identify them. (Birds)

10. Jaya, Olivia, and Mr. Vasquez crossed the street to get to the _____ entrance. (park)

Reading Skills

1. **Hyperbole** is an exaggerated statement that is used to make a point. For example, the sentence *I am so hungry I could eat a horse* means that the speaker is extremely hungry, not that she could actually eat a horse. Find the hyperbole in paragraph 3, and write it on the line below. Then, explain what you think it means.

   _____

   _____

2. Why do you think Mr. Vasquez says they should look for a trail that isn't too wooded and that has open areas and some water?

   _____

   _____

3. Find one sentence that shows that Mr. Vasquez is knowledgeable about birding.

   _____

   _____

4. Name two birds that Jaya and the Vasquezes saw on their walk.

   _____

5. Why is a bird's shape often a better clue to identifying it than its color?

   _____

   _____

6. Do you think that Olivia and Jaya will want to go birding again? Why or why not?

   _____

   _____

Bird Garden

What other living creatures might be attracted to a garden?

1   Olivia and Jaya sat at a table in the library with books spread out around them. They each had a notebook and a pen for recording interesting information about hummingbirds. Jaya's mom had allotted a portion of her garden for the girls to use as a hummingbird garden that summer. They couldn't wait to start planting, but they wanted to make sure they knew as much as possible about the tiny creatures before they began.

2   "Have you found anything yet that says how many species of hummingbirds there are?" asked Jaya.

3   Olivia nodded. "There are more than 300 species," she marveled. "The smallest one is the bee hummingbird, which lives in Cuba. It's just a little over two inches long and weighs only about a tenth of an ounce!"

4   "I'd love to see one," replied Jaya, "but I don't think there is much chance of us attracting one here in Colorado. How big are the ones that we might see in this area?"

5   "They're actually not too much bigger," said Olivia, turning the page in her book. "They only measure about four inches long. Their wings beat about 80 times per minute. The beating of their wings makes a humming noise, which is how they got their name. Their hearts beat more than 1,200 times per minute. Do you have any idea how that compares to the human heartbeat?" asked Olivia.

6   "Well, we took our heart rates in gym a few weeks ago. I think mine was about 65 beats per minute," said Jaya.

7   "Unbelievable," said Olivia shaking her head. "Okay, have we figured out how to attract these little hummers to our garden?"

8   It took Jaya a moment to locate the book she was searching for. "This one seems to have the most detailed information," she said, picking up a colorful paperback book. "It's called *Planting Your Hummingbird Garden*."

9   "I think I saw somewhere that hummingbirds are attracted to red flowers. Is that right?" asked Olivia.

10   Jaya nodded. "That's why hummingbird feeders are usually red. We should be able to find a simple, inexpensive one at a garden center. We just fill it with a mixture of four parts water to one part sugar. The book says that it's easiest to dissolve the sugar in hot or boiling water."

11   "I'm going to start a list of plants that hummingbirds like," said Olivia. "We know that red flowers appeal to them, and I remember reading that they like long, tube-shaped flowers too," she added. "I wonder if that's because of how long and thin their beaks are."

12   "You're right," said Jaya. "Other birds can't reach the sweet nectar in long, thin flowers. Neither can bees. That means that hummingbirds don't have much competition for the meals they get from those flowers. That's pretty important because they need to eat about every 10 minutes or so. They use up a lot of energy hovering over flowers, so they need to replenish it often."

13   "Do you think we're ready to ask my dad to take us to the nursery?" asked Olivia, beginning to gather up the books on the table.

14   "I think we're as ready as we're going to be," replied Jaya, her eyes dancing with excitement. "We'll just have to learn the rest from experience!"

Vocabulary Skills

Write the words from the story that have the meanings below.

1. distributed; set aside

   _____
   Par. 1

2. filled with surprise or astonishment

   _____
   Par. 3

3. to change from a solid to a liquid

   _____
   Par. 10

4. attraction

   _____
   Par. 11

5. staying in one place in the air

   _____
   Par. 12

6. to refill

   _____
   Par. 12

Find the compound words from the selection that contain the words below.

7. bird _____
   Par. 1

8. heart _____
   Par. 5

9. back _____
   Par. 8

The prefix **ir-** means *not*. Write the meaning of each word below. Then, use it in a sentence.

10. irregular _____

    _____

11. irresponsible _____

    _____

12. irresistible _____

    _____

Reading Skills

1. Check the phrase that best describes the author's purpose.

   _____ to entertain

   _____ to instruct

   _____ to persuade

2. Number the events below to show the order in which they happened.

   _____ Jaya says they'll have to learn the rest from experience.

   _____ Olivia began to gather up the books on the table.

   _____ Jaya's gym class took their heart rates.

   _____ Olivia tells Jaya that there are more than 300 species of hummingbird.

   _____ Olivia said she would start a list of plants that hummingbirds like.

3. How did hummingbirds get their name?

   _____

4. Why were Jaya and Olivia researching hummingbirds?

   _____

5. Why are hummingbird feeders usually red?

   _____

6. If you added one-quarter cup of sugar to a hummingbird feeder, how much water would you need to add?

   _____

7. How often do hummingbirds need to eat?

   _____

An Ancient Migration

Why do thousands of cranes stop at Nebraska's Platte River every spring?

1   A large flock of birds rising up to fill the sky can be a breathtaking sight, but imagine a place where you might see hundreds of thousands of birds all at once. For six weeks each spring, nearly 500,000 sandhill cranes stop along the Platte River in Nebraska as they make their annual northern migration. This unique, natural occurrence has happened for thousands of years and attracts large crowds of people each year to witness its beauty.

2   The sandhill crane has been in existence longer than any other crane. Fossil records show that they have been around for ten million years! Sandhill cranes stand nearly four feet tall and are mostly gray except for a bit of red on top of their heads. They also have a long, pointed bill and white feathers on the sides of their faces.

3   The most distinctive features of the sandhill crane can be seen when they fly. With long legs and a long neck extending out from their bodies, cranes create a graceful sight as they glide across the sky.

4   During the winter, sandhill cranes live in the wetter parts of Texas, New Mexico, and northern Mexico. Marshes and bogs provide the perfect habitat because the shallowness allows cranes to stand right in the middle of the water. This way they can easily forage for plants, insects, and fish. Because they eat both plants and animals, cranes are considered omnivorous. When sandhill cranes stop along the Platte River, their main food source is corn that can be found in the surrounding fields. Farmers benefit from the cranes because the birds help clean the fields for the next round of crops.

5   With the arrival of spring, cranes begin migrating north to their summer homes in Canada, Alaska, and even Siberia. Their flight pattern takes them across the central plains of the United States. For the most part these are arid states, but the Platte River provides a large area of shallow water that is perfect for the

cranes. In addition, the Platte is located approximately at the midpoint in the cranes' journey. Thousands and thousands of cranes land to take a break and socialize at this ideal resting place.

6   Originally called *Nebraskier*, an Oto word meaning *flat water*, the Platte was renamed by a French explorer because *platte* means *flat* in French. Its significance is not only for the birds. As Europeans traveled westward across the country, the Platte River was an important landmark. Both the Oregon Trail and the Mormon Trail ran alongside it.

7   If you are interested in traveling to see the cranes, Rowe Sanctuary in Gibbon, Nebraska, is one of the best places for viewing them. Run by the National Audubon Society, Rowe Sanctuary works for the conservation of the cranes and other migratory birds that stop along the Platte. They also provide blinds so visitors can watch the hundreds of thousands of sandhill cranes that land there without disturbing them.

Vocabulary Skills

Write the words from the passage that have the meanings below.

1. occurring once each year

   _____
   Par. 1

2. observe

   _____
   Par. 1

3. unusual; setting something apart from others

   _____
   Par. 3

4. to search for food

   _____
   Par. 4

5. dry

   _____
   Par. 5

6. perfect

   _____
   Par. 5

Read each pair of words listed below. If the words are synonyms, write **S** on the line. If the words are antonyms, write **A** on the line.

7. _____ graceful   clumsy

8. _____ important   significant

9. _____ shallow   deep

10. _____ unique   unusual

Reading Skills

1. Why are sandhill cranes classified as omnivorous?

   _____

2. The selection says that Rowe Sanctuary provides blinds for visitors. What do you think this means?

   _____

3. Where do sandhill cranes live during the winter?

   _____

4. What attracts the cranes to Platte River?

   _____

5. Check the sentence that best states the main idea of the passage.

   _____ Every spring, thousands of sandhill cranes stop at Nebraska's Platte River during their northern migration.

   _____ The most distinctive features of sandhill cranes are their long necks and legs.

   _____ Rowe Sanctuary in Gibbon, Nebraska, is one of the best places for viewing sandhill cranes.

Write **F** before the sentences that are facts. Write **O** before the sentences that are opinions.

6. _____ The summer homes of sandhill cranes are in places like Canada and Alaska.

7. _____ There is nothing as beautiful as a sandhill crane taking flight.

8. _____ Sandhill cranes like the environment of marshes and bogs.

9. _____ The best place to view sandhill cranes is Rowe Sanctuary.

10. _____ Large numbers of people come to watch the cranes migrate every spring.

A Trip to the Smithsonian

How will Ms. DeJohn's class decide which museums to visit during a class trip to the Smithsonian?

1   Ms. DeJohn stood at the front of the room. "Okay, everyone," she began, "as you all know, we'll be leaving for Washington, D.C. on Monday. We are going to spend some time this morning discussing what you would like to see when we visit the Smithsonian Institution. It will be possible for us to see only a fraction of all the Smithsonian has to offer, so we need to make some decisions about our priorities.

2   "We've done a little research as a class about the wide array of topics that the Smithsonian addresses in their museums. I know that during your free time many of you have also done some additional research on the Smithsonian's Web site."

3   Ty raised his hand. "How many museums are we going to have time to see?" he asked.

4   "That's a good question, Ty," replied Ms. DeJohn. "We're going to choose four museums. I'd like to hear some of your suggestions. What interests you most at the Smithsonian?"

5   "Can we go to the National Museum of Natural History?" asked Emma, consulting her notebook. "I'd like to see the dinosaur skeletons there."

6   "I want to see Anita and Arabella," said Calvin.

7   "Who?" asked Emma, turning around to look at Calvin.

8   "Anita and Arabella," he repeated. "They're the space spiders. A student wanted to know if spiders could spin webs in space, so NASA sent two spiders into space on *Skylab II*. Anita's and Arabella's bodies are housed at the National Air and Space Museum."

9   Ms. DeJohn began to list the students' suggestions on the board.

10   "If we go to the National Zoo," said Deepak, "we can see the three Sumatran tiger cubs. Only a few hundred of these tigers still in exist in the wild, and they all live in Indonesia. Also the giant pandas, Mei Xiang and Tian Tian, are on loan from the China Wildlife Conservation Association. I think that getting to see them in person would be really amazing."

11   "I'd like to go to the Museum of African Art," said Imani. "My parents emigrated from Kenya when they were children, but I've never been there to visit. My family collects African art, so I'd like to learn more about it."

12   "I think we should go to the National Museum of American History," said Chris. "They have a cool exhibit on the Information Age. It has some of the very first computers and even has some of Alexander Bell's telephones and Samuel Morse's telegraph machines."

13   "I like the idea of the American History Museum, too," agreed Emma. "They have a 'hands on history' room where you can actually try things from history, like sending a telegraph or riding an old-fashioned high-wheeled bicycle."

14   Ms. DeJohn smiled at the class. "I must say that I am extremely impressed by how knowledgeable you all are. You've done your research. Now, all we have to do is take a vote, and we'll be on our way to the Smithsonian!"

Vocabulary Skills

Write **S** if the possessive word is singular. Write **P** if it is plural.

1. _____ students' suggestions

2. _____ Ms. DeJohn's list

3. _____ spiders' webs

4. _____ the exhibit's location

5. _____ the pandas' cage

In each row, circle the word that does not belong.

6. rare   unusual   typical   uncommon

7. portion   fraction   part   whole

8. emigrate   visit   move   relocate

Reading Skills

1. Check the line beside the word or words that best describe what type of selection this is.

    _____ fiction

    _____ autobiography

    _____ biography

2. How can you tell that Ms. DeJohn's class is excited about their trip to the Smithsonian?

    _____

    _____

3. Why can't the class visit all of the Smithsonian's museums during their trip to Washington, D.C.?

    _____

    _____

4. What does Chris want to see at the National Museum of American History?

    _____

5. What problem does Ms. DeJohn's class have at the beginning of the story? How do they resolve it?

    _____

    _____

6. Who are Anita and Arabella?

    _____

7. Why do you think it might be interesting to visit a "hands on history" exhibit?

    _____

    _____

Study Skills

Write the name of the reference source you could use to answer each question below.

dictionary	thesaurus
atlas	encyclopedia

1. Where is Indonesia?

    _____

2. How does the telegraph work?

    _____

3. What does the root *tele* mean?

    _____

4. What is another word for *additional*?

    _____

The Mega-Museum

What are some different types of museums you have visited?

1   The Smithsonian Institution in Washington, D.C, covers so many subjects and contains so many objects that you would have to call it a super-museum. In fact, its collection of artifacts and memorabilia is so vast—more than 143 million items—the Smithsonian needs 17 separate museums to hold everything! Even more incredible is that the museums are free to the public because the institute is funded and managed by the Unites States government. Even though the Smithsonian is an American institution, it was because of an Englishman's generosity that it exists today.

2   In 1829, wealthy British scientist James Smithson died and passed his enormous fortune on to his nephew Henry Hungerford. However, Smithson stated in his will that if Henry died without having any children, all the money would be donated to the U.S. government. He wanted the government to establish an institution "for the increase and diffusion of knowledge."

3   As it turned out, Hungerford did not have any heirs, so the money—$500,000 in 1835, which would be equal to nearly $9,000,000 today—came overseas to America. Congress debated for many years about how exactly the money should be used, but in 1846 President James Polk signed a bill into law that founded the institution.

4   Today, almost 24 million people visit the Smithsonian museums each year, including the National Museum of Natural History, the National Portrait Gallery, the National Museum of American Indians, and the Anacostia Museum for African American History and Culture. The Smithsonian also runs the National Zoological Park. Among the zoo's 3,600 animals are two giant pandas, an endangered species that is rarely exhibited anywhere outside of China.

5   Another part of the Smithsonian Institution is the National Museum of American History, which covers all aspects of our history and culture. The museum displays fun artifacts, including sports memorabilia like Michael Jordan's basketball jersey, Muhammad Ali's boxing robe, and the goggles Gertrude Ederle wore when she swam across the English Channel.

6   There are also serious exhibits, like "The Price of Freedom," which shows objects from the wars in which the United States was involved. Among the many important artifacts you can see at this museum is the original Star Spangled Banner. This unique flag is the one that flew above Fort McHenry and inspired Francis Scott Key to write our national anthem.

7   One of the most popular Smithsonian sites is the National Air and Space Museum. This is where you can see the *Spirit of St. Louis*, the plane Charles Lindbergh flew across the Atlantic Ocean. The museum also houses the Wright brothers' airplane from 1903, as well as the *Columbia* space module, which landed on the moon carrying Neil Armstrong and Buzz Aldrin. You can even see a rock that was brought back from the moon!

Vocabulary Skills

Write the words from the passage that have the meanings below.

1. objects that are worth remembering

   _____
   Par. 1

2. enormous; wide-reaching

   _____
   Par. 1

3. financially supported

   _____
   Par. 1

4. the act of scattering or spreading out

   _____
   Par. 2

5. moved to action

   _____
   Par. 6

Circle the homophone that correctly completes each sentence below.

6. Henry Hungerford did not have an
   _____ to whom he could leave
   his wealth. (heir, air)

7. James Smithson _____ on his
   fortune to his nephew. (past, passed)

8. The Smithsonian is located in our nation's
   _____. (capital, capitol)

Divide the words below into syllables using a slash (/).

9. a m p l e

10. n o b le

11. g e n t l e

12. s i m p l e

Reading Skills

1. Approximately how many items are there in the Smithsonian's collection?

   _____

   _____

2. Do you think that the Smithsonian Institution will continue to accumulate more artifacts? Why or why not?

   _____

   _____

3. How is the Smithsonian's National Zoological Park different from its other museums?

   _____

   _____

4. What body of government decided how Smithson's money would be used?

   _____

   _____

5. Name two items you could find displayed in the National Museum of American History.

   _____

   _____

6. Does this selection take place in reality, or is it a fantasy? How can you tell?

   _____

   _____

7. Check the word or words that best describe what type of passage this is.

   _____ how-to

   _____ informative

   _____ biography

Always Have Hope

What are some precious stones besides diamonds?

1   What do you think is the most valuable piece of jewelry in the world? It depends on what standards the jewelry is judged by, but if you guessed the Hope diamond, there is a good chance you would be right.

2   The Hope diamond is an unusual blue-gray gem that is believed to have been mined in Golconda, India. The French jeweler Jean-Baptiste Tavernier bought a 112-carat stone, which he brought home to France. (A carat is a unit of weight for measuring the size of precious stones. It is equivalent to 200 milligrams.) Historians believe that King Louis XIV purchased the diamond in 1668 as part of the French crown jewels. The diamond was eventually recut, and a large portion of it, called the French Blue, disappeared in a robbery in 1792.

3   No one knows for certain the path of the diamond after its theft. However, a similar but smaller diamond was recorded as being part of the collection of a man named Henry Philip Hope. No record exists to verify where Hope got the diamond or how much he paid for it.

4   Relatives inherited the diamond after Hope's death. It was passed along through several generations when Lord Francis Hope decided to sell the diamond to pay off his debts. Subsequent owners also were driven to sell the diamond at times when they were in need of the money it would bring.

5   In 1912, the Hope diamond finally found a semi-permanent home with a woman by the name of Evalyn Walsh McLean. She had the stone reset among 16 pear-shaped white diamonds. Then, it was placed on a necklace that was strung with 45 smaller diamonds.

6   In 1949, after Mrs. McLean's death, the Hope diamond was sold to a well-known jeweler and diamond dealer named Harry Winston, in order to settle Mrs. McLean's debts. Winston exhibited the famous diamond at many events, but he never sold it. Instead, he decided to donate it to the Smithsonian Institution in 1958. How did Winston transport the fine piece of jewelry? By armored truck? Via special delivery, with the assistance of many security officers? No, Winston just chose to send it through the United States Postal Service!

7   Ever since then, the Hope diamond has been part of the Smithsonian Institution's National Museum of Natural History. Because of its size, 45.52 carats, and its unusual blue coloring, it is breathtaking to see in person. It also contains a phosphorescence that is uncommon in gemstones. When the Hope diamond is exposed to ultraviolet light, it will glow red for a few seconds.

8   It is no surprise that the Hope Diamond is the most popular exhibit in the museum. It has been seen by millions of visitors who are intrigued by the stone's mysterious history and the legends that the owners will be the victim of great misfortune. Everyone seems to want to catch a glimpse of this mysterious, sparkling beauty.

Vocabulary Skills

Write the words from the passage that match the abbreviations below.

1. mg. _____
   Par. 2

2. Nat'l _____
   Par. 7

3. UV _____
   Par. 7

The prefix **re-** means *again*. For example, *restart* means *to start again*. Underline the word with a prefix in each sentence, and then write the word's meaning on the line.

4. The diamond Tavernier bought was recut.

   _____

5. Mrs. McLean wanted her diamond to be reset.

   _____

6. Throughout history, the Hope diamond has been resold many times.

   _____

Reading Skills

1. On the lines below, write a summary for paragraph 5.

   _____

   _____

2. What happens when the Hope diamond is exposed to ultraviolet light?

   _____

3. According to legend, what happens to owners of the Hope diamond?

   _____

4. How did Harry Winston send the Hope diamond to the Smithsonian Institution?

   _____

5. Who owned the Hope diamond before Harry Winston?

   _____

6. Number the events below to show the order in which they happened.

   _____ Mrs. McLean had the Hope diamond reset.

   _____ Lord Francis Hope sold the Hope diamond.

   _____ Harry Winston donated the Hope diamond to the Smithsonian Institution.

   _____ Jean-Baptiste Tavernier traveled to India.

   _____ The French Blue diamond was stolen in a robbery of the French crown jewels.

Study Skills

Look at the following dictionary entry. Then, answer the questions that follow.

record (rek′ urd) (*noun*) 1. a disk on which music is recorded 2. a written history of something
(rē kŏ rd′) (*verb*) to store sound or pictures for later use

1. Which syllable is stressed when the word *record* is used as a noun?

   _____

2. What part of speech is *record* when it is used to mean *a disk on which music is recorded*?

   _____

Flying into History

Have you ever flown in a plane?

1   When you turn on the television or read a magazine, celebrities are everywhere. Although fame and the media play such major roles in our lives today, it has not always been that way. Eighty years ago, radio and movies were just beginning to have that kind of effect on Americans. Many historians agree that Charles Lindbergh was one of the first major celebrities, or superstars.

2   Lindbergh was born in Detroit, Michigan, in 1902, but he grew up in Little Falls, Minnesota. As a child, he was very interested in how things worked, so when he reached college, he pursued a degree in engineering. At the age of 20, however, the allure of flying captured Lindbergh's imagination. He quit school and moved to Nebraska where he learned to be a pilot. Soon after, Lindbergh bought his own plane and traveled the nation performing aerial stunts.

3   In 1924, Lindbergh became more serious about flying. He joined the United States military and graduated first in his pilot class. Lindbergh used this additional training to get a job as an airmail pilot, flying out of St. Louis, Missouri.

4   During the same time, a wealthy hotel owner named Raymond Orteig was offering a generous award to the first pilot who could fly nonstop from New York City to Paris, France. The Orteig Prize was worth $25,000—a large amount even by today's standards.

5   Lindbergh knew he had the skills to complete the flight, but not just any plane was capable of flying that far for that long. Working with an aviation company from San Diego, California, and with financial help from the city of St. Louis, Lindbergh got a customized airplane that could make the journey.

6   On May 20, 1927, Charles Lindbergh took off from Roosevelt Field in New York City and arrived the next day at an airstrip outside Paris. Named in honor of his sponsor, *The Spirit of St. Louis* carried Lindbergh across the Atlantic Ocean and into the record books. He became a national hero and a huge celebrity.

7   When he returned to the United States, Lindbergh rode in a ticker-tape parade held to celebrate his accomplishment. He also received a Medal of Honor, the highest United States military decoration. A very popular dance was even named for Charles Lindbergh—the Lindy Hop. Today, *The Spirit of St. Louis* is kept at the Smithsonian Institute's National Air and Space Museum in Washington, D.C.

Vocabulary Skills

Write the words from the passage that have the meanings below.

1. agencies of mass communication, such as news organizations

   _____
   Par. 1

2. tried to achieve; worked toward

   _____
   Par. 2

3. attraction

   _____
   Par. 2

4. of or in the air

   _____
   Par. 2

5. built to meet specific needs or according to specific guidelines

   _____
   Par. 5

Find the states in the passage that match the abbreviations below.

6. MI _____

7. MN _____

8. NE _____

9. MO _____

Read each word below. Then, write the letter of its antonym on the line beside the word.

10. _____ generous   **a.** minor

11. _____ wealthy   **b.** everywhere

12. _____ major   **c.** stingy

13. _____ nowhere   **d.** poor

Reading Skills

1. Check the word or words that best describe what type of passage this is.

   _____ historical fiction

   _____ historical nonfiction

   _____ legend

2. Check the words that best describe Charles Lindbergh.

   _____ adventurous

   _____ quiet

   _____ determined

   _____ kind

   _____ daring

3. What did Lindbergh have to do in order to win the Orteig prize?

   _____

4. Why was Lindbergh's plane named *The Spirit of St. Louis*?

   _____

5. Why do you think Lindbergh was one of America's first celebrities?

   _____

6. Where is *The Spirit of St. Louis* kept today?

   _____

7. Check the sentence that best states the main idea of the passage.

   _____ The dance called the Lindy Hop was named for Charles Lindbergh.

   _____ Lindbergh graduated first in his military pilot class.

   _____ Lindbergh, one of America's first celebrities, flew nonstop from New York City to Paris.

A Move to Safety

Will the Mahaulus have to move to stay out of the path of the Kilauea Volcano?

1   The Mahaulus sat at the kitchen table. The curtains fluttered in the gentle, fragrant breeze. The sun was shining and filled the kitchen with a warm, buttery light. It was a perfect day for having a picnic or going surfing. But in the Mahaulus' kitchen, no one seemed to be paying attention to the weather.

2   Leilani and Kala dejectedly picked at a bowl of pretzels. "Okay, girls," said Mrs. Mahaulu. "I can tell by the expressions on your faces that you have a pretty good idea of why we needed to have this family meeting." Leilani and Kala exchanged looks and slowly nodded.

3   "Your mom and I have been having many conversations lately about the possibility of moving," said Mr. Mahaulu. "We were hoping that it wouldn't come to this, but we don't see any alternative."

4   "But Dad," protested Kala, "Kilauea has been an active volcano since 1983! Nothing has happened to us or to our house yet. I know we'll be safe here."

5   "You're right in saying that Kilauea has been active for a long time, Kala," said Mrs. Mahaulu. "But your dad and I are concerned about all the recent evacuations. Even though we've been safe up to this point, there is no way to guarantee that a larger eruption isn't imminent."

6   "Mom, you've said yourself that the government's warning systems are efficient and effective. Doesn't that count for anything?" asked Leilani. "This is our home. I can't even remember living anywhere else!" she added, fighting back tears.

7   Leilani's mom put an arm around her daughter's shoulder. "This isn't going to be easy on any of us," she said. "Dad and I love this house, too. We have so many happy memories here. But we're tired of living with such uncertainty. The most important thing in the world to us is that our family stays safe."

8   Mr. Mahaulu nodded. "Volcanoes are a fact of life in Hawaii," he said. "I'm willing to accept that. I've never wanted to live anywhere else. But there are places in Hawaii where we'll feel safer. We'll have to give up our house, but you know as well as I do that home is wherever we go as a family. We'll make new memories, and we'll find things to love about our new home."

9   The girls were quiet for a moment as they considered what it would mean to move. "There are so many things I'll miss here," said Kala quietly.

10   "We all will," said Mrs. Mahaulu. "But one of the places that your dad and I have looked at has much more room for a garden than we have here. Another place is only a few minutes walk to the beach."

11   Kala and Leilani couldn't help smiling when they heard that. They both spent every spare minute they had surfing. If their parents told them that they could actually live in the water, they would have been perfectly happy.

12   Mr. Mahaulu walked around to the other side of the table. He put one large hand on each of his daughter's shoulders. "I'm proud of you two," he said. "Thank you for trying to understand why this is so important to your mom and me."

13   Leilani and Kala smiled and leaned back against their dad. He was right; home was wherever the family was.

Vocabulary Skills

Write the words from the story that have the meanings below.

1. gloomily; in a depressed way

   _____
   Par. 2

2. certain to happen

   _____
   Par. 5

3. without wasting time or energy

   _____
   Par. 6

4. producing the desired effect

   _____
   Par. 6

5. extra

   _____
   Par. 11

Write the idiom from paragraph 6 on the line next to its meaning.

6. trying not to cry _____

Write **S** if the possessive word is singular. Write **P** if it is plural.

7. _____ the Mahaulus' house

8. _____ the family's memories

9. _____ the girls' expressions

10. _____ the volcano's eruption

11. _____ the government's system

Find a synonym in the story for each of the words below.

12. option _____
    Par. 3

13. protected _____
    Par. 4

14. attempting _____
    Par. 12

Reading Skills

1. Why do Mr. and Mrs. Mahaulu think that the family needs to move?

   _____

   _____

2. Mr. Mahaulu says that volcanoes are a fact of life in Hawaii. What does he mean?

   _____

   _____

3. What problem do the Mahaulus have in the story?

   _____

   _____

4. Find a sentence in the story showing that one or both of the girls are not enthusiastic about moving.

   _____

   _____

5. What arguments to Leilani and Kala use to try to persuade their parents not to move?

   _____

   _____

   _____

6. Check the phrase that best describes the author's purpose.

   _____ to instruct

   _____ to persuade

   _____ to entertain

Home, Sweet Home

What is the strangest place you can think of to live?

1 Most people feel a strong attachment to their homes. It is not uncommon for people to do everything they can to protect their belongings and the place they call home from danger. But how far would you be willing to go? Would you choose to live in a place that was in a constant state of danger?

2 This isn't a hard question for Jack Thompson to answer. He lives in one of the most dangerous places on earth, but it's just home to him. Thompson lives in Hawaii near Kilauea, one of the most active volcanoes in the world. He owns a home in a subdivision called *Royal Gardens*. It is different than subdivisions that might be familiar to you. Thompson is the only resident. Everyone else evacuated more than 20 years before, when Kilauea began erupting in 1983.

3 Thompson has become accustomed to living in close quarters with the volcano. The flow of the 2,000-degree lava that eventually consumed many of the homes in Thompson's neighborhood no longer astonishes him. He still has a healthy respect for the power of Kilauea, but he does not live every day in fear. After all, it was Thompson's choice to stay in his home even though the environment he was used to changed so drastically.

4 Thompson's home is completely encompassed by the products of lava flow. Portions of it have cooled enough to allow Thompson a way out, either on foot or by motorcycle. However, his path is unreliable. Bubbling lava lies just below the surface of rock that Thompson crosses. Sometimes, it's hot enough to melt the rubber on his shoes. At any time, a sudden crack can open up, revealing the red-hot dangerous liquid. Thompson knows that he needs to keep moving because it is unsafe to linger for long on the quickly changing surface.

5 It takes an hour for Thompson to travel three miles over the unsteady rock. When he leaves his home to get supplies, he must be sure to purchase all the essentials because he never knows when he may be trapped for a period of time by a fresh lava flow. Thompson does not have a telephone line or electricity, so he has learned how to function using solar power, gas appliances, and rainwater that he collects and stores.

6 There is no doubt that the life Thompson leads isn't for everyone. But he loves the natural beauty of his home, and he even likes the isolation that comes with living in such an inaccessible location. Thompson runs the Lava-Side Inn, a bed-and-breakfast where adventurous guests can pay about $100 dollars a night to sleep in the path of an active volcano. But as you might imagine, Thompson's guests are few and far between. In the meantime, he goes about the business of daily life, happy to have had another day in his tropical paradise home.

Vocabulary Skills

Circle the word that best completes each sentence below.

1. Jack Thompson has become
   _____ to living in the path of
   an active volcano.

   related   accustomed   furious

2. Thompson enjoys living in a beautiful and
   _____ area.

   terrifying   common   remote

3. Thompson uses several _____
   energy sources.

   alternative   expensive   unrealistic

The suffix **-ous** means *full of*. For example,
joyous means *full of joy*. Write the definition of
the underlined word in each sentence.

4. Thompson must always be <u>cautious</u> of
   where he steps.

   _____

5. Thompson's story has become <u>famous</u>
   because it is so unusual.

   _____

6. Most people would feel <u>nervous</u> living in
   Jack Thompson's home.

   _____

Reading Skills

1. How is Royal Gardens different than other
   subdivisions?

   _____

2. What does it mean to live "in close
   quarters" with the volcano?

   _____

3. Why do you think that Thompson refused
   to move when everyone else sought shelter
   in safer places?

   _____

   _____

4. Check the sentence below that is the best
   summary for paragraph 3.

   _____ The lava that flows near Thompson's
   home averages about 2,000 degrees.

   _____ Thompson respects the power of the
   volcano but has become used to
   living so close to it.

   _____ The lava consumed many homes in
   Thompson's neighborhood.

Write **T** before the sentences that are true. Write
F before the sentences that are false.

5. _____ Kilauea stopped erupting about ten
   years ago.

6. _____ Thompson collects and stores
   rainwater.

Study Skills

A library's reference system can help you find a
book. Use the information below to answer the
questions that follow.

Call No:	866. 94 GI
Author:	Gilchrist, Alexander
Title:	Unusual Homes: People Who Live in Extreme Places
Publisher:	Hayberry Press, 2005

1. What is the author's last name?

   _____

2. In what year was the book published?

   _____

Moving Mountains

Where are most of the world's volcanoes located?

1   Have you ever heard of the *Ring of Fire*? It might sound like something straight out of science fiction, but it is a real place. The Ring of Fire is the name used by scientists to describe an area where frequent volcanic eruptions and earthquakes take place. In fact, about 75 percent of the world's 1,900 active and dormant, or inactive, volcanoes are located there.

2   In some parts of the world, giant pieces of Earth's crust, called *plates*, are constantly in motion. They collide and slowly slide over, under, and past one another. The Ring of Fire is located at the juncture of the Pacific plate with several other plates. The Ring of Fire is an arc-shaped region that runs along the coast of North and South America, along the eastern edge of Asia, across Alaska's Aleutian Islands, and along the coast of New Zealand in the South Pacific.

3   Sometimes, plates move past one another without creating much of a disturbance. Other times, when two plates collide, an earthquake occurs. This is exactly what happens at the well-known San Andreas Fault in California, and it is why earthquakes are so common in that part of the country.

4   Even though the plates move relatively slowly, at about the same rate that human fingernails grow, the friction they create as they slide into one another produces a great deal of energy. The heat from inside Earth is strong enough to melt rock and turn it into magma, or molten rock. Eventually, the magma rises because it is lighter, or less dense, than the rocky material that surrounds it. When it reaches the surface, it becomes known as lava and forms volcanoes.

5   The presence of dissolved gases in the magma determines whether or not the eruption will be explosive. Picture a bottle of soda that has been shaken. When the bottle is opened, the gases cause the liquid to explode from the bottle

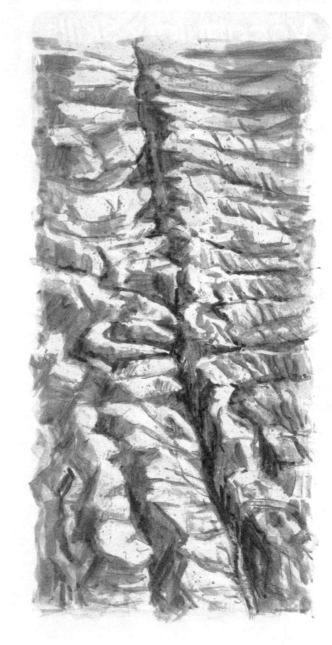

with force. In the same way, volcanoes that have a high concentration of gases will also explode with greater force.

6   Although most people view volcanoes as enormous and potentially dangerous mountains, scientists see them as temporary structures on earth's surface. They may not change much over the course of a lifetime, or even several lifetimes. Still, scientists know that over time volcanoes will move and shift, rise and fall with the movement of Earth's plates.

Vocabulary Skills

Write the words from the passage that have the meanings below.

1. fiction in which an element of science plays an important role; it often takes place in the future

   _____
   Par. 1

2. without stopping; all the time

   _____
   Par. 2

3. to crash or strike together

   _____
   Par. 2

4. the place where two things come together

   _____
   Par. 2

5. the rubbing together of two objects or surfaces

   _____
   Par. 4

6. heavy; having the parts packed tightly together

   _____
   Par. 4

Read each pair of words listed below. If the words are synonyms, write **S** on the line. If the words are antonyms, write **A** on the line.

7. _____ frequent   uncommon

8. _____ huge   enormous

9. _____ strong   powerful

10. _____ rise   fall

Words that have a single middle consonant are usually divided into syllables before the consonant. For example, *e/vil* or *o/pen*. Divide the words below into syllables using a slash *(/)*.

11. e r u p t

12. a l o n g

13. o v e r

Reading Skills

1. What is one difference between the way that scientists view volcanoes and most other people view them?

   _____
   _____
   _____

2. For what reason is the San Andreas Fault well known?

   _____
   _____

3. The author compares the rate at which Earth's plates move with something that is more familiar. What is the other element in the comparison?

   _____

4. Name two continents that border the Ring of Fire.

   _____

5. What percentage of the world's volcanoes are located in the Ring of Fire?

   _____

6. Why does magma rise to the surface?

   _____
   _____
   _____

7. What purpose would a reader have for reading this passage?

   _____ for pleasure or entertainment

   _____ for information

   _____ to learn how to solve a problem

Watery Giants

What are the oceans' most destructive waves, and what causes them?

1   If you have ever gone swimming in an ocean or in one of the Great Lakes, you may have some idea how powerful waves can be. Waves that are only a few feet tall hold enough energy to knock you off your feet. Now, try to imagine the power of a wave that is 50 feet tall and more than 100 miles wide, traveling at speeds of as much as 500 miles per hour. It's easy to see how such a wave could devastate an entire town.

2   The name for these enormous waves is *tsunami*, which means *harbor wave* in Japanese. Tsunamis are caused by a disturbance in the ocean, such as an earthquake or undersea volcanic eruption. Although underwater disturbances are the most common cause of tsunamis, they can also occur if a large meteorite crashes into the ocean.

3   Tsunamis may be relatively small when they are far out at sea. However, as they draw closer and closer to shore, they gather power. One sign of an approaching tsunami is water that recedes at the shore. This occurs because so much of the ocean water is sucked into the wave as it gathers strength.

4   Tsunamis do not consist of a single wave. One wave follows another in a series that may last several hours. A *period* is the length of time in between waves. For average wind-powered waves, a period may be about ten seconds long. Because a tsunami is so much larger, its period may be as long as an hour.

5   Tsunamis have destroyed homes, schools, and entire coastal towns in minutes. The force of a wave as it breaks can be strong enough to travel several hundred feet inland. That is exactly what happened to Hilo, a town on the island of Hawaii, in 1946. At that time, there was not yet an accurate warning system in place.

6   An earthquake registering 7.1 on the Richter scale occurred in Alaska's Aleutian Islands on April 1. About four hours later, Hawaii was struck with the first of seven waves. The waves measured between 24 and 32 feet in height and arrived at 15 to 20 minute intervals. By the time the tsunamis had run their course, 159 lives had been taken.

7   The devastation of the 1946 tsunamis led a team of scientists and government officials to create the Pacific Tsunami Warning System. They hoped that people would never again suffer such great losses because they were unaware of a tsunami's approach. They set up a system to monitor earthquakes that could cause tsunami. They also determined ways to predict the time of arrival of tsunamis so that people would have time to evacuate.

8   Unfortunately, there was no such warning system covering the Indian Ocean on December 26, 2004. An enormous earthquake took place and triggered the deadliest tsunami in history. Countries like Thailand, India, and Indonesia were especially hard hit. The loss of life was devastating, and people all around the world reached out to help the victims.

9   Plans are being made to create a global tsunami monitoring system. No system is perfect, but as technology advances, humans will learn better ways to protect themselves against some of the most incredible and powerful forces of nature.

Vocabulary Skills

Write the words from the passage that have the meanings below.

1. to ruin or destroy

   _____
   Par. 1

2. something that interrupts or alters events

   _____
   Par. 2

3. moves back; moves away from

   _____
   Par. 3

4. periods of time in between events

   _____
   Par. 6

5. watch; closely observe

   _____
   Par. 7

Read each word below. Then, write the letter of its abbreviation in the space beside it.

6. _____ hour   **a.** m.p.h.

7. _____ Alaska   **b.** HI

8. _____ miles per hour **c.** AK

9. _____ Hawaii   **d.** hr.

Reading Skills

1. Check the line beside the word that best describes what type of passage this is.

   _____ biography

   _____ informational

   _____ fiction

2. What does the word *tsunami* mean in Japanese?

   _____

3. What are two possible causes of tsunamis?

   _____

4. What is one way in which tsunamis are different than other waves?

   _____

5. What is one positive effect of the 1946 tsunamis?

   _____

6. Name three countries that were affected by the tsunami of 2004.

   _____

7. Why didn't the Pacific Tsunami Warning System alert people of the 2004 tsunami?

   _____

Circle the word that best completes each sentence below.

8. Tsunamis can cause great

   _____.

   accuracy   destruction   earthquakes

9. Scientists are looking for ways to be able to better _____ the arrival of tsunamis.

   explain   control   predict

10. Tsunamis are not _____ caused by meteorites.

    frequently   oddly   powerfully

Study Skills

Use a dictionary to help you divide the words below into syllables.

1. t s u n a m i

2. g o v e r n m e n t

3. d e v a s t a t i o n

4. t e c h n o l o g y

5. e n o r m o u s

6. m e t e o r i t e

Creatures of the Night

Do you have bats in your neighborhood? If you do, at what times of day have you seen them?

1   Charley and Mattie Rosen helped their parents clean up after dinner. Charley rinsed the dishes in a tub of clean water and then handed them to his mom to be dried. Mattie gathered firewood so that they could make s'mores and tell scary stories. Mattie loved the smell of wood smoke and the taste of gooey marshmallows melting the chocolate between crisp graham crackers.

2   "How much more wood do we need, Dad?" asked Mattie, setting a small stack beside her father.

3   "I think that should last us for a while, Mattie," replied Mr. Rosen. Mattie brushed her hands on her jeans and crouched beside her dad to watch as the fire grew larger and hotter.

4   "Look at those birds!" exclaimed Charley, pointing a soapy finger at the sky. His parents and Mattie followed his finger and saw what appeared to be a flock of birds swooping out of a tree into the deep blue sky of twilight.

5   "I don't think those are birds, Charley," said Mrs. Rosen, drying her hands on a dishtowel. "I'm pretty sure they're bats. You can tell by the way they fly. See how jerky their movements are? Birds seem to fly more gracefully than bats do."

6   "Shouldn't we get into the tent?" asked Charley nervously. "Vampire bats can suck your blood, can't they?"

7   Mr. Rosen chuckled. "I don't think we have to worry too much about that. There are only a few species of vampire bats in the world, and none of them live in North America. Besides, even vampire bats don't feed on human blood."

8   "What about rabies?" asked Mattie, leaning in closer to her dad.

9   "Bats can carry rabies, but it's quite unusual," said Mrs. Rosen. "We're not going to have close contact with the bats, so it's not anything we need to worry about.

10   "Didn't I ever tell you kids about my trip to Bracken Cave when I was in college?" Mrs. Rosen asked. Mattie and Charley shook their heads, but they kept an eye on the sky.

11   "Well," said Mrs. Rosen, "I was visiting a classmate from school who lived in San Antonio, Texas. She had told me all about a place called *Bracken Cave*. About 20 million Mexican free-tailed bats go there every year to give birth and raise their young."

12   "Twenty million bats?" said Mattie and Charley incredulously.

13   Mrs. Rosen nodded. "Watching them come out of the cave at night was one of the most remarkable things I have ever seen. The entire sky seemed to fill with them. Conservationists say that the bats from Bracken Cave eat about 200 tons of insects each summer evening."

14   The Rosens sat quietly, looking up at the sky as it darkened. The fire gave off a gentle glow as they patiently waited, hoping to catch another glimpse of the bats as they set out on their evening's activities.

Vocabulary Skills

Write the words from the story that have the meanings below.

1. a group of animals that lives or travels together

   _____
   Par. 4

2. the touching of two people or objects

   _____
   Par. 9

3. with amazement and disbelief

   _____
   Par. 12

Write the idiom from paragraph 10 on the line next to its meaning.

4. watched or observed _____

   _____

Find the compound words from the selection that contain the words below.

5. fire _____
   Par. 1

6. dish _____
   Par. 5

7. mate _____
   Par. 11

Check the meaning of the underlined word.

8. Mrs. Rosen looked calmly at the bats flying overhead.

   _____ not calm

   _____ in a calm way

   _____ capable of being calm

9. Charley and Mattie were unaware of their mother's experiences with bats.

   _____ not aware

   _____ aware again

   _____ wrongly aware

Reading Skills

Mark each sentence below **F** if it is in first-person point of view and **T** if it is in third-person point of view.

1. _____ I love making s'mores!

2. _____ Charley rinsed the dishes in a tub of clean water.

3. _____ I went to San Antonio to visit a friend from college.

4. _____ Mr. Rosen said that vampire bats don't live in North America.

Write **F** before the sentences that are facts. Write **O** before the sentences that are opinions.

5. _____ Mattie gathered wood for the fire.

6. _____ Everything is more enjoyable when you are camping.

7. _____ Mexican free-tailed bats come to Bracken Cave to give birth and raise their young.

8. _____ The sky is most beautiful at dusk.

9. How do you think Mattie and Charley will feel the next time they see a bat? Why?

   _____

   _____

10. What ingredients are used to make s'mores?

    _____

11. Find one sentence that shows that Mattie enjoys camping. Write it on the lines below.

    _____

    _____

12. Where is Bracken Cave located?

    _____

Going Batty

Keep reading to learn why many people try to attract bats to their yards and neighborhoods.

1   Some animals have good reputations. Most people think of dogs as being friendly and reliable. Kittens are sweet and cuddly. Everyone loves dolphins, seals, and chimpanzees. Other animals, such as bats, do not have nearly as positive a reputation. Many people are frightened of bats and believe that the small flying creatures will become tangled in their hair or give them rabies. There are many myths and superstitions surrounding bats. All of this makes it difficult for educators to get out the word that bats are actually wonderful, useful, and amazing creatures.

2   More than 1,100 species of bats can be found in almost every region of the world, except for the extreme polar and desert regions. Bats, the only flying mammals in the world, vary in size, coloring, and habits. The smallest bat in the world has a wingspan of only two inches and weighs less than a penny. The largest bat has a wingspan of about six feet. Most bats eat insects, but some species feed on fruit, pollen, and nectar, and others eat small animals like fish, frogs, and rodents. Although many scary stories tell of vampire bats, in reality, only three species out of more than one thousand survive on the blood of other animals.

3   Bats are useful creatures. They consume large quantities of insects every evening. A single common brown bat can eat as many as 2,000 insects a night. Imagine how many more mosquito bites you would have each summer if bats were not busy patrolling the night sky.

4   In addition, some bats pollinate plants and flowers. They suck the nectar from one plant and then transfer the plant's pollen when they move on to feed from another plant. In rain forests, bats drop plant seeds as they move, which allows new plants to grow. In regions where the rain forests are in danger, bats perform a very important task, because they insure that new growth will replace plants and trees that have been cut down or destroyed.

5   Because bats are nocturnal creatures, they have the difficult task of flying and catching all their meals in total darkness. This does not present much of a problem for them, though, because they use a special technique called *echolocation*. Bats emit very high-pitched sounds that bounce off objects, no matter how small they are. Bats use the reflected sounds to form pictures in their brains of where things are located. It might not sound like a simple process, but it is obviously very effective. After all, they can find a mosquito flying through the air in complete darkness.

6   The next time you see the flutter of wings in the sky at dusk, there is no need to run for cover. Instead, think about the good deeds that bats perform for human beings and think about their incredible diversity. Maybe you'll even decide to build a bat house in your backyard to encourage the furry flying creatures to take up residence nearby.

Vocabulary Skills

Write the words from the passage that have the meanings below.

1. the ways others judge the worth or quality of something

    _____
    Par. 1

2. amounts

    _____
    Par. 3

3. active at night

    _____
    Par. 5

4. sound, light, or heat that is sent back from a surface

    _____
    Par. 5

5. having the quality of being different, or unlike others

    _____
    Par. 6

6. a place where one lives

    _____
    Par. 6

Find a synonym in the story for each of the words below.

7. trustworthy _____
    Par. 1

8. incredible _____
    Par. 1

9. eat _____
    Par. 3

10. areas _____
    Par. 4

11. total _____
    Par. 5

Write **S** if the possessive word is singular. Write **P** if it is plural.

12. _____ animals' reputations

13. _____ trees' growth

14. _____ the plant's pollen

15. _____ the bat's wings

Reading Skills

1. Explain how *echolocation* works.

    _____

    _____

2. What is the author trying to persuade the reader of in this selection?

    _____

3. How can you encourage bats to live near your home?

    _____

4. Why do you think some people are afraid of bats?

    _____

    _____

5. Write two ways in which species of bats may differ from one another.

    _____

    _____

Write **T** before the sentences that are true. Write **F** before the sentences that are false.

6. _____ Some bats pollinate plants and flowers.

7. _____ More than 3,000 species of bats exist.

8. _____ Bats are nocturnal creatures.

9. _____ The smallest bat in the world weighs less than a penny.

10. _____ Bats feed only on insects.

11. Check the phrase that best describes the author's purpose.

    _____ to instruct

    _____ to inform

    _____ to entertain

A Natural Bath

What surprise will Charley and Mattie find on the trail?

1 The Rosens woke up early, even though they would have slept in at home if their alarm clocks weren't set. There was something about camping that made them feel wide-awake and excited to start the day as soon as their eyes were open.

2 They made breakfast over the propane stove. In just a few minutes, they sat down to a meal of coffee, hot cocoa, scrambled eggs, and granola with fresh blueberries.

3 As the Rosens ate, they discussed their plans for the day. "Dad and I looked at a map last night," said Mrs. Rosen. "We found a nearby hiking trail that looks like it will be challenging but not too difficult. It has some beautiful scenic views, and best of all, there will be a surprise at the end of the trail." She and Mr. Rosen exchanged secretive glances.

4 "What kind of surprise?" asked Mattie curiously.

5 "It wouldn't be a surprise if we told you," laughed her mom. "But the sooner you two get ready to go, the sooner you'll find out."

6 An hour later, everyone was ready to leave. They drove a short distance to the trailhead, gathered their hiking gear, and set out for the day. It was a good day for spotting wildlife. The trees were filled with birds, and dragonflies flitted along the path ahead of the Rosens. They stopped when they heard a rustle in the bushes and quietly watched as two deer delicately crossed the trail.

7 After they had been hiking for about an hour, the family stopped at a clearing and ate some dried apricots and almonds Mr. Rosen had packed. The snack gave them an energy boost, and just as they were about to get up, three quails wandered into sight. Charley reached for his camera and was able to snap a photo before the birds were startled and flew away.

8 Feeling refreshed, the Rosens continued their hike. Mattie and Charley were in the midst of a heated discussion about what kind of snake they had just seen when they came to another clearing. Charley's and Mattie's eyes grew wide. They looked at their parents.

9 "Is this the surprise?" asked Mattie.

10 Mr. and Mrs. Rosen smiled as they walked over to one of the small pools. Wisps of steam rose into the air, and there was a damp, earthy smell around them. "They're hot springs," explained Mrs. Rosen, reaching down to untie her hiking boots. "The water is heated by geothermal heat, which means that the heat is produced from inside Earth."

11 "Places where there are hot springs are usually places where magma lies close to Earth's surface," added Mr. Rosen. "It heats the water, which creates the hot springs."

12 "If we had our bathing suits, could we get in the water? asked Charley.

13 Mrs. Rosen nodded. "Your bathing suits are in my backpack," she said, lowering her feet into the steaming water.

14 Charley and Mattie rummaged through the backpack looking for their suits. "This is a great surprise, Mom and Dad!" exclaimed Mattie, as she headed behind a tree to change. "I never would have guessed in a million years!"

Vocabulary Skills

Underline the compound word in each sentence. Then, write the two words that make up each compound.

1. It was a good day for spotting wildlife.

   _____   _____

2. Dragonflies flew along the trail ahead of the Rosens.

   _____   _____

3. The Rosens put fresh blueberries on their granola.

   _____   _____

Circle the homophone that correctly completes each sentence below.

4. Mr. Rosen _____ a snack for the family. (pact, packed)

5. Three quails wandered into _____. (sight, site)

6. Mrs. Rosen dangled her _____ in the water. (feat, feet)

Reading Skills

1. Number the events below to show the order in which they happened.

   _____ The Rosens drove to the trailhead.

   _____ Mrs. Rosen lowered her feet into the water.

   _____ Charley and Mattie looked for their bathing suits.

   _____ The Rosens made scrambled eggs.

   _____ Charley took a picture of the quails.

2. Find the example of hyperbole in paragraph 14, and write it on the line below. Then, explain what you think it means.

   _____

   _____

3. **Dialogue** is what a character says. The words in dialogue are always in quotation marks. On the line below, write the words that are dialogue in paragraph 13.

   _____

   _____

4. Why do you think "Charley's and Mattie's eyes grew wide" in paragraph 8?

   _____

Study Skills

Use the table below to answer the questions that follow.

Spring	Temp (°F)	Area	State
Healing Spring	86	Roanoke	Virginia
Scenic Hot Springs	122	Seattle	Washington
Baker Hot Spring	108	Concrete	Washington
Caddo Gap Springs	95	Little Rock	Arkansas
Morning Mist Springs	205	Ashton	Wyoming

1. Which hot spring has the hottest water?

   _____

2. What is the name of the spring located near Seattle, Washington?

   _____

3. Where is Caddo Gap Springs located?

   _____

A Hot Topic

Have you ever visited a natural hot spring?

1   People visiting Hot Springs, Arkansas, get to take part in a tradition that is thousands of years old. Many years before the arrival of Europeans, Native Americans used the clean, fresh, hot water that burbled to the surface of Earth. Stone artifacts found in the vicinity led archaeologists to conclude that the springs were a place for different Native American tribes to bathe, relax, trade, and hunt.

2   In 1803, the United States purchased the Hot Springs area from France as part of the Louisiana Territory. Congress wanted to preserve the 47 natural springs in the area, so in 1832 they established the Hot Spring Reservation. In 1921, the reservation was renamed Hot Springs National Park.

3   People have long believed in the healing, therapeutic effects of hot springs. Temporary bathhouses were erected over individual hot springs so that people could soak in the warm waters. They even drank the water, hoping that it would heal their ailments. During the prosperous 1920s, bathhouses were built in Arkansas to draw wealthy tourists to visit the area. The bathhouses were beautiful, ornate structures, often having marble and tile walls and floors and decorative statues and fountains.

4   Visitors would come from near and far, hoping to benefit from the spas on Bathhouse Row. Today, it is not known whether the water can truly improve health. Any benefits it has are probably due to the high concentration of minerals and the high temperature—about 143 degrees Fahrenheit—at which the water rises to Earth's surface.

5   Although hot springs are commonly found in areas where magma, or molten rock, lies close to Earth's surface, that is not the case at Hot Springs National Park. In this area of Arkansas, there are two types of porous, or absorbent, rock. The rainwater soaks into the rocks, and they slowly carry it far underground. Scientists believe that the water produced by the hot

springs today is about 4,000 years old! That's how long it takes for the rainwater to travel 2,000 to 8,000 feet into earth and eventually rise again through underground cracks and faults.

6   One of the most remarkable things about the water is that it is sterile. This characteristic is so unique that NASA scientists stored samples of moon rock in water from the hot springs while they looked for signs of life.

7   If you visit Hot Springs National Park today, you can still go to one of the original bathhouses on Bathhouse Row. There, you can bathe in the warm, odorless water and imagine people doing exactly the same thing hundreds of years ago. You can even bring a jug on your trip so that you can collect water during your stay and bring it home with you. There's no need to worry about the springs running dry—they produce an average of about 850,000 gallons of water a day.

Vocabulary Skills

Write the words from the passage that have the meanings below.

1. area

   _____
   Par. 1

2. relating to a treatment or cure

   _____
   Par. 3

3. illnesses

   _____
   Par. 3

4. beautiful and decorative

   _____
   Par. 3

5. a large amount of something in one place

   _____
   Par. 4

6. free of germs

   _____
   Par. 6

The suffix **-less** means *to be without*. For example, *fearless* means *to be without fear*. Write a word to match each definition below. Then, write a sentence using each word.

7. to be without odor _____

   _____

8. to be without use _____

   _____

9. to be without a point _____

   _____

Reading Skills

1. What benefit do people expect to gain from drinking or bathing in the hot springs?

   _____

   _____

2. When were most of the bathhouses on Bathhouse Row constructed?

   _____

   _____

3. What is the average temperature of the water?

   _____

4. How did NASA scientists use water from the hot springs?

   _____

   _____

5. Do you think the hot springs at Hot Springs National Park will ever run out of water? Explain your answer.

   _____

   _____

6. Number the events below to show the order in which they happened.

   _____ Many bathhouses were built in Hot Springs, Arkansas.

   _____ Hot Spring Reservation was renamed Hot Springs National Park.

   _____ Native Americans used the hot springs for many years before Europeans discovered them.

   _____ Hot Spring Reservation was established.

   _____ The U.S. purchased the Louisiana Territory.

Study Skills

Write the entry word you would look for in a dictionary next to each word below.

1. established _____

2. healing _____

The Little Giant

Have you ever heard of the basketball player Yao Ming?

1   There is no doubt that it is difficult to move to another country at any age. But imagine moving to a country where the language and customs are very different than those of your homeland. Now, imagine that you are the National Basketball Association's first pick, and only the third player ever to make the NBA from your country.

2   These were the expectations that Yao Ming, the Houston Rockets' basketball star, faced when he moved to Texas from Shanghai, China, at the age of 22. The stress and pressure might have proven to be too much for many young athletes, but Yao Ming's good nature and levelheaded attitude allowed him to quickly become one of the most popular and well-respected young basketball players today.

3   Yao Ming was born in China on September 12, 1980. Although he is often referred to in America by his full name, technically the order is reversed. *Yao* is his last name, or surname, and *Ming* is his first name.

4   Both of Yao's parents played basketball professionally in China. Yao's father is 6 feet 7 inches tall, and his mother is 6 feet 3 inches tall. That is probably why it didn't come as much of a surprise when Yao reached his present height of 7 feet 6 inches.

5   In spite of his height and his parents' background in professional sports, Yao was not destined to become a basketball player. His parents had hoped for a different life for their son, and Yao had not shown much interest in basketball as a small child. However, Yao was accepted into junior sports school in China. Yao's parents allowed him to go because they knew his chances of eventually being accepted by a good university would increase.

6   It turned out that Yao showed so much promise as a basketball player that he never made it to college. Today, this is one of his greatest disappointments. Yao is aware that his basketball career won't last forever, and he plans to earn his degree when he retires from basketball.

7   In the meantime, Yao has been dazzling fans with his skills on the court. During his first year in the NBA, Yao scored an average of 13.5 points, 8.2 rebounds, and 1.74 blocks per game. He earned NBA All-Rookie First Team honors. He has also made the cover of many magazines and has appeared in television commercials for several different products.

8   All the fame and success hasn't changed Yao Ming, though. He is the same generous, humble, and likable person he was before his basketball career took off and placed him in the spotlight. He is grateful for the opportunities he has had but doesn't see basketball as his only purpose in life. Yao will be remembered for his success on the basketball court, but he hopes to someday make a difference in the world off the court, too.

Vocabulary Skills

Write the words from the passage that have the meanings below.

1. sensible; having good judgment

   _____
   Par. 2

2. changed the order of

   _____
   Par. 3

3. meant to be

   _____
   Par. 5

4. gives up a career, usually at a certain age

   _____
   Par. 6

5. not speaking too highly about one's abilities or accomplishments

   _____
   Par. 8

Write the words from the story that match the abbreviations below.

6. NBA _____
   Par. 1

7. TX _____
   Par. 2

8. Sept. _____
   Par. 3

9. pts. _____
   Par. 7

Find the compound words from the selection that contain the words below.

10. land _____
    Par. 1

11. ground _____
    Par. 5

12. mean _____
    Par. 7

13. light _____
    Par. 8

Reading Skills

1. Check the word that best describes what type of passage this is.

   _____ autobiography

   _____ biography

   _____ fantasy

2. Check the words that best describe Yao Ming.

   _____ sensible

   _____ creative

   _____ athletic

   _____ rude

   _____ hardworking

3. Why weren't Yao's parents surprised when he grew to be 7 feet 6 inches tall?

   _____

   _____

4. What do you think Yao will do when he retires from his career in basketball? Explain your answer.

   _____

   _____

5. What persuaded Yao's parents to allow him to attend the junior sports school?

   _____

   _____

6. Why do you think Yao Ming gained fame and popularity so quickly?

   _____

   _____

Rolling to Victory

1 After World War II, many injured veterans returned home needing wheelchairs for mobility. These former soldiers tended to be young and mentally fit, so they were not about to let their physical disabilities make them idle. In Veteran's Association hospitals across the country, vets needed an outlet for their energy and athleticism. It was this desire for activity that gave birth to wheelchair basketball.

2 In 1946, two different chapters of the Paralyzed Veterans of America, one in California and one in New England, began hosting wheelchair basketball games in VA hospitals. Word spread about this new sport, and soon there were veterans' teams forming all over the United States and Canada. The excitement even crossed the Atlantic Ocean, and a team was formed in England. At the first PVA wheelchair basketball tournament, the original California team, the Birmingham Flying Wheels, won the series.

3 In 1948, the Flying Wheels received sponsorship to travel the U.S. and play other VA teams. The popularity of these wheelchair basketball competitions inspired the first civilian, or nonmilitary, team to form in Kansas City. They were originally called the *Kansas City Wheelchair Bulldozers,* but today they are known as the *Rolling Pioneers.*

4 The next year, a group of students at the University of Illinois, helped by the university's director of rehabilitation, developed a more organized wheelchair basketball league. They held the first National Wheelchair Basketball Association tournament in 1949. Today, the NWBA has grown to include 22 conferences with 165 teams!

5 So, what makes wheelchair basketball different than the game you usually see on television or at the school gym? Aside from a few rules concerning the wheelchairs, it is mostly the same. The most obvious difference is that to be an eligible player you must have a

physical disability that requires the use of a wheelchair.

6 However, even this requirement allows for a wide range of physical abilities with advantages and disadvantages for each player. To compensate, points are awarded to each player depending on how severe his or her disability is. Each team is allowed to have a maximum of twelve points, ensuring that teams are fairly matched.

7 Another rule that helps keep the game fair is the *physical advantage foul*. Someone with a spinal cord injury might not be able to move his or her legs, but another player might still have use of part of his or her leg. This foul rule states that all players must remain firmly seated and may not use a physical advantage to raise themselves up in the wheelchair. Three physical advantage fouls will cause the offending player to be removed from the game.

8 There are also specific requirements for the shape and size of the wheelchair, including a roll bar that protects the player if the chair tips over. During intense moments of play, it is not unusual for a player to fall out of his or her wheelchair. As long as the fallen player is not hurt and the fall does not interfere with play, the game keeps rolling!

Vocabulary Skills

Write the words from the passage that have the meanings below.

1. ability to move

   _____
   Par. 1

2. happening earlier in time

   _____
   Par. 1

3. not active or busy

   _____
   Par. 1

4. the condition of restoring to health

   _____
   Par. 4

5. qualified; fit to be chosen

   _____
   Par. 5

Write the words from the story that match the abbreviations below.

6. WWII _____
   Par. 1

7. VA _____
   Par. 1

8. PVA _____
   Par. 2

9. IL _____
   Par. 4

10. The Latin root **mob** means *move*. Find a word in paragraph 1 with the root **mob**.

    _____

11. The Latin root **act** means *do*. Find a word in paragraph 1 with the root **act**.

    _____

12. The Latin root **form** means *shape*. Find a word in paragraph 2 with the root **form**.

    _____

Reading Skills

Write **T** before the sentences that are true. Write **F** before the sentences that are false.

1. _____ The first military wheelchair basketball team was called the *Kansas City Wheelchair Bulldozers*.

2. _____ Today, there are more than 160 NWBA teams.

3. _____ The first NWBA tournament was not held until the 1990s.

4. _____ All participants in wheelchair basketball games must have a physical disability.

5. How does the physical advantage foul rule help keep the game fair?

   _____

6. Why was wheelchair basketball first invented?

   _____

7. What was the name of the original California wheelchair basketball team?

   _____

8. Why are points awarded to each player depending on the severity of his or her disability?

   _____

9. Check the phrase that best describes the author's purpose.

   _____ to persuade the reader to attend a wheelchair basketball game

   _____ to explain the origins and rules of wheelchair basketball

   _____ to instruct the reader on how to join a wheelchair basketball league

The Racing Gloves

What special equipment do you think a wheelchair athlete needs?

1   Julio and Tasha sat on the porch drinking lemonade and eating pretzels that Julio's Uncle Jorge had made earlier that morning. Tasha popped the last bite of pretzel in her mouth and dusted the salt from her hands. "Your pretzels are great," Tasha told Uncle Jorge when she saw him wheel into the doorway. "I've never eaten homemade soft pretzels before."

2   "They're easy to make," said Uncle Jorge. "Next time you come over, I'll show you and Julio how to make them," he added, maneuvering his wheelchair down the ramp that led from the front door to the porch.

3   A mail truck pulled up in front of the house, and a moment later, the postal carrier came up the front walk carrying a stack of mail and a small brown package.

4   "Who is the package from, Uncle Jorge?" asked Julio eagerly.

5   Uncle Jorge opened the box and removed a pair of odd-looking gloves from the crumpled brown wrapping paper. "I've been waiting for these," he said, trying on the gloves. He flexed his fingers back and forth several times. "I'm going to be racing in the Boston Marathon this spring," he told Tasha and Julio.

6   "I don't think I knew that the race in Boston was a marathon," said Julio, inspecting one of his uncle's gloves. "You haven't raced in a marathon before, have you?"

7   "This will be my second," said Uncle Jorge. "I've completed plenty of shorter races during the past ten years. Last year, I did my first marathon, and I qualified for the Boston Marathon. My best friend, who is a wheelchair racer too, placed third in his age group in last year's Boston Marathon. We have a friendly competition going, so that's given me incentive to stick to my training schedule."

8   "Is your racing chair very different from your everyday chair?" asked Tasha.

9   Uncle Jorge nodded. "It has two large wheels like this chair does," he said, gesturing to his wheelchair, "but it also has a third, smaller wheel in front. Sports tires are also different than my everyday tires." He grinned. "It's kind of like the difference between wearing running shoes and loafers."

10   "Do a lot of wheelchair racers compete in the Boston Marathon?" asked Julio, dipping a piece of pretzel in some spicy mustard.

11   "It's considered one of the most prestigious races," replied Uncle Jorge. "Other than the Olympic and Paralympic Games, the Boston Marathon is the only race in the world for which you have to meet a qualifying time in order to participate."

12   Tasha and Julio exchanged glances. "I wish it was closer to home so we could go along and cheer for you," said Julio.

13   Uncle Jorge looked at him thoughtfully. "Let me talk to your parents," he said. "Maybe you can drive up with Aunt Amelia and me the night before the race." He smiled at Julio and Tasha. "I'm going to need the biggest cheering section I can get!"

Vocabulary Skills

Write the words from the story that have the meanings below.

1. moving carefully and skillfully

   _____
   Par. 2

3. something that motivates a person to behave in a certain way

   _____
   Par. 7

4. highly admired and respected

   _____
   Par. 11

5. a minimum level to be reached before acceptance

   _____
   Par. 11

Find an antonym in the story for each of the words below.

6. few _____
   Par. 7

7. mild _____
   Par. 10

8. farther _____
   Par. 12

Compound words are divided into syllables between the two words that make the compound. For example, *eye/sight*. Divide the words below into syllables using a slash (/).

9. w h e e l c h a i r

10. h o m e m a d e

11. m i d d a y

12. d o o r w a y

Reading Skills

1. What analogy does Uncle Jorge make when he is talking about his everyday tires as compared to his racing tires?

   _____

2. How is a racing wheelchair different from a regular wheelchair? How are they similar?

   _____

   _____

Write **F** before the sentences that are facts. Write **O** before the sentences that are opinions.

3. _____ Uncle Jorge has completed a marathon before.

4. _____ Uncle Jorge will probably complete the marathon in less time than his friend.

5. _____ Tasha and Julio ate the pretzels Uncle Jorge baked.

6. _____ The package contained Uncle Jorge's racing gloves.

7. _____ Uncle Jorge makes the best soft pretzels.

8. Check the words that best describe Uncle Jorge.

   _____ impatient

   _____ competitive

   _____ determined

   _____ lonely

   _____ enthusiastic

Study Skills

Use the pronunciation key on the inside back cover of this book to write the words that match these pronunciations.

1. /thôt ɜ fůl lē/ _____

2. /lō͞ɜ ferz/ _____

3. /trāɜ ning/ _____

4. /mârɜ ə thon ɜ/ _____

5. /pär tis ɜ i pāt ɜ/ _____

A Reason to Run

Have you ever participated in a charity event?

1   Julio and Tasha sat on the sun-warmed grass at the park. They were stretching before they set out on their afternoon run. As they stretched, they spoke about the upcoming race. Neither Julio nor Tasha had raced before, but they had been training together for nearly three months and felt prepared.

2   "Do you have any sponsors yet?" asked Tasha. Her voice was a bit muffled as she bent over and gripped her ankles in a deep stretch.

3   "Not really," replied Julio. He stood up and leaned to one side, reaching as far as he could over his head with the opposite hand. "My parents and my grandma have both signed up. I know my aunts and uncles will help out, too, but I haven't actually asked them yet. What about you?"

4   Tasha took a quick drink from her water bottle and stood up. "I haven't asked anyone but my parents yet," she said. "I'm really nervous about asking other people to sponsor me for this race," she confessed. "I really want to run, and I want to help support the Leukemia Society, but I'm dreading the whole process of asking for sponsors."

5   Tasha and Julio started down the bike path at a medium jog. "What are you worried about?" asked Julio. "I think that people will be willing to help out a good cause. We're not asking them to buy anything. All we want is a donation to the Leukemia Society in exchange for the time and effort we put into training."

6   "I know," agreed Tasha. "It shouldn't be a big deal, but I'm just afraid that no one will want to participate, or that they'll pledge to support me and I won't be able to finish the race for some reason."

7   Julio and Tasha ran single file for a few seconds as they passed a family on roller blades. When Julio caught up to Tasha, he said, "Listen, I completely understand why it's hard for you to ask people you don't know for donations. I can help you with that part. But you have to have a little more confidence in yourself about the race. We've both been able to run the entire three miles for the last month. You're practically not even out of breath anymore when we finish. This race is going to be a piece of cake for you."

8   The two runners were quiet for a moment. The only sound was the gentle thudding of their shoes hitting the path. "You're right," said Tasha finally. "Running the race isn't going to be the hard part for me. Do you have any ideas about whom we could ask for pledges?"

9   Julio, who was starting to become a bit short of breath, nodded. "Could you ask the parents of the players on your soccer team?" he asked. "Also, the neighborhood block party is going to be next weekend. That could be a great time to ask our neighbors. Everyone will be in a good mood, so they'll probably be pretty receptive to helping us out."

10   Tasha smiled. "We make a good team, Julio," she said. "I definitely feel like I can do this now."

11   Julio smiled back. "Good," he said, picking up the pace, "because the last one to make it to the finish today has to buy ice cream on the way home!" Tasha laughed as the two friends sprinted toward the park's gates.

Vocabulary Skills

Write the words from the story that have the meanings below.

1. admitted

   _____
   Par. 4

2. not looking forward to

   _____
   Par. 4

3. a feeling of sureness in one's abilities

   _____
   Par. 7

4. open to ideas or suggestions

   _____
   Par. 9

5. raced at a high speed for a short distance

   _____
   Par. 11

6. Check the sentence in which *spoke* has the same meaning as it does in paragraph 1.

   _____ The writer spoke about her career during the school assembly.

   _____ One spoke on my bicycle wheel is broken.

7. Check the sentence in which *cause* has the same meaning as it does in paragraph 5.

   _____ My sister is selling magazines to raise money for a good cause.

   _____ I think that eating too much candy is the cause of my stomachache.

Write the idiom from paragraph 7 on the line next to its meaning.

8. easy; simple to do _____

Reading Skills

1. What problem does Tasha have in the story?

   _____

2. How does Julio help her resolve the problem?

   _____

3. Name one way in which Tasha and Julio are similar.

   _____

4. Name one way in which Tasha and Julio are different.

   _____

5. What charitable organization will Julio and Tasha help by running the race?

   _____

6. Why does Julio think that it would be a good idea to ask their neighbors to pledge money during the block party?

   _____

7. The **theme** of a story is its subject. It tells what idea the story is mostly about. Check the word below that best describes the theme of "A Reason to Run."

   _____ fitness

   _____ friendship

   _____ loyalty

Circle the word that best completes each sentence below.

8. Tasha feels that she can _____ with Julio's support.

   win   succeed   apply

9. Julio _____ Tasha to have more confidence in herself.

   encourages   discourages   requests

Getting Up to Speed

Where can you go running safely in your neighborhood?

Before you begin training:

- Find a running "buddy" to train with you. Ask a friend from school or from your neighborhood, your brother or sister, or a parent or other relative.

- Make sure you have a good pair of running shoes that fit you properly.

- Stay hydrated! Even if you aren't perspiring visibly, exercise uses up a great deal of your body's water. Be sure to drink water frequently to keep your energy level up and your body working.

- Snack on healthful foods. Fruits and vegetables, whole grains, and low-fat dairy products all help maintain a healthy body. Have an apple and a piece of cheese, some yogurt sprinkled with granola, or an orange and a handful of whole-grain pretzels. You'll find that you have plenty of energy to complete the goals you set for yourself.

- Get in the habit of taking a few minutes to stretch before you begin running. Stretching helps you stay flexible. It can also help protect your body from injury.

1   The best way to begin training is by alternately walking and running. This allows your body to become accustomed to the challenge of running without overdoing it. Begin your first week with running for two minutes and walking for four minutes. Do this sequence five times in a row, four times a week.

2   If you feel comfortable doing this sequence after a week, you're ready to progress to the next level. If it still feels challenging, continue with it for another week.

3   When you decide to move to the next level, you'll run three minutes and walk for three minutes. Continue to progress each week, increasing the time you spend running and decreasing the time you spend walking, until you reach 30 minutes of continuous running.

4   When you are running, you should be able to comfortably talk with your running buddy. If you are pushing yourself too hard, talking will be difficult because you'll be short of breath.

5   The days of the week that you don't run, try some different kinds of fitness activities, like hiking, ice skating, jumping rope, or playing basketball. You'll find that these activities use different muscles than running does. This kind of cross-training can help you get into even better shape than only repeating a single activity. Don't forget to schedule at least one day of rest every week. It's always a good idea to give your body a chance to recover from your daily workouts.

6   Consider keeping a runner's log or journal. You can record the weather, your route, the distance you ran, and how you felt. You might notice that you prefer running early in the day or that eating an orange before you go for a run gives you a good boost in energy.

7   Most of all, remember to have fun. Running is just one of many different activities you can do to stay in shape. Vary your routine enough to keep it interesting, and bring along a friend to keep you company.

Note: Children under the age of 14 should not regularly run more than three miles at a time. Children's bones are still growing, and the cartilage at the ends of the bones is softer than adult cartilage, which means that it is easier to injure.

Vocabulary Skills

Write the words from the passage that have the meanings below.

1. supplied with water

_____
Bullet 3

2. to keep in a certain condition

_____
Bullet 4

Circle the homophone that correctly completes each sentence below.

3. The lengths of ribbon _____ by about four inches. (vary, very)

4. Can you pack another _____ of fruit in my lunch? (piece, peace)

5. The seafood chowder contained fish, lobster, clams, and _____. (muscles, mussels)

Use a dictionary to help you place the words below into the correct category of origin.

spaghetti	bouquet
debris	coyote
rodeo	piano
fiancé	

6. French   7. Italian   8. Spanish

_____   _____   _____

_____   _____   _____

_____

Reading Skills

1. What are some types of fitness activities mentioned in the selection besides running?

_____

_____

2. What do you think cross-training is?

_____

_____

3. Why shouldn't children under the age of 14 regularly run more than three miles at a time?

_____

_____

4. What purpose would a reader have for reading this selection?

_____ for pleasure or entertainment

_____ to form an opinion about running

_____ to learn how to become a runner

5. Write a summary sentence for paragraph 5.

_____

_____

6. What kind of information could you record in a runner's log?

_____

_____

7. Do you think the author is trying to persuade the reader of anything in this selection? Explain.

_____

_____

_____

A Mysterious Glow

Have you ever seen an organism that glows? Where were you?

1 It was the Taylors' first night at the beach. Miles, Sophie, and their parents sat outside and enjoyed a big seafood dinner that included fresh fish, scallops, crab, coleslaw, and corn on the cob. The sun was a ball of fire as it slipped into the ocean and left a peach-colored glow in the sky. They played several board games, and by nine o'clock, everyone had caught their second wind.

2 "How does an evening stroll along the beach sound?" asked Mrs. Taylor, stretching as she stood up. "It's a beautiful night, and I don't think you kids have ever seen stars the way they look over the ocean at night."

3 "Sounds good to me," said Mr. Taylor, collecting the game pieces on the coffee table and putting them back in the box.

4 Sophie used a flashlight to guide the group down the sandy path in between the cottages, and in just a few minutes the Taylors found themselves on the beach. Miles and Sophie took off their flip-flops and let the sand squish between their toes.

5 "The sand is so much cooler than it was earlier today!" exclaimed Sophie, remembering how she had danced across the beach to the water to keep from burning the soles of her feet.

6 Mrs. Taylor nodded. "The sand absorbs the sun's heat during the day, but it cools off quickly as soon the sun goes down."

7 Miles and Sophie walked ahead of their parents, wading in the gentle waves along the shore as they tried to pick out constellations in the cloudless sky. "Miles," said Sophie after a few minutes, "do you notice anything weird about the water? Doesn't it seem like it's almost glowing?" She stopped walking and kicked her bare foot in the water. There was an explosion of milky-green light where Sophie kicked. Miles and Sophie looked at one another. "This is totally bizarre," said Sophie.

8 She and Miles crouched at the water's edge and ran their hands back and forth rapidly in the cool water. Swirls of light traced the pattern their hands had made.

9 Their parents had finally caught up to Miles and Sophie. "Did you find something?" inquired Mrs. Taylor, kneeling beside Sophie. Before Sophie even had time to answer, Mrs. Taylor gasped. "This is incredible," she said swirling her hands in the water. "I've read about it, but I've never seen it myself. Ian, did you see this?" she asked Mr. Taylor.

10 He nodded, and even in the dim light Sophie and Miles could see the look of amazement on their dad's face. "What is it, Mom?" asked Sophie. "Why is the water glowing?"

11 "It's called *bioluminescence*," said Mrs Taylor. "You're not actually seeing the water itself glow. There's just a high concentration of tiny organisms in it that create light. It's similar to the type of light that fireflies produce."

12 "I think we were all too busy looking at the stars in the sky to see the ones in the ocean," marveled Mr. Taylor.

Vocabulary Skills

Write the idiom from paragraph 1 on the line next to its meaning.

1. felt refreshed _____

A **metaphor** is a comparison of two things without using the word *like* or *as*. For example, *Her fingers were icicles*. Find the metaphor in paragraph 1, and write it on the line.

2. _____

The suffix **-est** means *most*. For example, *highest* means *most high*. Write a word to match each definition below. Then, write a sentence using each word.

3. most bright _____

_____

4. most young _____

_____

5. most happy _____

_____

Reading Skills

1. Write one sentence from the story that indicates how the Taylors felt about discovering the bioluminescence.

_____

_____

2. What happened when Sophie kicked the water?

_____

3. What explanation does Mrs. Taylor have for why the water is glowing?

_____

_____

4. Why do you think the Taylors didn't notice the glowing water right away?

_____

5. Do you think that Sophie and Miles will try to learn more about bioluminescence when they get home? Why or why not?

_____

Read the sentences below. Write **B** next to the sentence if it tells about something that happened before Miles and Sophie noticed the water was glowing. Write **A** if it describes something that happened after.

6. _____ Mrs. Taylor swirled her hands in the water.

7. _____ Mr. Taylor collected the game pieces from the coffee table.

8. _____ Miles and Sophie picked out constellations in the night sky.

9. _____ Miles and Sophie took off their flip-flops.

10. _____ Mrs. Taylor knelt beside Sophie.

Study Skills

Guide words are printed at the top of each page in a dictionary. The guide word at the left is the first word on the page. The guide word at the right is the last word on the page. Check each word that could be found on a page having the guide words shown in dark print.

1. **error—estimate**

_____ essence   _____ escalator
_____ eucalyptus

2. **acute—administer**

_____ activist   _____ acre
_____ adhesive

3. **rugged—rupture**

_____ ruin   _____ rumor   _____ rustle

Living Lights

What would it be like to glow in the dark?

1   Very few organisms that live on land have the ability to glow in the dark, but it is a surprisingly common characteristic among deep-sea marine creatures. In fact, about 90 percent of animals that live 200 to 1,000 meters below the surface of the ocean are bioluminescent.

2   The word *bioluminescence* (bīз ō lüз mi nes з ens) comes from the Greek word *bios*, which means *living*, and the Latin word *lumen*, which means *light*. It refers to organisms that produce light as a result of a chemical reaction. Bioluminescence is a cool light. In a lightbulb, about 97 percent of the energy is used to create heat, and only 3 percent is used to create light. When bioluminescence is produced, very little energy is used to create heat. This is one reason that scientists are so interested in learning about bioluminescence and how it might be used to create more efficient, less wasteful light sources.

3   Ocean animals use bioluminescence in various ways. You might think that light would not be very effective as camouflage because it would draw attention to an animal instead of helping it hide. However, if you were a predator hunting a bobtail squid and you looked up at the squid's belly, its bioluminescence would allow it to blend with the stars of the night sky.

4   Other animals use bioluminescence to attract mates. This is the case with fireflies on land, who use light signals to attract others of the same species. It is also true of ocean animals like the Bermuda fireworm.

5   One species of squid uses bioluminescence to confuse predators. If it feels threatened, it spews a cloud of bioluminescent chemicals. While the predator is surprised and confused, the squid has time to quickly escape.

6   Another possible use of bioluminescence is to lure prey. The cookie cutter shark is one animal that uses its light in this way. Patterns of bioluminescence on the shark's underside may resemble small fish to predators like tuna or mackerel. When they come closer to investigate, the shark attacks. The anglerfish uses a similar method to capture prey. It extends a glowing lure from an appendage on its head. Other fish mistake the glowing lure for a meal and venture closer. When they do, the anglerfish moves quickly and snaps them up.

7   Because many bioluminescent animals live deep underwater, most people don't have the opportunity to observe them. However, tiny one-celled creatures called *dinoflagellates* (dīз nō flagз ə lets) live in the sea and produce much of the visible bioluminescence near the ocean's surface. In areas that have large numbers of dinoflagellates, the motion of waves, a boat, a porpoise, or even a hand can easily disturb them and cause them to glow. On a dark night, this eerie but beautiful sight can create quite a light show in the ocean!

Vocabulary Skills

Write the words from the passage that have the meanings below.

1. to hide by blending into one's surroundings

   _____
   Par. 3

2. an animal that hunts other animals

   _____
   Par. 3

3. something that attracts

   _____
   Par. 6

4. a body part that extends out from the body

   _____
   Par. 6

5. to move forward in spite of risk

   _____
   Par. 6

6. odd or mysterious; causing an uneasy feeling

   _____
   Par. 7

7. The Latin root **mar** means *sea*. Find a word in paragraph 1 with the root **mar**.

   _____

8. The Latin root **fic** means *make* or *do*. Find a word in paragraph 2 with the root **fic**.

   _____

9. The Latin root **tract** means *pull* or *drag*. Find a word in paragraph 4 with the root **tract**.

   _____

Read each pair of words listed below. If the words are synonyms, write **S** on the line. If the words are antonyms, write **A** on the line.

10. _____ attract   repel

11. _____ helping   assisting

12. _____ investigate   explore

13. _____ create   destroy

Reading Skills

1. Write a sentence that tells the main idea of the passage.

   _____

   _____

2. Explain one way in which an animal can use bioluminescence to lure prey.

   _____

   _____

3. What kind of creature produces much of the visible bioluminescence near the ocean's surface?

   _____

   _____

4. How does bioluminescence help camouflage the bobtail squid?

   _____

   _____

5. How is bioluminescence different from the light produced by a lightbulb?

   _____

   _____

6. What can cause dinoflagellates to glow?

   _____

   _____

7. Check the line beside the word or words that best describe what type of selection this is.

   _____ science fiction

   _____ informative

   _____ fantasy

A Stinging Surprise

What happens when Miles has an unexpected encounter with a jellyfish?

1   Sophie, Miles, and Mr. Taylor walked along the beach. The late afternoon sun reflected off the water and made it sparkle like a sea of diamonds.

2   "Quick, kids, look at the seagull!" exclaimed Mr. Taylor. He pointed toward a gull that had just swooped down and plucked a large fish from the water. The fish wriggled, and they could see that it was a struggle for the seagull to hold its catch firmly without dropping it.

3   "I can't believe that a bird that size can carry such a...ouch! Dad, help! I think I stepped on something!" Miles hopped on one foot, trying to shake the stinging sensation from his other foot. Mr. Taylor reached him quickly and helped Miles take a seat on the warm sand.

4   "I think that's what you stepped on," said Sophie, pointing to a sand-covered, jelly-like blob on the beach. "Is it a jellyfish, Dad?"

5   Mr. Taylor nodded. Then, he looked at Miles who was wincing in pain. "You're all right, Miles," he said, giving his son a gentle squeeze on the shoulder. He turned to Sophie. "Do you see that lifeguard tower down the beach?" he asked. Sophie nodded. "Can you run over there and tell the lifeguard that we think your brother was stung by a jellyfish?"

6   Sophie nodded and headed for the tower. Meanwhile, Mr. Taylor emptied the bucket of seashells and used it to gently rinse the sand from Miles's foot with seawater.

7   "How does that feel?" he asked Miles.

8   "About the same," replied Miles. "It burns and stings."

9   In just a few minutes, Sophie returned with the lifeguard, a friendly-looking man with deeply tanned skin and curly black hair.

10   He opened a small red and white box and removed some rubbing alcohol. "First, we're going to clean the area with a bit of alcohol," he began. "Vinegar works too, just in case you're ever stung again."

11   "Now what are you going to put on it?" asked Sophie curiously.

12   "Well, it might sound funny, but I'm making a paste using meat tenderizer and water." He smeared the paste on the heel of Miles's foot, which had become red and slightly swollen. "Meat tenderizer is an enzyme that breaks down protein. Jellyfish poison is a protein, so it works on the poison the same way it does on meat."

13   "It actually feels better already," said Miles in surprise.

14   The lifeguard smiled. "If you don't have any meat tenderizer at home, a paste made of baking soda and water will also soothe it. If the area becomes any more irritated in the next couple of hours, I'd suggest seeing a doctor. Otherwise, you'll probably be feeling much better by morning."

15   "Thank you for all your help," said Mr. Taylor, shaking the lifeguard's hand. "Come on, Miles. This is probably the last piggyback ride you're going to get before you get taller than me!"

Vocabulary Skills

Write the words from the story that have the meanings below.

1. something that is felt or sensed

   _____
   Par. 3

2. making a face to indicate pain or discomfort

   _____
   Par. 5

3. make something feel better or less painful

   _____
   Par. 14

Find the simile in paragraph 1, and write it on the line below.

4. _____

Fill in the blanks below with the possessive form of the word in parentheses.

5. _____ foot swelled and turned red when he was stung. (Miles)

6. The _____ tower was located nearby. (lifeguard)

7. The _____ colors and sizes were quite diverse. (seashells)

8. The Latin root **flect** means *bend*. Find a word in paragraph 1 with the root **flect**.

   _____

9. The Latin root **claim** means *shout*. Find a word in paragraph 2 with the root **claim**.

   _____

10. The Latin root **doc** means *teach*. Find a word in paragraph 14 with the root **doc**.

    _____

Reading Skills

1. Number the events below to show the order in which they happened.

   _____ Mr. Taylor shook the lifeguard's hand.

   _____ The Taylors watched a seagull catch a fish.

   _____ The lifeguard cleaned the sting with alcohol.

   _____ Sophie pointed to the sand-covered jellyfish.

   _____ The lifeguard smeared meat tenderizer on Miles's foot.

2. If you don't have alcohol and meat tenderizer at home, what else can you use to treat a jellyfish sting?

   _____

3. Under what circumstances does the lifeguard recommend that Miles see a doctor?

   _____

4. Why does meat tenderizer soothe a jellyfish sting?

   _____

5. What were the Taylors looking at when Miles was stung?

   _____

6. How did the Taylors determine what Miles had stepped on?

   _____

7. The **climax** of a story is the point of highest excitement. What is the climax in "A Stinging Surprise"?

   _____

   _____

Curious Creatures

Have you ever seen a jellyfish in the wild or at a zoo or an aquarium?

1   What kind of animal has no brain, no bones, and no circulatory system? This might sound like a riddle, but it isn't. The jellyfish is one of the ocean's most unusual creatures. Instead of having all the organs that are typical of most animals, jellyfish have specialized tissues that carry out the various functions they need to survive.

2   The term *jellyfish* is inaccurate because these animals are neither fish nor made of jelly. They are invertebrates, which means that they do not have backbones. They are also relatives of corals and sea anemones. Scientists believe that there may be as many as 2,000 types of jellyfish in the world's oceans. Most species are found in saltwater, though a few freshwater varieties do exist.

3   Because there are so many different species of jellyfish, it is not surprising that there is such variety in their appearance. The smallest jellyfish are less than an inch in length, while the largest may grow to be 200 feet long! Shape and color are two more ways in which jellyfish differ. Typically, jellyfish have little color because their bodies are composed of 95 to 99 percent water. Some species are more colorful and may be brown, pink, white, or blue.

4   Most jellyfish have the same basic shape. From the top, they look similar to an umbrella or a mushroom, with long thin tentacles that extend below their "heads." The tentacles are lined with stinging cells called *nematocysts* that the jellyfish uses to capture food such as small fish, plankton, and other small sea creatures.

5   These same stinging cells are what cause people such pain if they accidentally step on a jellyfish that has washed up on shore or brush against a tentacle as they swim in the ocean. The sting from most species of jellyfish is relatively harmless, though it can be painful. However, there are several species of jellyfish whose sting can be fatal.

6   For the most part, jellyfish are transported by ocean currents and the wind. They have some ability to move through the water by contracting muscles in the main part of the body. These contractions can push the jellyfish vertically through the water at a slow pace. For the most part, though, jellyfish are content to float through the waves, waiting for the next potential food source to become tangled in their tentacles.

7   The next time you go to the beach, keep your eyes open for a colorless blob gently floating on the water's surface. If you're lucky, you'll get a close-up view of one of the ocean's strangest creatures.

Vocabulary Skills

Check the meaning of each underlined word.

1. Many jellyfish are <u>colorless</u> because their bodies are made mostly of water.

   _____ in a colorful way

   _____ without color

   _____ capable of color

2. <u>Typically</u>, jellyfish are not dangerous to people.

   _____ in a typical way

   _____ not typical

   _____ typical again

Underline the compound word in each sentence. Then, write the two words that make up each compound.

3. Most of these creatures are found in saltwater.

   _____ _____

4. Invertebrates do not have backbones.

   _____ _____

5. There are about 2,000 species of jellyfish.

   _____ _____

Reading Skills

1. Why does the author say that the description of a jellyfish might sound like a riddle?

   _____

2. How much of a jellyfish's body is composed of water?

   _____

3. What are nematocysts?

   _____

4. Check the phrase that best describes the author's purpose.

   _____ to entertain

   _____ to inform

   _____ to persuade

Write **T** before the sentences that are true. Write **F** before the sentences that are false.

5. _____ All species of jellyfish are totally harmless to humans.

6. _____ Jellyfish do not have most of the organs that are common in other animals.

7. _____ Jellyfish can move only where the wind and the tides take them.

8. _____ Only about one-third of a jellyfish's body is water.

9. _____ A few freshwater species of jellyfish do exist.

Study Skills

Write the name of the reference source you could use to answer each question below.

encyclopedia dictionary	phone directory thesaurus

1. How do you pronounce the word *nematocysts*?

   _____

2. Where do coral and sea anemones live?

   _____

3. What is another word for *potential*?

   _____

4. How can you reach the information line at the National Oceanic Institute?

   _____

Catching a Wave

What kind of surfing tips will Kerry and Dylan give their cousins?

1 Sophie and Miles sat on the shore and let the waves wash over their toes. They were watching their cousins surf. Dylan and Kerry were a few years older than Sophie and Miles, and they had started surfing almost before they were able to walk.

2 Kerry rode a wave into shore, and then hopped off her board and jogged over to where Sophie and Miles were sitting. Her dark hair, which was as sleek and glossy as an otter's fur, was plastered against her head. "Are you two ready to give it a try?" she asked, squinting through the sun at her cousins.

3 Miles took a deep breath and nodded. He was worried about looking silly in front of his cousins, but he had a feeling he was going to love surfing. He expected it to feel like flying through the water or riding his bike down a steep hill without using the brakes.

4 "Don't go out too far!" shouted Mrs. Taylor into the wind, and Sophie cheerfully waved back to her parents. Sophie was usually good at the things she tried. She learned quickly and wasn't afraid to plunge right in, even if she had never done something before. Miles admired these characteristics in his sister, but knew he just wasn't as adventurous as she was.

5 "Okay," Kerry began, "we're going to start you two out on longboards. They are easier to paddle, and they catch waves more easily, which is good when you are a beginner because it gives you more time to stand up.

6 "There are a few surfing fundamentals that are pretty important. First, never paddle your surfboard out farther than you can swim back in without it. Know the beach you're surfing, and know what weather conditions to expect. Never surf alone, and always remember your limitations. Don't forget that as much fun as you have surfing, the ocean isn't something to take lightly." Kerry paused for a moment and looked at the serious expressions on her cousins' faces.

7 "Now for the fun part," Kerry said. She waved her arms at Dylan, who waved back and began to paddle into shore. "You need to position yourself in the center of your board, between the nose and the tail. When you're positioned the right way, the nose should be a couple of inches above the water's surface. When a wave catches the tail of the board, start paddling. Try to remember the sweet spot on your board, because you'll want to position yourself the same way each time you go out, no matter what kind of wave you're trying to catch."

8 Sophie grinned at Kerry. "I had no idea that surfing was so technical. I thought you just catch a big wave and try to ride it without falling off."

9 Just then, Dylan walked up, shaking himself the same way the Taylors' dog did after she had had a bath. "Is she still explaining things?" he asked Sophie and Miles, winking at Kerry.

10 Kerry swatted at her brother. "They're almost ready to get started," she said, turning back to Sophie and Miles. "We're just going to practice standing up a few times on the sand where the board will be on a stable surface. Then, you can try to paddle out and catch a wave."

11 "Who wants to go first?" she asked.

12 Miles put up one hand. "This is the easy part," he said. "Sand surfing doesn't worry me a bit. Besides, I think I'm going to need all the practice I can get!"

Vocabulary Skills

Write the words from the story that have the meanings below.

1. pressed tightly against

   _____
   Par. 2

2. looked up to; respected

   _____
   Par. 4

3. basic principles or skills

   _____
   Par. 6

4. restrictions; the act or quality of being limited

   _____
   Par. 6

5. sturdy; firm

   _____
   Par. 10

Read each word below. Then, write the letter of its synonym on the line beside the word.

6. _____ worried   a. middle

7. _____ anticipated   b. novice

8. _____ beginner   c. concerned

9. _____ center   d. expected

10. Find the simile in paragraph 2, and write it on the line below.

    _____

11. What two things were compared to one another in question 10?

    _____   _____

12. Choose one of the answers to number 11, and use it to create your own simile on the lines below.

    _____

    _____

Reading Skills

1. Why does Kerry think that Sophie and Miles should start out using longboards?

   _____

   _____

2. What do you think Kerry means when she refers to the "sweet spot" on a surfboard?

   _____

   _____

3. What is one way in which Miles and Sophie are different?

   _____

4. What does Miles think surfing will feel like?

   _____

   _____

5. What are the surfing terms for the front and back ends of a surfboard?

   _____

6. Check the line beside the word or words that best describe what type of selection this is.

   _____ poetry

   _____ fiction

   _____ science fiction

Mark each sentence below F if it is in first-person point of view and T if it is in third-person point of view.

7. _____ I wish I was as adventurous as my sister.

8. _____ Sophie waved to her parents.

9. _____ I've been surfing since I was only five years old.

10. _____ Dylan shook himself off when he got out of the water.

Wave-Sliding

How did surfing become the popular sport it is today?

1   Who first had the idea of shaping a piece of wood into a long narrow board and using it to ride ocean waves? No one knows for sure, but we do know that Hawaiians have been surfing since the 1400s. The Hawaiian word for *surfing* translates to *wave-sliding*, a fairly accurate description of this sport in which a surfer stands on a board and gets propelled across the water by the energy of the waves.

2   Surfers are fond of saying that surfing isn't a sport, it's a lifestyle. This was true for the relatively small numbers of surfers who participated in the sport before the 1950s. Then, new types of surfboards became available. They were made of fiberglass and foam instead of wood. This made them less expensive, as well as much easier to use and maneuver. Suddenly, surfing became enormously popular in the United States, and surfing culture was born.

3   Movies and magazines that featured surfing became trendy, as did beach music and surfing fashion. But nothing changed what was most important to serious surfers—enjoying the beach and the ocean as they went on a quest for the perfect wave.

4   Surfing appeals to people for several reasons. Surfers have an inherent love and respect for the ocean. They like participating in a sport in which the challenges constantly change and the environment is somewhat unpredictable. Surfers also seek the adrenaline rush that comes with riding the waves. It is the same feeling that draws people to other high-speed activities, like downhill skiing, hang-gliding, or car racing.

5   In 1953, the Waikiki Surf Club hosted the first international surfing championships. This competition led surfing to be regarded as a sport. Judges based their decisions on elements such as the length of ride, the number of waves a surfer caught, skill, sportsmanship, and grace. Today, the Association of Surfing Professionals, or ASP, holds annual world championship series at different beaches around the country. Some surfers participate happily in such competitions, but others feel that this goes against the true nature and "soul" of surfing.

6   Other than Duke Kahanamoku, the Hawaiian surfer who is thought to have introduced the sport to the rest of the world, Laird Hamilton is probably the most well known and respected surfer today. Large waves are his specialty, and Hamilton has been known to surf 70-foot-tall waves at speeds of approximately 50 miles per hour.

7   Hamilton also popularized a form of the sport called *tow-in surfing*. He wanted to have access to some of the oceans' largest waves, but he knew surfers could not reach those waves just by paddling their boards. The solution was to use jet skis to tow surfers to areas that were farther from shore, where they could wait for enormous waves to crest nearby.

8   The tow-in method is controversial among serious surfers, but most people couldn't help being impressed when Hamilton used it to surf a well-known Tahitian surf spot called *Teahupoo*. Wipeouts at Teahupoo are likely to be fatal, but Hamilton took the challenge and survived.

Vocabulary Skills

Write the words from the passage that have the meanings below.

1. pushed or moved forward

   _____
   Par. 1

2. a search

   _____
   Par. 3

3. attracts; interests

   _____
   Par. 4

4. a basic part of one's character or nature

   _____
   Par. 4

5. a hormone that causes a rush of energy and feeling of excitement

   _____
   Par. 4

6. relating to a subject about which there are opposing views

   _____
   Par. 8

Find the compound words from the selection that contain the words below.

7. style _____
          Par. 2

8. boards _____
           Par. 2

9. down _____
          Par. 4

Circle the homophone that correctly completes each sentence below.

10. Many surfers prefer one type of
    _____ over another.
    (board, bored)

11. Let's go to the _____ and watch the storm roll in. (beach, beech)

12. I will _____ the turkey again in about an hour. (baste, based)

Reading Skills

Write **F** before the sentences that are facts.
Write **O** before the sentences that are opinions.

1. _____ Laird Hamilton is the most talented surfer alive today.

2. _____ Surfing became very popular in the 1950s and 1960s.

3. _____ The surfing spot Teahupoo is located near Tahiti.

4. _____ No one can appreciate the power of the ocean the way a surfer does.

5. _____ Laird Hamilton has surfed at speeds of up to 50 miles per hour.

6. Why did the new fiberglass and foam surfboards cause a rise in surfing's popularity?

   _____

   _____

7. What draws people to high-speed activities?

   _____

   _____

8. What is tow-in surfing?

   _____

   _____

9. What do you think the surfing term *wipeout* means?

   _____

   _____

10. Write a summary sentence for paragraph 4.

    _____

    _____

The Father of Modern Surfing

Who was Duke Kahanamoku, and how did he change the world of surfing?

1   The word *Duke* brings to mind royalty. Duke Kahanamoku was not royalty, but he might as well have been a king in Hawaii. He was a talented swimmer, an actor, and even the mayor of Honolulu, Hawaii, for nearly 30 years. But what Duke Paoa Kahinu Makoe Hulikohoa Kahanamoku will be most remembered for is bringing surfing to the world outside of Hawaii.

2   Kahanamoku was a native Hawaiian, born in 1890 in Honolulu. From an early age, he felt most at home at the beach and in the ocean. He attended school but rushed home every afternoon, knowing that the ocean was patiently waiting for him.

3   Kahanamoku went to the Olympics as a swimmer in 1912 and 1920, where he won a total of three gold medals for the United States. He also traveled around the world as a water safety instructor for the Red Cross in between Olympics.

4   Kahanamoku was so enthusiastic about the water that he was able to successfully encourage others to take an interest in water sports. As he traveled, Kahanamoku spoke about surfing and demonstrated the sport to audiences around the globe. Surfing, which had had little publicity outside of Hawaii, started gaining in popularity.

5   Kahanamoku's favorite type of board was made from a koa tree. It was quite long by today's standards—16 feet in length—and it weighed 114 pounds. As a point of comparison, boards today are only 6 to 9 feet long and weigh between 6 and 15 pounds. Kahanamoku's preferred board was fashioned after the ancient Hawaiian *olo* boards. Kahanamoku was convinced that it was the best because he believed that big boards were for big waves. One of Kahanamoku's early boards can be viewed today in Honolulu's Bishop Museum.

6   Duke Kahanamoku was the first person to be inducted into both the Swimming Hall of Fame and the Surfing Hall of Fame. Yet all the

celebrity surrounding his achievements seemed to have little effect on Kahanamoku's personality. The ocean remained his first love, and he stayed true to the roots of his Hawaiian culture, speaking the language, following the customs, and eating the foods as often as possible.

7   Kahanamoku died in 1968 at the age of 77. He had a burial at sea, accompanied by a 30-person police escort. Kahanamoku's ashes were scattered in the water off Waikiki Beach, the place he had felt most at home in the world, while a group of beach boys sang traditional Hawaiian songs. The world would never forget the man who shared his love of the ocean and surfing with people all around the globe.

Vocabulary Skills

1. The Latin root **nat** means *born*. Find a word in paragraph 2 with the root **nat**.

   _____

2. The Latin root **duc** means *lead*. Find a word in paragraph 6 with the root **duc**.

   _____

In each row, circle the word that best completes each sentence below.

3. People who listened to Kahanamoku speak found his enthusiasm for the ocean and for surfing to be _____.

   common   contagious   annoying

4. Celebrity did not seem to _____ Kahanamoku's personality.

   display   create   alter

Reading Skills

1. What are two jobs that Kahanamoku held that were unrelated to swimming or surfing?

   _____
   _____

2. Do you think that surfing would have spread to other areas of the world without Duke Kahanamoku's encouragement and enthusiasm? Why or why not?

   _____
   _____

3. Find a sentence in the selection showing that Kahanamoku was a talented and successful swimmer, and write it on the lines below.

   _____
   _____
   _____

4. Check the sentence that best states the main idea of the selection.

   _____ Duke Kahanamoku's full name was Duke Paoa Kahinu Makoe Hulikohoa Kahanamoku.

   _____ Duke Kahanamoku was the first person to be inducted into both the Swimming Hall of Fame and the Surfing Hall of Fame.

   _____ Duke Kahanamoku was known as the "father of modern surfing" because he helped bring the sport to areas of the world outside of Hawaii.

Study Skills

Use the timeline of Duke Kahanamoku's life to answer the questions that follow.

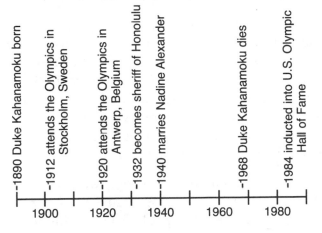

1. In what year were the Olympics held in Antwerp, Belgium?

   _____

2. Was Kahanamoku inducted into the U. S. Olympic Hall of Fame before or after his death?

   _____

3. In what year did Kahanamoku marry?

   _____

It's All Academic

Keep reading to find out more about the experiences of the Schuyler Middle School students who appear on an academic quiz show.

1 The bus was filled with energy and excitement. Students were talking and laughing, but there was also a bit of nervous energy in the air. As the bus rounded the corner and pulled into the parking lot at the television studio, Mr. Ishikawa cleared his throat.

2 "I want to thank each one of you for your hard work. I know that many of you have had to put other activities on hold for the intensive training we've done in the past weeks.

3 "Whether or not Schuyler Middle School wins today's competition, I'm proud of you all," Mr. Ishikawa continued. "It's a great honor just to have qualified to be on *Quiz Power*. Schuyler is proud to have you represent our school. Just do your best, and enjoy yourselves today. No matter what, we're all going home winners."

4 The members of the team cheered as Mr. Ishikawa finished his speech. As they headed for the doors of the bus, several students paused to thank Mr. Ishikawa for his commitment to the team and all the time he had spent coaching. The students knew they were ready for almost any question the quizmaster might pose. They couldn't wait to get started.

5 Inside the studio, the students were met by Annette Cane, the show's executive producer. Ms. Cane was a tall, friendly woman with thick auburn hair and an infectious laugh. Within a few minutes, she had put all the contestants at ease. When the competing team from Brighton Park arrived, Ms. Cane made quick introductions and passed out drinks.

6 "I'm sure you've already heard this a hundred times today," she told the room of expectant students, "but the most important thing you can do during the competition is to relax and have fun. Do your best to ignore the cameras and the microphones. Once the announcer has finished asking a question, you will want to ring your buzzer as soon as you think you have the answer. You may not ring in until the entire question has been read.

7 "People tend to speak more quickly when they are nervous, so just try to answer slowly and calmly when it's your turn." Ms. Cane paused and took a sip from a bottle of water. She smiled sympathetically at the students who were beginning to look tense. "Do you have any questions before we begin taping?"

8 Gabriel, a seventh-grader from Schuyler, waved his hand. "Will the winning team come back to compete for the championship?" he asked.

9 Ms. Cane nodded. "The championships are held in the spring. The winning teams from the rest of the year will participate in playoffs to determine the final four teams. Each member of the winning team will receive a $1,000 college savings bond. The winning school will also receive two brand-new, fully-equipped computers."

10 "Who chooses the questions that are used during the show?" asked Monique, an eighth-grader from Brighton Park.

11 "We have a panel of researchers who compile a list of questions. They come together to narrow down the list of questions and determine which ones will actually be used in the show. Each question is given a rating to ensure that the level of difficulty progresses as the game goes on." Ms. Cane glanced at the platform where there were places for each team and a podium for the announcer.

12 "Any more questions?" she asked. The students were silent, focused on the task ahead of them. "Then, let the game begin!"

Vocabulary Skills

Write the words from the story that have the meanings below.

1. very strong; thorough

_____
Par. 2

2. an agreement or pledge to a certain event or activity

_____
Par. 4

3. present or put forward

_____
Par. 4

4. freedom from worry; a feeling of comfort

_____
Par. 5

5. put together

_____
Par. 11

Use a dictionary to help you place the words below into the correct category of origin.

mosquito	confetti
ballet	gourmet
cello	bizarre
avocado	tortilla

6. French   7. Spanish   8. Italian

_____   _____   _____

_____   _____   _____

_____   _____

Reading Skills

1. What prize will the team that wins the championship receive?

_____

2. Do you think that Mr. Ishikawa is a good coach? Why or why not?

_____

_____

3. In paragraph 5, the author describes Ms. Cane as having "an infectious laugh." What do you think this means?

_____

_____

4. What are three words you could use to describe Ms. Cane's personality?

_____

_____

5. What purpose would a reader have for reading this selection?

_____ for pleasure or entertainment

_____ for information

_____ to learn how to be on an academic game show

Study Skills

Read the television studio's rules and regulations, and answer the questions that follow.

• Student must currently be enrolled in classes at the school he/she is representing.
• Student must be between the ages of 11 and 14 at the time of taping.
• No cameras or videotaping devices are allowed in the studio at time of taping.
• Students' names may be used for promotional purposes before the airing of the show.

1. How old must a student be at the time of taping in order to be a contestant?

_____

2. Can students or their families record the show as it is being taped?

_____

Tune in to History

Do you know who invented television?

1   Television is such a familiar part of our daily lives that you probably never think about its history or the fact that as recently as 70 years ago many people had never even heard of it. The word *television* comes from the Greek word *tele*, which means *far*, and the Latin word *visio*, which means *sight*. It's the perfect description for this electronic device that receives images and sound transmitted from another place.

2   Early in the 20th century, many experiments were attempted to transmit moving images from one place to another. Because there were so many contributors, it is hard to pinpoint exactly who gets credit as the inventor of TV. However, television as we know it today was developed in the 1920s by two men working separately.

3   Philo Taylor Farnsworth, a farm boy from Idaho, demonstrated the first electronic television in 1927. It was a prototype of the TVs we use today. During the late 1920s, a Russian-born scientist named Vladimir Zworykin worked with the electronics company RCA to develop the first marketable televisions. Because of this pivotal role in bringing TV to the public, he was regarded for many years as the "inventor" of television. Historians disagree about which man deserves more credit, but today, Farnsworth's contribution is seen as the crucial first step in the technological developments made by Zworykin.

4   The first TVs were not too impressive by our standards. In fact, they were actually radios with an extremely small television device attached. The screen was lit by a reddish neon light, and the image was only the size of a postage stamp.

5   By the 1930s, TVs became available to the public, but they were very expensive—about $7,000 each in today's money. After World War II, however, the price dropped significantly and televisions became a much more common sight. By the late 1950s, color televisions became available, and the Western series *Bonanza* became the first TV show to be regularly shown in color.

6   Television is similar to radio in the way that it uses an antenna to pick up signals sent over the airwaves. Local TV stations still send signals that can be picked up by your TV's antenna, but increasing numbers of people use cable to receive their television broadcasts.

7   In 1949, John Watson, a television salesman in rural Pennsylvania, was having a hard time selling his TVs. Television signals were weak by the time they reached his town, and people did not think it was worthwhile to buy a TV. Watson put up a giant antenna to get better reception and offered his customers a free connection to the stronger signal. Eventually, he started to charge for the service, and cable TV was born.

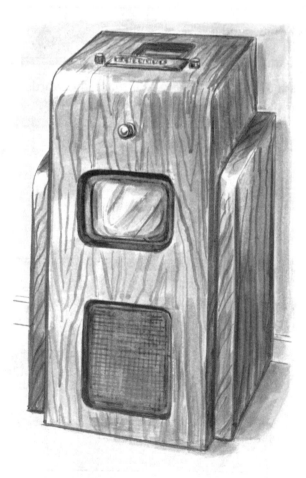

Vocabulary Skills

Write the words from the passage that have the meanings below.

1. sent from one place to another

   _____
   Par. 1

2. identify with certainty

   _____
   Par. 2

3. an original model

   _____
   Par. 3

4. important; the thing on which something else depends

   _____
   Par. 3

5. very important; essential

   _____
   Par. 3

6. of or relating to the country or country living

   _____
   Par. 7

Read each word below. Then, write the letter of its antonym on the line beside the word.

7. _____ separate   **a.** cheap

8. _____ expensive   **b.** national

9. _____ weak   **c.** together

10. _____ local   **d.** strong

Divide the words below into syllables using a slash (/).

11. p e r f e c t

12. w o r t h w h i l e

13. s i g n a l

14. c a b l e

15. e q u a l

Reading Skills

1. What was the first TV show to be regularly shown in color?

   _____

2. Who are the two people that are often given credit for inventing television?

   _____

3. What Latin and Greek roots are found in the word *television*? What do they mean?

   _____

   _____

4. About how much would a 1930s television have cost in today's dollars?

   _____

5. Check the phrase that best describes the author's purpose.

   _____ to entertain

   _____ to inform

   _____ to persuade

Circle the word that best completes each sentence below.

6. Televisions became _____ priced after World War II.

   significantly   reasonably   highly

7. John Watson's _____ thinking led to the invention of cable TV.

   creative   unimaginative   selfish

8. Farnsworth and Zworykin both _____ to the invention of the modern television.

   developed   requested   contributed

Moving Images

What is the most important event you have seen on TV?

1   With at least one television in nearly every home in the United States, TV has become the major source for news. In recent memory, September 11, 2001, and the days that followed kept people glued to their television sets for information and comfort. During the more recent war in Iraq, Americans turned on their TVs for similar reasons. Many historical events from the past 50 years would not be remembered the same way without the televised images. Some events were even shaped by the powerful influence these images have on the public.

2   The "Checker's Speech" by vice-presidential candidate Richard Nixon was an early example of how television can change the public's perception of someone. Nixon had been accused of accepting gifts for his campaign and was viewed negatively by the public.

3   On September 9, 1952, Nixon went on TV to defend himself. He claimed that the only questionable gift he had received was the family dog, Checkers, and he was not about to give the pet back. The public was moved to tears by Nixon's speech, and he redeemed himself. However, television would not be so kind to Nixon in the future.

4   In 1959, television played an important role in the presidential debate between Richard Nixon and John F. Kennedy. Viewers saw a younger, smiling Kennedy trading viewpoints with Nixon, who was scowling and looked uncomfortable. Radio listeners, who had heard only the words and ideas, thought that Nixon had won the debate. However, television viewers declared Kennedy the winner. The power of televised images in politics was never underestimated again.

5   During the tragedy of JFK's assassination, television allowed the citizens of our nation to grieve together. People across the country saw Kennedy's coffin as it was loaded onto *Air Force One* while Jackie Kennedy, the First Lady, stood by watching. Millions who were still in shock over these unbelievable events viewed JFK's funeral procession. Many citizens were also reassured about the power of our democracy as they watched Vice-President Lyndon Johnson quickly sworn in as the new president.

6   Not all historical moments on television involve politics. For instance, the Beatles' appearance on the *Ed Sullivan Show* on February 9, 1964, changed American pop culture. Viewers across the nation saw their goofy grins and goofier haircuts, as well as the crowd's frenzied cheering, and "Beatlemania" was born.

7   In July of 1969, 94 percent of Americans who owned televisions watched a live broadcast and saw Neil Armstrong and Buzz Aldrin become the first humans on the moon. Around the world, nearly one billion people watched this event on TV.

Vocabulary Skills

Write the words from the passage that have the meanings below.

1. the way in which one is viewed or perceived

   _____
   Par. 2

2. changed for the better; reformed

   _____
   Par. 3

3. estimated as being less in size or importance

   _____
   Par. 4

4. to mourn; to feel very sad about a loss

   _____
   Par. 5

5. felt comforted and less anxious

   _____
   Par. 5

6. wildly excited

   _____
   Par. 6

Check the meaning of the underlined word in each sentence.

7. Today, television is a <u>major</u> source of news.

   _____ important; significant

   _____ a military rank

8. The family was <u>glued</u> to the television as the story unfolded.

   _____ watched closely

   _____ attached with a sticky substance

Circle the homophone that correctly completes each sentence below.

9. Will you be _____ to stay up late to see the end of the movie? (allowed, aloud)

10. Television has played an important _____ in American history. (roll, role)

Reading Skills

Write **T** before the sentences that are true. Write **F** before the sentences that are false.

1. _____ Nixon stated that he did not receive any questionable gifts.

2. _____ About 75 percent of Americans who owned televisions watched Armstrong and Aldrin walk on the moon.

3. _____ The Beatles appeared on the *Ed Sullivan Show* in 1964.

4. _____ Lyndon Johnson became president after Kennedy's assassination.

5. Do you think that television as a source of news will be as important in the future as it has been in the past? Explain.

   _____

   _____

6. How did the "Checker's Speech" change the way people thought of Richard Nixon?

   _____

   _____

7. Do you think it is fair for people to base their opinions on what they see as well as what they hear? Explain.

   _____

   _____

8. What kind of effect did television have on the popularity of the Beatles?

   _____

9. How did Kennedy and Nixon appear to be different from one another during their televised debate?

   _____

   _____

A Reservoir of Memories

Have you ever gone canoeing?

1   Meghan sat in the canoe, patiently waiting for her sister and grandma to join her. She watched Becca cautiously step into the canoe as her grandma coached her.

2   "Remember not to stand up all the way or make any abrupt movements," said Grandma, holding the canoe steady.

3   Once Becca was safely in the canoe, Grandma passed the girls the camera, which was sealed in a waterproof bag. She confirmed that both paddles were in the canoe, and then she deftly climbed in and settled herself at the head of the small craft.

4   "How did you learn to canoe, Grandma?" asked Becca, once Meghan and their grandmother had established a rhythm for paddling.

5   "It was such a long time ago," she said thoughtfully, "in a reservoir much like this one. When I was 18 years old, I worked as a camp counselor at a girls' summer camp in Vermont. I learned how to canoe that summer, but I also learned how to build a fire, treat snake bites, and survive in the woods for a week on my own. At least in theory," she chuckled.

6   "There was a boys' camp nearby, and we scheduled activities or events with them several times during the summer. That's actually how I met your grandfather," she said, smiling fondly.

7   "I love him dearly, but your grandpa is one of the most uncoordinated people I've ever known," Grandma continued. "The day we met, he was paddling a canoe across the reservoir, and he kept overturning it. He'd reach for something in the canoe, or stand up when he got excited and lose his balance. He asked me to give him canoeing lessons, but I think it was just because he wanted to get to know me." Grandma smiled at the memory.

8   "How is a reservoir different than a lake?" asked Meghan.

9   "It is a type of a lake," said Grandma, resting her paddle across her knees. "Most lakes are naturally formed, but reservoirs are made by humans. I've brought you to see Dillon Dam before, haven't I?" she asked. The girls nodded. "Dillon Dam was built about 30 years ago to control the flooding in this area. When a dam is built, an artificial lake is created by flooding the land behind the dam."

10   Becca furrowed her eyebrows. "I still don't understand how that controls flooding," she said.

11   "The dam can be emptied when flooding is expected," said Grandma. "Making space for flood waters helps, because the water can be held in the reservoir and gradually released later. The reservoir is also hundreds of times wider than the river, so water that would flood the banks of a river only causes the water level in the reservoir to rise a small amount." Grandma picked up her paddle, and she and Meghan began paddling again.

12   Becca looked around at the high valley walls surrounding the reservoir and the serene water that stretched as far as she could see. "I'm glad that reservoirs aren't only used for controlling floods," she said.

13   Grandma laughed. "Me, too," she said. "I might never have met your grandpa otherwise!"

Vocabulary Skills

Write the words from the story that have the meanings below.

1. taking place without warning

   _____
   Par. 2

2. made sure of

   _____
   Par. 3

3. quickly and skillfully

   _____
   Par. 3

4. with affection

   _____
   Par. 6

Add a prefix or suffix from the box below to each word to form a new word.

-ly	-est	re-
mis-	-able	

5. patient _____

6. comfort _____

7. arrange _____

8. funny _____

9. gradual _____

10. step _____

Reading Skills

1. What do you think Grandma means when she says she learned to survive in the woods, "at least in theory"?

   _____

   _____

   _____

2. Who do you think is older, Becca or Meghan? Why?

   _____

   _____

3. How did Grandma learn to canoe?

   _____

   _____

4. What advice does Grandma give Becca when Becca is climbing into the canoe?

   _____

5. What is one difference between a natural lake and a reservoir?

   _____

6. Why does Grandma think that Grandpa wanted canoeing lessons?

   _____

   _____

7. What is the setting for this story?

   _____

Study Skills

Check each word that could be found on a page having the guide words shown in dark print.

1. **grudge—guitar**

   _____ guardian   _____ groundhog
   _____ grumpy

2. **decipher—deer**

   _____ defend   _____ dedicate
   _____ decorate

3. **sherbet—shipyard**

   _____ shelter   _____ shear
   _____ shingle

Blocking Water

Is there a dam located near you?

1   If you are hiking through the woods and notice a pile of timber, mud, and stone blocking a stream, you just might have stumbled upon a beaver dam. Beavers build dams so they can construct their lodges in the middle of the pond that forms as a result of the blocked water. The entrance to the lodge is located under the surface of the water, allowing the pond to function as a natural defense against predators. The pond also allows the beavers to live right on top of water lilies, their favorite meal.

2   However, the biggest builders of dams are humans, and they have been doing it for a long time. Some of the earliest structures built by humans are dams dating back nearly 5,000 years. At the beginning of civilization, dams were built in the Middle East so that people could stay in one place and farm. The water captured by dams enabled the first farmers to irrigate crops in areas that were otherwise too dry. The Ma'rib Dam in Yemen, originally built 2,700 years ago, is still in use today, although many parts of it have been rebuilt during that time.

3   Irrigation is just one reason people build dams. Water that pools behind these structures can also supply drinking water to cities and towns. Dams allow large populations to live in places where water is scarce. Lake Mead is a reservoir, or artificial lake, created by Hoover Dam. It provides water for more than 16 million people in Nevada, Arizona, and California. The Colorado River feeds Lake Mead, which holds enough water to cover the entire state of Pennsylvania!

4   Dams are also used to help ships and barges navigate rivers that would otherwise be too shallow. Canals are built alongside the dam so that boats can travel around it. In addition, the canals usually contain locks because the area around the dam is higher than the river, meaning the boat needs to travel up and over the surrounding area.

5   A lock is part of the canal that can be blocked off and filled with water. Each lock is flooded or drained, depending on whether the boat needs to be raised or lowered. The front of the lock is then opened, allowing the boat to float into the next lock. The process is repeated until the boat has traveled up or down the area needed to pass the dam.

6   Many modern dams harness the power of flowing water, transforming its energy into electricity. These dams are hydroelectric dams. The largest hydroelectric dam in the world is under construction right now in China. It is expected to have a reservoir 370 miles long. The Three Gorges Dam on the Yangtze River is designed to control flooding but will also produce enough energy to fill a good deal of China's electrical needs.

7   Three Gorges Dam has created controversy, for many of the same reasons that other large dams have. Land that has always been dry will now be underwater, altering the environment drastically. Dams especially affect migratory fish, like salmon and trout, because they need to move upstream and downstream for feeding and reproduction. Three Gorges Dam has also displaced millions of people because their homes have been destroyed to make space for the dam.

Vocabulary Skills

Write the words from the passage that have the meanings below.

1. allowed; made possible

   _____
   Par. 2

2. to supply with water using artificial means

   _____
   Par. 2

3. not enough to meet a demand

   _____
   Par. 3

4. to direct the course or path of something

   _____
   Par. 4

5. to bring under control and put to use

   _____
   Par. 6

6. took the place of

   _____
   Par. 7

Write the abbreviation for each state in the space beside it.

7. Nevada _____

8. Arizona _____

9. Pennsylvania _____

10. Colorado _____

Check the meaning of the underlined word.

11. The earliest dams may date back 5,000 years.

    _____ in an early way

    _____ most early

    _____ not early

12. Parts of the Ma'rib Dam have been rebuilt.

    _____ built again

    _____ not yet built

    _____ capable of being built

Reading Skills

1. What is one benefit to beavers of having the entrance to a lodge located underwater?

   _____

   _____

2. How old is the Ma'rib Dam?

   _____

   _____

3. Why do dams cause problems for migrating fish?

   _____

   _____

4. Why do canals often contain locks?

   _____

   _____

5. What are two reasons the Three Gorges Dam is being constructed in China?

   _____

   _____

6. What purpose would a reader have for reading this selection?

   _____ for pleasure or entertainment

   _____ for information

   _____ to learn how to build a dam

7. On the lines below, write a summary for paragraph 2.

   _____

   _____

   _____

   _____

The Eighth Wonder of the World

Why is Washington's Grand Coulee Dam considered to be such an impressive structure?

1   The Grand Coulee Dam, on the Columbia River in Washington State, is one of humankind's most amazing structures. There is enough concrete in the dam to build a four-lane highway between Los Angeles and New York City. The dam is more than a mile long, and at 550 feet tall, it is about twice as tall as the Statue of Liberty or Niagara Falls!

2   If you are thinking that it must have been a time-consuming project to build the dam, you are correct. Work on the Grand Coulee Dam was begun in 1933 during Franklin D. Roosevelt's administration. When the dam was finally completed in 1942, nine years after it was begun, it was the largest dam in the world.

3   Initially, the Grand Coulee Dam was built as part of an irrigation system for desert areas in the Pacific Northwest. However, World War II was beginning just as the dam was completed, and it became necessary to use the energy created by the flow of water.

4   Hydroelectric power uses the energy created by falling water to produce electricity. The type of energy produced by falling water is called *mechanical energy*. It is converted into electrical energy by a generator and a water turbine. As the country's need for electricity increased during the war, the Grand Coulee Dam was able to fill some of that need with the massive amounts of energy it produced.

5   Although the dam proved to be beneficial to the area and to the nation, there were also drawbacks to its existence. The land of Native American tribes who lived along the Columbia River was flooded after the construction of the dam, and they were forced to move to new areas. In addition, the dam disrupted the migration of salmon, a staple of their diet.

6   In the 1990s, the government was required to offer a large sum of money to the Colville tribe in payment for the disturbances and suffering the dam had caused. Although the tribe received millions of dollars, the money could not buy back what its members and their relatives had lost.

7   Today, the dam is a popular tourist attraction. It continues to function as a source of irrigation and as a powerful electrical generator. Franklin Delano Roosevelt Lake, the reservoir created by the dam, has more than 500 miles of shoreline. Residents and visitors enjoy a variety of recreational activities there, including fishing, swimming, hiking, and boating. The public can tour the inside of the dam. During the summer months, they can watch a laser light show on the dam's wall.

8   If you ever happen to visit Washington, put the Grand Coulee Dam on your list of places to see. With its enormous size and incredible power, no wonder it is often considered to be the Eighth Wonder of the World.

Vocabulary Skills

Check the meaning of the underlined word in each sentence.

1. Salmon were a <u>staple</u> of life for the Colville tribe of the Pacific Northwest.

   _____ a small piece of metal used for attaching sheets of paper to one another

   _____ something basic and necessary

2. The dam can <u>produce</u> an enormous amount of hydroelectric power.

   _____ create

   _____ fresh fruits and vegetables

Read each word below. Then, write the letter of its synonym on the line beside the word.

3. _____ essential   **a.** disturb

4. _____ disrupt   **b.** regarded

5. _____ variety   **c.** necessary

6. _____ considered   **d.** assortment

Reading Skills

1. On the lines below, write a sentence that describes the main idea of the selection.

   _____

   _____

2. Why does the author say that the money the government paid could not buy back what the Colville tribe had lost?

   _____

   _____

3. How long did it take to complete construction on the Grand Coulee Dam?

   _____

4. Is Franklin Delano Roosevelt Lake a natural or human-made lake? How do you know?

   _____

   _____

5. In paragraph 1, the author compares the height of the dam to the height of two well-known landmarks. What are they?

   _____

6. Check the phrase that best describes the author's purpose.

   _____ to share information about the Grand Coulee Dam

   _____ to entertain

   _____ to persuade the reader to visit the Grand Coulee Dam

Study Skills

Use the schedule below to answer the questions that follow.

Grand Coulee Dam Visitors' Center Schedule
September 7–November 30 9 A.M.–5 P.M. (every day)
December and January CLOSED
February 1–Memorial Day Weekend 9 A.M.–5 P.M. (every day)
Memorial Day Weekend–July 31 8:30 A.M.–11 P.M. (every day)

1. What will the visitors' center hours be on March 8?

   _____

2. During which two months will the center be closed?

   _____

3. When will the center extend its daily hours?

   _____

Book Fair Brainstorming

Does your school hold an annual book fair?

1   "This is a lot of responsibility, Caleb," said Tanika, twirling her pen. "I don't have much experience planning an event like this. I'm glad Mr. Rutledge trusted us to work out all the details, but I'm still worried that we'll forget something important."

2   Caleb leaned back in his chair. "I'm not worried, Tanika," he said. "We just have to be organized. I have no doubt that this will be the best annual book fair George Washington Middle School has ever seen. We'll raise so much money for the library that they'll have to build a new room to accommodate all the books they'll be able to buy," he joked.

3   Tanika grinned at Caleb. "You might be just a bit too optimistic, but I agree with you that somehow we'll manage to make this book fair a success."

4   Caleb took out a pad of paper. "Do we have the list of books the librarians ordered?" he asked.

5   Tanika handed Caleb some papers that he quickly leafed through. "We should think of some interesting display ideas," he said thoughtfully. "The book fairs that we've had in the last few years have been kind of dull. I want this one to make everyone feel excited about reading."

6   "What if we set up areas with different themes?" suggested Tanika. "We can borrow different kinds of sports equipment from Ms. Spisak and make a display near the sports books."

7   Caleb was sitting up in his chair writing furiously. "That is a fantastic idea, Tanika!" he said excitedly. "We can have a different exhibit for each area. My class has a turtle and some fish that we could display in the area with books about animals."

8   "The librarians ordered quite a few winter and holiday books, as well," said Tanika, consulting the list again. "We could make a festive winter scene in one area. I know where there are some little white lights from the school play. I can bring in my ice skates and a few pairs of mittens for the display."

9   "What about trying to see if we could get a few writers to come in on the day of the book fair? They could sell autographed copies of their books and answer questions students have about being a writer."

10   "Rachael Weinstock's mom wrote a picture book a few years ago," said Tanika. "She's done several author events around town, and there's a good chance she'd be willing to help us."

11   "And Carson Davies's dad used to be an editor for a children's book publisher. He might know some local authors, too," added Caleb. He made a few more notes on his pad of paper. "Are you still worried about being able to pull off this book fair, Tanika?" he asked.

12   Tanika shook her head. "Now I just can't wait for it to get here," she said. "I think a little of your optimism has started to rub off on me!"

Vocabulary Skills

1. The Latin root **ann** means *year*. Find a word in paragraph 2 with the root **ann**.

   _____

2. The Greek root **graph** means *write*. Find a word in paragraph 9 with the root **graph**.

   _____

3. The Latin root **loc** means *place*. Find a word in paragraph 11 with the root **loc**.

   _____

4. Check the sentence in which *fair* has the same meaning as it does in paragraph 2.

   _____ All the booths for the fair have been set up.

   _____ Few people thought that the referee's call was fair.

5. Check the sentence in which *dull* has the same meaning as it does in paragraph 5.

   _____ Remind me to have this dull knife sharpened.

   _____ I expected the movie to be dull, so I was surprised to find it so interesting.

Reading Skills

Write **F** before the sentences that are facts. Write **O** before the sentences that are opinions.

1. _____ Tanika worries too much.

2. _____ This year's book fair will be better than previous fairs.

3. _____ Rachael Weinstock's mom is the author of a picture book.

4. _____ Caleb's class has a turtle and some fish.

Mark each sentence below **F** if it is in first-person point of view and **T** if it is in third-person point of view.

5. _____ I think this book fair will be a success.

6. _____ Caleb looked through the list books the librarians ordered.

7. _____ My sister might have some sports equipment we could use.

8. What are two ideas that Tanika and Caleb have to make this year's book fair more exciting?

   _____

   _____

   _____

   _____

9. Why does Caleb think that Mr. Davies might be able to help?

   _____

   _____

   _____

Read the descriptions below. Write **C** next to the phrase if it describes Caleb. Write **T** if it describes Tanika.

10. _____ feels calm and confident about the success of the book fair

11. _____ suggests setting up areas with different themes

12. _____ offers to bring in ice skates and mittens for the winter display

Book Fair Funds

How will Tanika and Caleb decide to spend the proceeds from the book fair?

1   Tanika and Caleb sat at a large round table in the library with their teacher, Mr. Rutledge, and one of the school librarians, Mrs. Angley. The adults were grinning widely at Tanika and Caleb, who smiled back uncertainly.

2   "You are probably wondering why we asked you both to stay a few minutes after school today," began Mr. Rutledge. "We have the totals from last weekend's book fair, and we wanted to share them with you," he continued. "Mrs. Angley, will you do the honors?" he asked, turning to the librarian.

3   Mrs. Angley nodded. "This has been the most successful book fair in the nine years that Washington has held book fairs," she said, passing out a sheet of paper that showed the results of previous book fairs. "Much of the credit goes to you two," she added, gesturing to Tanika and Caleb, who still had expressions of awe on their faces. "Mr. Rutledge is also deserving of some credit since it was his idea to involve such creative and motivated students in planning the fair."

4   "This is great news," said Caleb. "We could see that people were enjoying themselves at the fair, but we had no idea how that would translate into profits."

5   "The planning required a lot of work," added Tanika, "but we had so much help. It really was a team effort."

6   "Because you both put so much energy and enthusiasm into this event," said Mr. Rutledge, "we've decided that we could use your help in allocating the money we raised. The principal and the library staff have already set aside funds for items that are necessities. However, it has not yet been decided how the remaining money will be used. Do you have any ideas?"

7   Caleb and Tanika were quiet for a moment as they thought about the possibilities. Then, Caleb spoke up. "I agree with what Tanika said about the fair being a team effort. Students from every class contributed, and it would be nice if there was a way we could show our appreciation. Could they help decide which books will be added to the library's collection?" he asked.

8   "That's an excellent idea," agreed Mr. Rutledge.

9   "If there's any money leftover," said Tanika, "do you think we could use it to bring authors and illustrators to the school more often? Everyone I talked to seemed to think that was the best part of the fair."

10   Mrs. Angley nodded. "We've already put some money aside for that," she said. "The school received several donations from parents during the fair, and the principal thinks that the money would be well spent just as you've suggested."

11   "There's just one more thing," said Mr. Rutledge, turning to Tanika and Caleb. "Would you consider helping to plan next year's book fair? We could use your expertise."

12   Tanika and Caleb exchanged glances. "With an invitation like that, how could we resist?" said Caleb.

Vocabulary Skills

Write the words from the story that have the meanings below.

1. amazement

   _____
   Par. 3

2. distributing; dividing up

   _____
   Par. 6

3. money marked for a specific purpose

   _____
   Par. 6

4. items that are needed or necessary

   _____
   Par. 6

5. gratitude

   _____
   Par. 7

6. the skill and knowledge of someone experienced

   _____
   Par. 11

Circle the homophone that correctly completes each sentence below.

7. Do you know what the taxicab _____ will be? (fair, fare)

8. The winning _____ will receive a trophy. (teem, team)

9. The building on the corner will be _____ to make room for the new mall. (raised, razed)

10. Which word in paragraph 1 has a prefix and a suffix? _____

11. Write the prefix, suffix, and word's meaning on the lines below.

    _____

    _____

Reading Skills

1. Why do Caleb and Tanika think that the students should be able to vote on the books that will be added to the library?

   _____

   _____

2. Do you think that Caleb and Tanika work well together as a team? Why or why not?

   _____

   _____

3. Why did Mr. Rutledge and Mrs. Angley decide to ask for Caleb and Tanika's help?

   _____

   _____

   _____

4. What is the setting for this story?

   _____

   _____

   _____

5. Do you think that Caleb and Tanika will choose to work together on future projects? Explain.

   _____

   _____

6. Check the line beside the word or words that best describe what type of selection this is.

   _____ a tall tale

   _____ realistic fiction

   _____ historical fiction

A Writer's Life

Who are your favorite authors? Do you know how they became writers?

1 Louis Sachar is one of the most well-known writers of children's books today. He is the author of more than 20 books that are loved by children, parents, teachers, and critics alike. You might recognize Sachar's name from the series of *Wayside School* books or *Marvin Redpost* books. You might also know him as the author of the Newbery Award-winning book *Holes*.

2 As successful as Louis Sachar is at writing funny, touching books that kids can relate to, he didn't always know he wanted to be a writer. Sachar remembers enjoying his writing assignments in school, but writing wasn't something he did on his own. When he was in college, he studied economics, and even briefly studied Russian language and literature.

3 Sachar spent time as a teacher's aide when he was in college because he thought it would be an easy way to earn class credit. Although the work was not as easy as he thought it would be, Sachar found that he really enjoyed working with young people. In fact, Hillside Elementary, where Sachar worked as an aide, eventually became the inspiration for his popular *Wayside School* books. The kids in the books are even named after students that Sachar worked with in real life!

4 Even after his experiences teaching and working with children, Sachar still hadn't made a decision about what career path to follow. After college, he decided to go to law school. He graduated several years later with a law degree. By this time, Sachar had published his first children's book, but he didn't feel confident about making a living as a writer.

5 About ten years later, after the publication of several more books, Sachar finally felt that his books were successful enough for him to devote himself to writing full time. In 1989, Sachar quit his job as an attorney and became a writer.

6 Sachar spends about two hours writing each morning, when he feels most fresh and sharp.

He likes to be alone when he writes, except for the company of his two dogs, Tippy and Lucky. Some writers base their stories closely around the people and events in their lives, and others create characters and places that are entirely fictional. Sachar uses a combination of the two. He tries to remember what it was like to be a child and to use those memories and feelings in his novels. He also uses his teaching experiences, as well as moments from his daughter's life.

7 Sachar doesn't sit down with an organized plan or outline when he starts a new book. Instead, he begins with just a seed of an idea—maybe a character trait or a funny event. He starts writing and finds that the act of writing produces more ideas. Those ideas branch out into other ideas, and before he knows it, a new book is well on its way.

8 Sachar doesn't worry too much about perfecting his story, plot, characters, and setting the first time around. In fact, he may rewrite his story five or six times before he even sends it to his publisher. That might seem like a lot of work, but one thing is for sure—Louis Sachar seems to have hit on a winning formula for writing!

Vocabulary Skills

Write the words from the passage that have the meanings below.

1. the field of study dealing with the development and use of money, goods, and services

   _____
   Par. 2

2. something that moves one to action

   _____
   Par. 3

3. to give one's time or attention completely

   _____
   Par. 5

4. made up; imaginary

   _____
   Par. 6

Rewrite the phrases below in the possessive form.

5. the novels of Louis Sachar

   _____

6. the aide of the teacher

   _____

7. the habits of the writers

   _____

8. the characteristics of the person

   _____

Reading Skills

1. Check the words that best describe Louis Sachar.

   _____ creative

   _____ humorous

   _____ unpredictable

   _____ intelligent

   _____ nosy

2. What purpose would a reader have for reading this selection?

   _____ for information about the life and work of Louis Sachar

   _____ to learn how to solve a problem

   _____ to form an opinion about the work of Louis Sachar

3. Check the line beside the word or words that best describe what type of selection this is.

   _____ autobiography

   _____ historical nonfiction

   _____ biography

4. Name two series of books that Louis Sachar has written.

   _____

   _____

5. Why didn't Sachar become a full-time writer as soon as his first book was published?

   _____

   _____

6. What happens after Sachar has completed the first draft of a book?

   _____

   _____

7. Name two sources of ideas for Sachar's stories and characters.

   _____

   _____

So, You Want to Be a Writer?

What are some tips on becoming a writer?

1. Read everything you can. Most writers are voracious readers. They read because they love to lose themselves in books. They like the sounds of language and the way that reading a good description can feel as satisfying as winning a baseball game or eating a banana split.

As you read, pay attention to what speaks to you. Do you like stories that are fast-paced and full of unexpected twists? Do you prefer to read books with characters who seem like someone you might know? Do you like tales that take you on faraway adventures, or ones that explain the mysteries of the natural world? Do you like to feel scared when you read under the covers, or do you like a story that makes you laugh until you cry? Think about the types of writing you like best, and try to identify the qualities that appeal to you.

2. Keep a notebook. It's easy to forget a good idea if you do not record it immediately. If you get in the habit of carrying a notebook or journal with you everywhere you go, you can write down anything you want to remember. When you are talking to friends in the cafeteria or waiting for the bus, something might spark an idea for a character or a scene in a story. You might have a dream you don't want to forget, or you might just write down the lyrics of a song you love. These everyday thoughts and observations can be material for a story, poem, or essay that you write one day.

3. Write every day. One piece of advice that nearly all writers agree on is that writers must write. It doesn't matter if you feel like you have nothing to say; the important thing is that you write every single day. Sometimes, you need to give yourself permission to write things you know won't be your best work. Once you start writing, you'll see that this is a good way to clear your mind and make room for more of the "good stuff."

4. Join or start a writing group. Do you have any friends who enjoy writing? Think about starting a writing group with other people who have similar interests. It helps to have the support of other writers. You will also receive valuable feedback, or suggestions, about how to make your work better.

5. Do your homework. If you decide that you would like to submit your work for publication, make sure to do your research. If you are sending your writing to a magazine, look through old issues. Does it seem like your writing fits in with the other stories or articles? If you are submitting to a book publisher, explore their Web site to make sure your material is similar to (but not exactly the same as) other books they publish.

Also make sure that you pay attention to the guidelines. Present your work to them exactly the way they have requested it. If your work doesn't conform to their guidelines, the publisher may not even look at it.

6. Stay positive. A writer's life can be frustrating. Sometimes it's hard to sit down and write. You may get many rejections before you receive a single acceptance. This is why perseverance is an important quality for a writer to have.

Writing can also be one of the most satisfying jobs in the world. Most writers feel lucky to do what they do and wouldn't trade their career for any other. You could be one of them someday.

NAME _____

Vocabulary Skills

Write the words from the passage that have the meanings below.

1. very eager; having a large appetite

   _____
   Num. 1

2. the words to a song

   _____
   Num. 2

3. to put forward or turn in for consideration

   _____
   Num. 5

4. to follow a set of rules

   _____
   Num. 5

5. refusals of acceptance

   _____
   Num. 6

6. the quality of continuing to do something in spite of hardship or difficulties

   _____
   Num. 6

Reading Skills

1. Check the phrase that best describes the author's purpose.

   _____ to instruct

   _____ to entertain

   _____ to inform

2. Name three things you might record in a writer's notebook.

   _____

   _____

3. What does the author mean by "Do your homework"?

   _____

   _____

4. Why is perseverance an important quality for a writer to have?

   _____

5. Why do you think that most writers like to read?

   _____

6. On the lines below, write a summary of Step 3.

   _____

   _____

Study Skills

Use the submission guidelines below to answer the questions that follow.

**Willow Lake Press
Guidelines for Submission**

Currently accepting: fiction picture books; nonfiction early readers (especially about sports, animals, and science); young adult fiction

Format: Submission must be typed and printed on plain white 8 1/2 x 11 paper. Your name should appear on the top right corner of each page.

Send your manuscript and a self-addressed stamped envelope (SASE) to—Submissions Editor, Willow Lake Press, 445 Rockbridge Way, Daleville, WI 28556.

1. What is a SASE?

   _____

2. What nonfiction early reader topics is Willow Lake Press interested in?

   _____

3. Where should your name appear on your manuscript?

   _____

Spectrum Reading Grade 6

121

A Lone Adventure

Will Tyler be able to survive all alone on a faraway island?

1   When I woke up, my mouth was full of sand and the sun was glaring angrily at me from high in the cloudless sky. I sat up and spit the sand from my mouth. I could feel every sore muscle as I walked the few feet to the water. The salt stung my dry, cracked lips, but the water helped remove the last bits of sand that lay gritty and unpleasant below my tongue and in my teeth.

2   As I stood in the water to soothe my sunburned skin, I tried to piece together the events of the past few days. Try as I might, I could remember very little. I knew that my boat had capsized because I could see its remains lying not far down the beach. I knew that the crew had escaped in the lifeboats when they became sure the ship was sinking. They had begged me to come with them, but I insisted that a captain must always remain with his ship.

3   A few minutes later, I decided to walk down the beach and see what remained of my beloved vessel. My stomach was an animal, growling and rumbling hungrily. As bright as the day was, I knew that night would fall quickly. I needed to build a shelter for myself before dark, and I would need a source of fresh water and food.

4   It would be hard to call the bits of wood that were strewn about the beach a boat. Luckily, I found a canvas bag that was tied to a large, flat piece of wood that I must have used as a makeshift raft. I worked at the knot for a few minutes before I was able to loosen it enough to untie the bag.

5   Inside, I was pleased to find a knife, a wool blanket, a small bottle of water, and four cans of food—fish, beans, corn, and stewed tomatoes. There was also a box of matches, but my heart sank when I saw how soggy they were. I would place them on the beach to dry in the sun, but I was skeptical that they would be of much help in producing fire.

6   I chose a spot just off the beach to make my shelter. The sandy ground would provide a bit more comfort than the land farther up in the wooded area, which was knotted with the roots of trees and covered with twigs and branches. I used my knife to split pieces of bamboo that I planned to use as the walls and roof of my hut.

7   I was sweating with the effort of my work when I felt a cool breeze that chilled my damp skin. I stood quietly, enjoying a moment of relief from the sun's glare, when I noticed dark clouds gathering in the sky. I quickly resumed my task, hoping that the storm would not move in too rapidly. Another gust of wind caught the edge of my blanket and carried it down the beach. I raced after it as the first sounds of thunder rumbled around me.

8   The garbage truck growled and rumbled as it chugged down the street. Tyler lay on his bed with his eyes open for a moment before he could identify the sound. He sat up quickly, and the book that had been resting on his covers dropped to the floor with a thud. The bearded face of Robinson Crusoe stared up at Tyler from the cover of the book as he fumbled for his glasses. He glanced at his bedside clock. Eight o'clock! He had overslept again. Tyler jumped out of bed and headed for the bathroom.

Vocabulary Skills

Write the words from the story that have the meanings below.

1. overturned

   _____
   Par. 2

2. a boat or ship

   _____
   Par. 3

3. spread or scattered around

   _____
   Par. 4

4. something that is used as a temporary substitute

   _____
   Par. 4

5. went back to something that was already begun

   _____
   Par. 7

Circle the homophone that correctly completes each sentence below.

6. My back was _____ for a week after I helped Aliya move. (soar, sore)

7. We planted a row of _____ trees beside the driveway. (beach, beech)

8. Do _____ ride your bicycle without wearing a helmet! (not, knot)

Underline the word with a prefix or a suffix in each sentence. Then, write the meaning of the word on the line.

9. The sand felt unpleasant in my mouth.

   _____

10. The day was warm, and the sky was cloudless.

    _____

Find the metaphor in paragraph 3, and write it on the line.

11. _____

Reading Skills

1. Why didn't the narrator escape from the sinking ship on one of the lifeboats?

   _____

   _____

2. Name three items the narrator found in the canvas bag.

   _____

   _____

3. **Personification** is a literary device in which human characteristics are given to inanimate objects. In the sentence *Sam's bed beckoned to him invitingly*, Sam's bed is personified. Find an example of personification in the story, and write it on the line below.

   _____

   _____

4. What do you think the book Tyler was reading when he fell asleep was about?

   _____

   _____

5. From what point of view are the first seven paragraphs of the story told?

   _____

   _____

6. From what point of view is the last paragraph told?

   _____

   _____

7. What purpose would a reader have for reading this selection?

   _____ for information

   _____ for entertainment

   _____ to answer a specific question

The Real Crusoe

How long do you think you could go without human company?

1   *Robinson Crusoe* by Daniel Defoe is one of the most well-known and widely-read books ever written. It was published in 1719, and by the end of the next century, more than 700 versions, translations, sequels, and imitations had been published.

2   *Robinson Crusoe* is a fascinating adventure tale of a man who is shipwrecked on an island and survives until his rescue 28 years later. There is no doubt that Defoe was an imaginative and gifted storyteller, but the idea for the fictional character of Crusoe didn't come solely from Defoe's imagination. That is why it is believed that the story of Robinson Crusoe was actually based on the real life adventures of Alexander Selkirk.

3   Selkirk was a Scottish sailor on a ship called the *Cinque Ports*. He had had frequent disagreements with the ship's captain, William Dampier, about the safety of the craft and the decisions the captain had made during the expedition. Selkirk demanded to be left ashore at the Juan Fernández Islands (about 400 miles off the coast of Chile) when he became convinced that the *Cinque Ports* was no longer seaworthy.

4   Captain Dampier was not sorry to see Selkirk go and happily left him on one of the islands. Selkirk seemed to have had a moment of regret as the ship left, but it was too late; no one heard his cries for the ship to return.

5   Selkirk quickly learned what he needed to do to survive on the uninhabited island. He had brought several items with him from the ship, including a musket, gunpowder, a knife, carpenter's tools, clothing, and a few books.

6   Selkirk used native trees and his tools to construct two huts for shelter, which he then covered with long grasses. There were plenty of goats on the island, so he was assured a steady supply of milk and meat. There were even vegetables that had been planted by Spanish sailors who had stopped at the island in years past.

7   At first, Selkirk had a serious problem with the island's rats, which gnawed at him at night while he slept. However, sailors had also left cats on the island. Selkirk found that he could easily control the rat population by using meat to entice the cats to remain nearby.

8   Selkirk managed to survive on the island for four years. Loneliness and depression were as much a problem for him as food and shelter. Eventually, though, Selkirk came to enjoy living alone with only his books, cats, and goats for company.

9   When he was finally rescued by a ship called the *Duke*, Selkirk found that it was difficult to adjust to being around people again and that he had lost some of his language skills. He became accustomed to living in society again, but a part of him always missed the peace of the island.

10   In 1712, Woodes Rogers, captain of the *Duke*, published *A Cruising Voyage Round the World*, which included an account of Alexander Selkirk's experiences in the Juan Fernández Islands. This book, as well as Defoe's *Robinson Crusoe*, has given readers a chance to experience the life and adventures of an island castaway— adventures they could otherwise only imagine.

Vocabulary Skills

Check the correct meaning of the underlined word.

1. *Robinson Crusoe* appeals to people <u>regardless</u> of age or nationality.

   _____ full of regard

   _____ without regard for

   _____ capable of regarding

2. Selkirk could <u>easily</u> control the rat population by feeding the island's cats.

   _____ most easy

   _____ not easy

   _____ in an easy way

In each row, circle the word that does not belong.

3. construct   break   build   assemble

4. imaginative   creative   inventive   precise

5. difficult   lonely   challenging   hard

Reading Skills

1. What nationality was Selkirk?

   _____

2. Why do you think Selkirk called out to the *Cinque Ports* as it sailed away from the island?

   _____

   _____

3. How do we know so many details about Selkirk's experiences on the island?

   _____

   _____

5. What is one difference between Robinson Crusoe and Alexander Selkirk?

   _____

   _____

   _____

6. Is *Robinson Crusoe* fantasy, or does it take place in reality?

   _____

7. Is *A Cruising Voyage Round the World* fantasy, or does it take place in reality?

   _____

Circle the word that best completes each sentence below.

8. Selkirk's use of _____ thinking allowed him to survive on the island.

   optimistic   creative   frequent

9. It was difficult for Selkirk to _____ to life in society.

   readjust   communicate   accustom

10. Woodes Rogers's book _____ Selkirk's experiences.

    neglected   ridiculed   detailed

Study Skills

Use the pronunciation key on the inside back cover of this book to write the words that match these pronunciations.

1. /sûr vīvɜ/ _____

2. /ad ven ɜ chûr/ _____

3. /pôpɜ yə lāɜ shən/ _____

4. /ri mān ɜ/ _____

5. /lōn ɜ lē nes/ _____

A Desert in Bloom

Will Chiara and her mom be able to make themselves feel at home in their new house?

1 Chiara made her way down the hallway, past the neatly stacked cardboard boxes, and into the kitchen, where the early morning sunlight streamed through the windows. She stepped over another stack of boxes and slid open the glass door that led to a small deck. Chiara's mom was sipping a cup of coffee, wisps of steam drifting into the air.

2 "What are you doing, Mom?" asked Chiara, staring out at the turquoise sky and clumps of plants that dotted the backyard.

3 "Well," began Mrs. Giardini, "I was just noticing how strange and unfamiliar the landscape is here. Arizona and Massachusetts could be different planets, as far as the landscape is concerned. I was missing all the greenery in our backyard at home, but I was also appreciating how blue the sky is here. It really contrasts with the red earth, doesn't it?" she asked, taking a sip of coffee.

4 Chiara nodded. "I see what you mean," she said. "It doesn't look like we could grow much here, does it?" she said gesturing to the few dusty looking plants in the yard.

5 "I have an idea," said Mrs. Giardini suddenly. "Have you had your breakfast yet?" she asked. Chiara shook her head. "Grab a muffin and some fruit, and come with me."

6 Half an hour later, Chiara and her mom pulled into a nursery on the outskirts of town. As they entered the greenhouse, both Chiara and her mother took a deep breath, inhaling the familiar green, damp scent of growing plants. "Can I help you?" asked a man wearing a tag with the nursery's logo and the name *Joseph* printed on it.

7 Mrs. Giardini smiled. "We've just moved here from Massachusetts," she began. "We need some help starting a desert garden."

8 "Welcome to Arizona!" said Joseph. "The weather and the landscape here might take a little getting used to, but once you fall in love with it, you won't want to live anywhere else.

9 "My first recommendation is that you primarily plant native plants. They thrive in this climate for a reason, and you won't have to spend all your time watering plants that were meant to live somewhere else."

10 "That makes sense," said Mrs. Giardini. "I've never grown cacti or other succulents before, but I think that it could be fun to experiment with them."

11 Joseph nodded in agreement. "You can create some beautiful cacti gardens, but you aren't limited to planting only succulents in the desert." He pointed to several nearby pots. "I'll show you a few of my favorites. The desert willow has beautiful blooms that some people think resemble orchids. Indian paintbrush can provide bright bursts of color in your garden."

12 Chiara and her mom grinned at each other. "I don't think we had any idea what a lush, colorful garden we could have in the desert!" exclaimed Mrs. Giardini. "I'm not even going to worry about our stacks of boxes until we get a good start on the garden."

13 "I can't wait to begin," said Chiara, already loading plants into the cart.

Vocabulary Skills

Write the words from the story that have the meanings below.

1. the edge or outer limits of a city or town

   _____
   Par. 6

2. breathing in

   _____
   Par. 6

3. for the most part

   _____
   Par. 9

4. to grow successfully; flourish

   _____
   Par. 9

Find the compound words from the selection that contain the words below.

5. board _____
   Par. 1

6. land _____
   Par. 3

7. green _____
   Par. 6

8. brush _____
   Par. 11

Reading Skills

1. Number the events below to show the order in which they happened.

   _____ Joseph showed Chiara and her mom several of his favorite desert plants.

   _____ Chiara ate her breakfast in the car.

   _____ The Giardinis moved to Arizona from Massachusetts.

   _____ Mrs. Giardini said she missed the greenery in her old backyard.

   _____ Chiara found her mother sitting on the deck sipping coffee.

2. What problem do Chiara and her mom have at the beginning of the story?

   _____

3. Do you think that planting a garden will help the Giardinis feel more at home in Arizona? Why or why not?

   _____

   _____

4. What is one way in which Massachusetts and Arizona are different?

   _____

5. What does Mrs. Giardini mean when she says, "Arizona and Massachusetts could be different planets"?

   _____

   _____

6. Name the two different settings in this story.

   _____

Study Skills

Write the name of the reference source you could use to answer each question below.

| atlas | dictionary |
| newspaper | encyclopedia |

1. What will the weather be like in Phoenix on Saturday?

   _____

2. Which five states surround Massachusetts?

   _____

3. What are the characteristics of a desert?

   _____

4. What is the origin of the word *cactus*?

   _____

A Dry, Hot Land

Where is the world's largest desert?

1   Unless you live in the Western part of the United States, you may consider deserts to be exotic, rare places. Actually, deserts are very common, covering nearly one-third of Earth's land surface. Although lack of precipitation is the most obvious characteristic of desert regions—they receive less than ten inches per year—deserts also have high rates of evaporation. What little precipitation does fall is quickly absorbed back into the atmosphere.

2   Because of this lack of moisture, deserts can be very hot during the day. Water has a natural cooling effect, but without it, the sun cooks the land. In some deserts, temperatures are regularly as high as 130 degrees Fahrenheit. However, after the sun goes down, all that heat escapes from the desert ground and the temperatures drop quickly, sometimes all the way to freezing!

3   Some deserts are not hot, even during the day. Areas with low precipitation and high evaporation rates located in the extreme Northern Hemisphere are called *tundras*, a type of frozen desert. Because of the tundra's extremely low temperature, any moisture that is present remains frozen.

4   Sandy deserts are the most familiar, probably because they are filmed and photographed so often for their natural beauty. Looking like giant, frozen ocean waves, sand dunes reach up to meet the brilliant blue sky. In fact, the dunes are not frozen at all. They are constantly moving and act more like the ocean than you might think.

5   Winds in the desert are very powerful because there is so little in the landscape to slow them down. The sand gets pushed around, just like water in the sea, and shifted and shaped into constantly changing wave-like forms. However, only about 20 percent of Earth's deserts are made of sand. Most deserts consist of larger rocks like pebbles and stones.

6   The largest desert on Earth is the Sahara in northern Africa. Covering more than three-and-a-half million square miles, the whole United

States could fit within this arid region. The Sahara is one of the driest places on earth. It receives almost no rainfall during the year and has basically no surface water. However, there is water flowing underground that occasionally reaches the desert surface. An area of moisture and plant life within a dry desert is called an *oasis*. Although there are some natural oases, most of them are artificially created by irrigation or wells.

7   The Gobi is a major desert found in Asia. It sits on a plateau that stretches between two higher mountains. Even though part of the Gobi is as harsh as any desert, most of it is covered in a thin layer of bushes and grass that allows people to live there. The famous Venetian (və nē₃ shən) traveler Marco Polo made his way across the Gobi in 1275, becoming the first explorer to describe this arid region to Europeans.

8   The largest desert in the United States is the Mojave Desert, which covers parts of California, Utah, Nevada, and Arizona. An area of the Mojave, called *Death Valley*, is the lowest and hottest point in North America. Despite its reputation for hot temperatures, the Mojave does get quite cold during the winter, regularly dropping to 20 to 30 degrees Fahrenheit, and it sometimes even snows there.

Vocabulary Skills

Write the words from the passage that have the meanings below.

1. the process by which liquid changes into vapor or gas

   _____
   Par. 1

2. water that falls to Earth in the form of rain or snow

   _____
   Par. 3

3. hills of sand that are pushed into shape by the wind

   _____
   Par. 4

4. dry; having little rainfall

   _____
   Par. 6

5. an area of flat land that is higher than the surrounding land

   _____
   Par. 7

Reading Skills

1. How much of Earth's land surface do deserts cover?

   _____

2. Who was Marco Polo?

   _____

   _____

3. Why do some people compare sand dunes to ocean waves?

   _____

   _____

4. What is an oasis? What is the plural form of oasis?

   _____

   _____

Write **T** before the sentences that are true. Write **F** before the sentences that are false.

5. _____ Most of Earth's deserts are made of sand.

6. _____ The Sahara receives almost no rainfall.

7. _____ The Mojave Desert is the largest American desert.

8. _____ The Gobi is located in northern Africa.

Study Skills

A **bibliography** is a list of articles or books that an author referred to when writing his or her own work. Use the bibliographic entries below to answer the questions that follow.

Chin, Cynthia. *Deserts of the World*. New York: McNaughton Publishers, Inc., 2001.

Gordon, Oliver. "The Effects of Global Warming on Desert Temperatures." *EnviroWorld*. (January 2005): 45–52.

1. Who is the author of the magazine article?

   _____

2. In what year was *Deserts of the World* published?

   _____

3. On which pages of the January 2005 issue of *EnviroWorld* would you find the article referenced above?

   _____

Calling Nowhere

Why would there be a phone booth in the middle of the desert?

1   At some point following World War II, a phone booth was installed in the Mojave Desert, 12 miles from the nearest interstate. It seems like an odd location for a phone booth, but there are two mines in the area, and the phone was originally installed for use by the miners and their families.

2   Godfrey Daniels, a computer programmer from Arizona, heard about the phone from a friend. He had the number and decided to call it one day, just to see if anyone might answer. He didn't really expect a response, and sure enough, there was no answer when he called.

3   After dialing the number periodically, he was shocked to hear a busy signal one day. He assumed that there was a problem with the line, but he kept calling anyway. After several tries, someone actually answered the phone. Daniels spoke with a woman who worked at one of the mines. She lived in a remote area without phone service and used the phone for making calls.

4   Daniels loved the idea of a phone in the middle of nowhere. He was even more fascinated with the idea that someone might actually be available to answer the phone in such a remote place. He posted the phone's number on the Internet, and people began calling it. Just as Daniels was intrigued by the idea of the phone booth in the middle of the desert, so were the callers who had visited his Web site.

5   Daniels eventually traveled to Southern California to visit the booth himself. Evidently, he wasn't the only person to have that idea. As more people heard about the Mojave Desert phone booth, tourists decided to visit the secluded location. People who called the phone began to frequently hear a busy signal. When someone answered the phone, he or she had the opportunity to speak with callers from all around the United States, as well as Germany, England, Italy, France, Australia, and South Africa.

6   What did strangers find to talk about during these unusual calls? They usually identified themselves and discussed where they were calling from and how they had heard about the phone booth. One thing people love about the Internet is how it seems to make the world feel smaller. Maybe in some small way, the Mojave Desert phone booth accomplished the same thing.

7   In May of 2000, the National Park Service and Pacific-Bell, the owner of the phone booth, made the decision to remove the booth. The National Park Service felt that the area was receiving too much traffic as a result of all the publicity surrounding the booth. They were worried that it might somehow damage the environment, and they felt that it was their responsibility to protect the land of the Mojave Desert National Preserve.

8   Today, the place where the booth once stood is marked by a simple tombstone. People who don't know that it was removed still call the number. There is no disconnect message on the line. The number just rings and rings, as the caller waits patiently for someone to answer.

Vocabulary Skills

Write the words from the passage that have the meanings below.

1. put in position for use

   _____
   Par. 1

2. from time to time

   _____
   Par. 3

3. supposed

   _____
   Par. 3

4. faraway; isolated

   _____
   Par. 4

5. far removed

   _____
   Par. 5

Use a dictionary to help you place the words below into the correct categories.

finale	fiasco
bouquet	suite
tornado	pasta
chef	fiesta

6. Spanish   7. Italian   8. French

   _____   _____   _____

   _____   _____   _____

   _____   _____

Write **S** if the possessive word is singular. Write **P** if it is plural.

9. _____ the phone booth's location

10. _____ the callers' nationalities

11. _____ Godfrey Daniels's interest

12. _____ the tourists' visits

Reading Skills

1. How did Godfrey Daniels publicize the Mojave Desert phone booth?

   _____

2. Do you think the National Parks Service and Pacific-Bell made the right decision to remove the phone booth? Explain.

   _____

   _____

3. What happens if someone calls the phone booth today?

   _____

4. Why was the phone booth originally installed?

   _____

   _____

5. On the lines below, write the main idea of paragraph 6.

   _____

   _____

Write **T** before the sentences that are true. Write **F** before the sentences that are false.

6. _____ The phone booth was originally intended to be used by miners.

7. _____ The phone booth is still in working order today.

8. _____ Godfrey Daniels posted the number of the booth on the Internet.

9. _____ The phone booth was located in Arizona.

10. _____ People seemed to like the idea of connecting with others in faraway places.

A Paper Surprise

Keep reading to learn more about Aunt Suki's interesting hobby.

1   Emi and Ken were sitting on the floor of the guest bedroom talking to their aunt. Their parents had gone out for the evening, and they were trying to decide if they should rent a movie, play a game, or make Aunt Suki's special chocolate-chunk oatmeal cookies.

2   "What are those, Aunt Suki?" asked Emi, pointing to two brightly-colored paper animals sitting on top of the dresser.

3   "Last night, I couldn't sleep, probably because I was still adjusting to the time difference between California and New Jersey," replied Aunt Suki. "I was rummaging through my suitcase, looking for a book or a crossword puzzle, when I found my origami papers."

4   "Origami is paper folding, right?" asked Ken.

5   Aunt Suki nodded. "There is more to it than that, though. The nature of origami appeals to many people. You must concentrate when you do origami, but it doesn't require a great deal of thought.

6   "In a way, it reminds me of counting. Once you know your numbers, counting is a simple task. But when you are counting a large number of things, you must concentrate or you will lose your place. Counting isn't as productive, or nearly as enjoyable, as origami, though," Aunt Suki added, smiling and showing the dimple in her right cheek.

7   Emi reached up and touched the small indentation on her aunt's face. "Mom has one just like it," she said.

8   "I know," said Aunt Suki. "Your mother's dimple is in her left cheek, and mine is in my right cheek. When we were little, we used to pretend it meant that we were twins."

9   Emi and Ken grinned. They liked the idea of their mother and Aunt Suki as little girls, pretending to be twins. "Does Mom know how to do origami?" asked Ken.

10   Aunt Suki shook her head. "Even though we grew up in Japan, I didn't learn origami until I moved to the United States. Your mother has mentioned that it is a tradition she would like to learn one day, so I thought I might give her a few lessons while I'm here."

11   "Can you give us a few lessons, too?" asked Emi. She cupped the delicate origami bird gently in her hand. "I can't believe you made this just by folding paper."

12   "Of course," said Aunt Suki. "I'd love to." She gestured to the bird in Emi's hands. "Pull his tail gently." When Emi did, the bird's wings flapped up and down. Emi looked amazed.

13   "When can we start?" asked Ken, pulling the origami frog from the dresser to examine it more closely.

14   Aunt Suki shrugged. "Whenever you'd like."

15   "You can teach us first," suggested Emi, "and we'll help you teach Mom. We'll be passing the tradition up instead of down."

16   Aunt Suki smiled again, showing her dimple. "I think your mom will love the surprise," she said.

Vocabulary Skills

Write the words from the story that have the meanings below.

1. getting used to; becoming accustomed to

   _____
   Par. 3

2. to focus one's thoughts or think deeply about

   _____
   Par. 5

3. a dent

   _____
   Par. 7

4. placed one's hands in the shape of a cup

   _____
   Par. 11

Circle the homophone that correctly completes each sentence below.

5. When Emi pulled the bird's _____, it flapped its wings. (tail, tale)

6. Please _____ down the following information. (right, write)

7. The _____ family will be attending the reunion. (whole, hole)

Underline the compound word in each sentence. Then, write the two words that make up each compound.

8. Aunt Suki discovered some origami papers in her suitcase.

   _____   _____

9. She was looking for a crossword puzzle to work on because she couldn't sleep.

   _____   _____

10. Oatmeal with cinnamon and bananas is my favorite way to start the day.

    _____   _____

Reading Skills

Mark each sentence below **F** if it is in first-person point of view and **T** if it is in third-person point of view.

1. _____ Can we rent a movie tonight?

2. _____ I moved to the United States when I was 19 years old.

3. _____ Ken examined the origami frog.

4. _____ I find origami to be a relaxing hobby.

5. _____ Emi and Ken liked hearing stories about their mother as a little girl.

6. How is Aunt Suki related to Emi and Ken's mother?

   _____

   _____

7. Where did Aunt Suki grow up?

   _____

8. What does Emi mean when she says they'll pass the tradition "up instead of down"?

   _____

   _____

9. What does Aunt Suki do when she can't sleep?

   _____

10. What feature do Aunt Suki and her sister share?

    _____

11. What purpose would a reader have for reading this selection?

    _____ to learn

    _____ to form an opinion

    _____ for entertainment

Fascinating Folders

Have you ever tried folding paper into interesting shapes?

1   What can you do with a simple sheet of paper? You could write a note to a friend, type a story, or make a paper airplane. But if you learn a few basic folding techniques, you could be making a variety of interesting objects, such as a grasshopper, a stegosaurus, a giraffe, a pick-up truck, or even the White House. There's a good chance that an expert folder somewhere in the world has made an origami version of almost anything you can imagine.

2   Origami is the art of folding paper into three-dimensional figures of people, animals, and objects. The word *origami* is Japanese. It comes from the word *oru*, meaning *to fold*, and *kami*, meaning *paper*. The origin of origami itself, however, is unclear. Some historians believe that it was first practiced in China around the second century A.D. Others think that there is not enough evidence to support this theory and that the practice of origami was begun in Japan several hundred years later. What we do know is that origami was clearly developed in Japan, where it is considered a part of the culture and lifestyle of the people.

3   One of the most fascinating aspects of origami is the way in which something as simple as a sheet of paper can be transformed into something beautiful and complex. Origami begins with sheets of special paper that are usually six inches on each side. The paper is generally white on one side and colored or marked with a decorative pattern on the other side. It is thin, which allows it to be folded many times, and creases easily.

4   Although origami paper is traditionally used in this ancient craft, modern-day folders have experimented with many other materials, such as tissue paper, silk, foil, and even bubblegum wrappers. Folders usually avoid scissors and glue, two taboos in the world of paper folding.

5   Beginners are often taught several folds and bases which are the starting shapes for other, more complicated figures. Some basic folds are the valley fold, mountain fold, petal fold, rabbit ear, squash fold, and reverse fold. These folds are used to create bases, such as the kite, fish, bird, and frog. Once a folder has learned these basic elements, he or she can progress to more elaborate figures.

6   Diagrams are important to people who take origami seriously because they show the folds needed to make a particular figure. In the early 1950s, Akira Yoshizawa, a Japanese origami master, began publishing books that provided illustrations showing others how to re-create the designs he had invented. He also created a set of diagram symbols that could be used when someone wanted to share with others a figure he or she had created.

7   For some people, origami is a hobby. Others view it as an art form and a means of creative expression. It is not uncommon for people to spend a great deal of time creating original pieces of origami in designs they have invented themselves. For example, one man created an origami model of the *Starship Enterprise* from the popular television show *Star Trek*. It took him a month to design the piece. If someone else wishes to duplicate it, they can use the 72 diagrams and 11 pages of directions the designer created to explain the process.

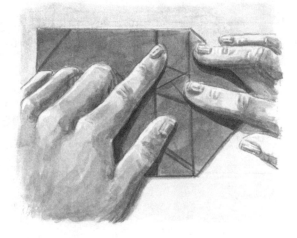

Vocabulary Skills

Write the words from the passage that have the meanings below.

1. made of many parts

   _____
   Par. 3

2. like a custom that has been passed down

   _____
   Par. 4

3. things that are forbidden and should be avoided

   _____
   Par. 4

4. detailed; fancy

   _____
   Par. 5

5. copy

   _____
   Par. 7

6. The Greek root **saur** means *lizard*. Find a word in paragraph 1 with the root **saur**.

   _____

7. The Latin root **var** means *different*. Find a word in paragraph 1 with the root **var**.

   _____

8. The Latin root **form** means *shape*. Find a word in paragraph 3 with the root **form**.

   _____

9. The Latin root **lab** means *work*. Find a word in paragraph 5 with the root **lab**.

   _____

Find an antonym in the story for each of the words below.

10. novice _____
    Par. 1

11. complicated _____
    Par. 1

12. boring _____
    Par. 3

Reading Skills

1. What does the word *origami* mean in Japanese?

   _____

2. Name two materials other than origami paper that have been used in modern origami.

   _____

3. Why do you think that serious origamists do not use scissors or glue?

   _____

4. How many diagrams would you have to follow to create an origami model of the *Starship Enterprise*?

   _____

Write **T** before the sentences that are true. Write **F** before the sentences that are false.

5. _____ Origami paper tends to be thicker than regular paper.

6. _____ People have experimented with using materials other than paper to create origami figures.

7. _____ Akira Yoshizawa was the first person to practice origami in Japan.

8. _____ The kite, fish, bird, and frog are four origami bases.

9. _____ Some historians believe origami has its origins in China.

10. Check the sentence below that is the best summary for paragraph 6.

    _____ Yoshizawa published origami books during the 1950s.

    _____ Origami diagrams are important because they allow people to share their designs for particular figures.

    _____ Diagrams show the folds needed to make origami figures.

Seeing Differently

Do you think you would have a hard time coping with losing your eyesight?

1   "Hi, Grandpa," said Pablo, taking a seat across from his grandfather at the breakfast table. Pablo knew that his grandfather's eyesight had been going downhill for the past year. Still, it was a shock to realize that his grandfather could now see only occasional shadows and changes in light.

2   "Morning, Pablo," said Grandpa, with the same old grin he had always had. "Here, try a bite of this." Grandpa neatly scooped up a piece of omelet from his plate and offered it to Pablo.

3   Pablo ate the piece of omelet and made a face. "The eggs aren't too bad, Grandpa," he said, "but I don't know how you can eat all that hot sauce for breakfast."

4   Grandpa laughed. "It keeps me young!" he said.

5   Pablo was surprised to see Grandpa walk over to the computer a few minutes later and flip it on. "Do you need some help, Grandpa?" asked Pablo.

6   "I don't think so," replied Grandpa. "I just wanted to get a little dose of morning news," he said.

7   "How will you do that?" asked Pablo curiously, pulling up a chair next to his grandfather.

8   "Well, I'm going to go to a special Web site where I can hear an audio clip of the news. I listen to the headlines and then choose a story I want to hear more about." Pablo's grandfather began typing at the keyboard.

9   "How do you know where all the letters are?" asked Pablo.

10   "I've been typing for a long time," answered Grandpa. "After 60 years of typing, I think I have the location of the keys committed to memory. But if I didn't, I could use a Braille keyboard to guide me."

11   "Do you use Braille to read books?" asked Pablo.

12   "Sometimes," replied Grandpa. "Usually, I just do it to stay in practice though. Books in Braille can be very large and awkward to use because spelling out words in Braille takes up more space than using the Roman alphabet. That's why a type of Braille called *Grade 2 Braille* is used in almost all books. In Grade 2 Braille, contractions are used to represent frequently used words. For example, *b* stands for *but*, *c* stands for *can*, and *d* stands for *do*. Using contractions makes a Braille book easier to read and hold.

13   "I prefer listening to audio recordings of books. There are some marvelous readers. The range of voices a single reader can do is quite impressive." Grandpa paused to adjust the volume on the computer's speakers. He looked surprised when Pablo grabbed him in a bear hug.

14   "I'm glad you're here, Grandpa," said Pablo. "And I'm glad that you've adjusted to the changes in your eyesight so well."

15   "Losing my eyesight just made all my other senses sharper," said Grandpa. "It sounds like a cliché, but it's true." He smiled at his grandson. "I'm happy to be here, too," he added. "I can never get enough time with my grandkids."

Vocabulary Skills

Write the words from the story that have the meanings below.

1. an amount or serving of something taken at one time

   _____
   Par. 6

2. dedicated to a particular purpose

   _____
   Par. 10

3. a saying or expression that is overused

   _____
   Par. 15

Write the idiom from paragraph 1 on the line next to its meaning.

4. declining; getting worse _____

In each row, circle the word that does not belong.

5. hear   audio   explain   listen

6. memory   believe   remember   reminisce

7. marvelous   interesting   great   fantastic

Divide the words below into syllables using a slash (/).

8. a f t e r

9. b r e a k f a s t

10. a c r o s s

11. s i n g l e

12. e y e s i g h t

Reading Skills

1. Why does Pablo make a face after he tries his grandpa's omelet?

   _____

   _____

2. How are the Braille contractions that Grandpa talks about different from the contractions you are familiar with?

   _____

   _____

3. How can Grandpa type without seeing the keyboard?

   _____

   _____

4. Name two reasons that Grandpa prefers audio books to Braille books.

   _____

   _____

5. Number the events below to show the order in which they happened.

   _____ Grandpa explained Grade 2 Braille to Pablo.

   _____ Pablo hugged his grandpa.

   _____ Pablo sat down at the breakfast table.

   _____ Grandpa turned on the computer.

Study Skills

Use the letters of the Braille alphabet to decode the words below.

A B E I L M O P R T

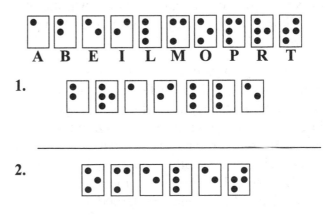

1. _____

2. _____

Looking Into the Eye

Do you know how the human eye functions?

1   As you begin reading this, you probably aren't thinking about how your eyes allow you to see the letters, the book, and everything else in the room. But your eyes are the complex organs that perform this very specific function, and without them you would not see. Your eyes change the light patterns surrounding you into information the brain can use to form a visual image.

2   Light is the key to vision. Light waves coming from the sun or a lightbulb bounce off objects and surfaces, creating unique patterns and colors for your eyes to detect. Light enters the eye first through the cornea, the tough, clear outer layer of your eyeball. The cornea protects the fragile parts located inside the eyeball. It is also the first place where light is refracted so that the image you see is in focus. When someone has laser eye-surgery, it is a defective cornea that is cut and reshaped so that the person can see clearly without glasses.

3   Directly behind the cornea is a watery fluid, called the *aqueous humor*, that keeps the moving parts of the eye flexible and hydrated. The iris, the colored part of your eye, is the first of these moving parts. The black dot in the middle of your iris is an opening called the *pupil*, and it controls the amount of light entering the eye. Muscles in the iris contract and relax to change the size of the pupil. When you walk indoors on a sunny day and notice that it takes time for your eyes to adjust, it is because you are waiting for your pupils to open wide enough to make up for the reduced light.

4   Human beings have round pupils, but many animals have pupils of different shapes. Cats and snakes, for instance, have slit-shaped openings in their irises, allowing them to see in a wider range of light and dark circumstances. No matter what their shape, pupils appear black because they are the hole leading into the dark interior of the eyeball where light is absorbed.

5   Sitting right inside the pupil's opening is the lens, the other moving part of the eye. The lens is a flattened, transparent disc that works with the cornea to focus images onto the back of your eyeball. Although the shape of the cornea is fixed, the lens is attached to muscles that make it rounder or flatter, depending on what is needed for focusing.

6   Inside the eyeball is a clear, jelly-like substance that keeps it round, like air filling a balloon. The back wall of the eyeball contains a very important area called the retina. The retina is covered with two kinds of light-sensitive nerve cells. Six million of them are *cones*, the cells that read color. Cone-shaped cells are divided into three types that detect only specific colors—yellow, green, or blue—but combine to let you see an incredible array of different colors. Color blindness is caused by a lack of one or more of these specific cone cells.

7   The most abundant cells in the retina, nearly 120 million of them, are the *rods*. These rod-shaped cells are much more sensitive to light than the cones, but they only produce black and white imagery. Most of the cones are located in the center of the retina, where you have the sharpest focus and sight. The edges of the retina, however, contain more rods that can detect very subtle amounts of light.

8   If you go out on a clear night, you might notice that the faintest stars are very hard to see when you look directly at them. Try looking slightly to the side of the star. The light-sensitive rods on the edges of your retinas will allow you to see the star more clearly!

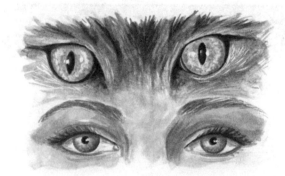

Vocabulary Skills

Write the words from the passage that have the meanings below.

1. to notice or discover something

   _____
   Par. 2

2. delicate; easy to break or harm

   _____
   Par. 2

3. faulty; not working properly

   _____
   Par. 2

4. an impressive group

   _____
   Par. 6

5. not obvious

   _____
   Par. 7

Find the compound words from the selection that contain the words below.

6. light _____
           Par. 2

7. ball _____
           Par. 2

8. in _____
           Par. 3

9. Check the sentence in which *glasses* has the same meaning as it does in paragraph 2.

   _____ Do you like my new glasses?

   _____ I need four coffee mugs and four juice glasses.

10. Check the sentence in which *pupil* has the same meaning as it does in paragraph 3.

    _____ The pupil determines how much light is allowed into the eye.

    _____ The best pupil in the class received a perfect grade on her spelling test.

11. Check the sentence in which *cells* has the same meaning as it does in paragraph 6.

    _____ Bees' honeycomb contains hundreds of cells.

    _____ The cells reproduced at a rapid rate.

Reading Skills

1. What do pupils control?

   _____

   _____

2. What is the colored part of the eye called?

   _____

   _____

3. If you walked from a dark room into a brightly-lit room, how would the size of your pupils change?

   _____

   _____

4. What colors do the cone-shaped cells in your eyes detect?

   _____

   _____

5. What kind of cells are missing from the eyes of a person who is colorblind?

   _____

   _____

6. Name two ways in which cone-shaped cells and rod-shaped cells are different from one another.

   _____

   _____

7. What is the purpose of the cornea?

   _____

   _____

8. What purpose would a reader have for reading this selection?

   _____ to form an opinion

   _____ to learn

   _____ for entertainment

Eyes on the Ends of Your Fingers

Have you ever seen anything written in Braille?

1   Think about how many things you read every day. Even when you are not in school, doing homework, or reading a book for fun, you read almost constantly. You read the writing on a cereal box to decide what to have for breakfast. You read the label on a bottle of shampoo, the newspaper headlines, billboards, street signs, and the sides of buses. You read menus, e-mails, and the weather report. Everywhere you go, words surround you.

2   Going about the tasks of daily life would be much more difficult for some people if it weren't for the creative thinking of a man named Louis Braille. Even though Braille translations are not provided everywhere, the availability of the Braille system in many public places opens up a new world for people who cannot see.

3   Louis Braille was born in France in 1809 and became blind in an accident when he was three years old. When Braille was ten, he was sent to a school for the blind in Paris. At that time, the only material that was available for blind students to read was carved in wood, cut in cardboard, or made from lead, a heavy metal. This severely limited what students could read. In addition, there was no way for them to write using this system.

4   Braille became aware of a system of military communication that was invented by Charles Barbier, a French cavalry officer. Barbier had devised a system based on the arrangement of dots in groups of 12. He wanted military personnel to be able to communicate with one another at night when vision was limited. In Barbier's system, the dots were punched into cardboard, which could be read by touch.

5   Braille modified this system for use by the blind when he was only 15 years old. Instead of 12 dots, Braille's system used only six dots, arranged in three rows of two dots each. The presence or absence of dots, and the way in which they were arranged, was used to symbolize specific letters and numbers.

6   During the next 20 years, similar systems of reading, using dots arranged in different patterns, were developed in the United States. In 1916, Louis Braille's system was officially accepted in the United States. Sixteen years later, English Braille became the universal system for the English-speaking world.

7   Even as the Braille system gained acceptance around the world, the development of a good printing process was slow and often tedious. The first books in Braille were printed using a sharp instrument that punched holes in thick paper to form the patterns of dots. Over time, progress was made with the presses that printed Braille materials. The process became quicker and more efficient. Today, computer programs translate written words into Braille code, which is then sent to machines that electronically make the printing plates that are used to produce the books.

8   Once you start paying attention, you'll notice Braille in places you've never seen it before—in elevators, on doors to public restrooms, on keypads of automated banking machines. It's impressive to see how far the idea of a 15-year-old boy from France has spread since 1824.

Vocabulary Skills

Write the words from the passage that have the meanings below.

1. seriously; extremely

   _____
   Par. 3

2. created; invented

   _____
   Par. 4

3. changed; altered

   _____
   Par. 5

4. long and boring; time-consuming

   _____
   Par. 7

5. automatic; working without human assistance

   _____
   Par. 8

Read each pair of words listed below. If the words are synonyms, write **S** on the line. If the words are antonyms, write **A** on the line.

6. _____ surround   encompass

7. _____ presence   absence

8. _____ specific   general

9. _____ available   accessible

10. The Latin root **commun** means *common*. Find a word in paragraph 4 with the root **commun**.

    _____

11. The Latin root **vis** can mean *see*. Find a word in paragraph 4 with the root **vis**.

    _____

12. The Latin root **ver** can mean *truth*. Find a word in paragraph 6 with the root **ver**.

    _____

Reading Skills

1. What was the problem with materials intended for blind people before the creation of the Braille system?

   _____

   _____

2. How was Braille's system different from Barbier's?

   _____

   _____

3. How old was Braille when he invented his dot-reading system?

   _____

4. How are Braille books produced today?

   _____

   _____

   _____

   _____

5. Check the line beside the word or words that best describe what type of selection this is.

   _____ historical fiction

   _____ historical nonfiction

   _____ fiction

6. Check the words that best describe Louis Braille.

   _____ cheerful   _____ outgoing

   _____ inventive   _____ determined

   _____ original

7. Check the word below that best describes the theme of "Eyes on the Ends of Your Fingers."

   _____ disability   _____ creative thinking

   _____ friendship   _____ honor

The Quarreling Colors

Do you have a favorite color? Why do you like that color?

1   Long, long ago, when Earth was young, there was a terrible quarrel among the colors. Each believed he or she was superior to all other colors, and no color was willing to admit defeat.

2   Red claimed to be the most important of all because she was the color of life. "Red is the color of blood," she proclaimed, "and what life is possible without blood? Red is the color of love, of anger, and of heat. What would life be without me?" She did not believe that any other color could make so strong an argument.

3   Orange stood up. "It is thoughtless to state that red is the most important color. Have you never tasted the juice of an orange or the flesh of a pumpkin? And what color are the most breathtaking sunrises and sunsets? They are orange, of course! There is no question that orange is the most important color."

4   "I suppose you have all dismissed the importance of yellow." Yellow smiled, content with her place in the world. "Can you imagine Earth without the yellow sun? The sun is as responsible for life as blood is," she reminded the others. "Without the sun, nothing could grow. You would all live in a world of darkness. It is folly to suggest that any color but yellow is most needed and most beloved."

5   "Look around you," said Green. "Do you see anything at all that has not been touched by my hand? Green is truly the color of life. It is grass and trees, toads and salamanders, beans and spinach. The survival of any living creature on Earth would be brief were it not for me. I see no reason to dispute my importance."

6   Then, there came the cry of a high-pitched voice. "If you think that I am not needed, all you must do is point your face to the sky. In any direction you look, you will see a brilliant blue. Turn your gaze to the water, the root of all life, and you will see me. Without my wide-open spaces, you would be lost." Having said his piece, Blue settled back to listen to the others.

7   Violet stood up, proud and tall. "I am the color of royalty," he said. "I am the color of power and authority. No one questions my wisdom or superiority." With confidence he nodded and turned to Indigo, who had remained quiet until it was her turn to speak.

8   "Have you forgotten me?" she asked quietly. "Indigo is the color of twilight. It is the color of the mountains at night and of the sky just before a storm. Indigo is the color of peace and of quiet times. You would not want to live in a world without me."

9   As the colors argued, a jagged streak of lightning lit the sky. A moment later, there was a giant clap of thunder and a steady rain began to fall. The colors drew closer together, sheltering one another from the storm. They could hear the voice of Rain over the thunder's rumblings.

10   "You are all so foolish," Rain scoffed. "Why would you think that one of you is superior to another? Look around," she said. "Each one of you is unique and essential. Aside from your quarreling, I would not want to live in a place that even one of you didn't inhabit."

11   The colors were silent as they listened to the wise words. "Each time it rains," added Rain, "I would like you all to come together and stretch across the sky in a giant bow of color. You will be a reminder to us all of how to live with one another in peace—a reminder of how each individual contributes something to the whole."

Vocabulary Skills

Write the words from the story that have the meanings below.

1. better than others

   _____
   Par. 1

2. the state of having lost or been beaten

   _____
   Par. 1

3. declared

   _____
   Par. 2

4. treated as unimportant

   _____
   Par. 4

5. a foolish idea

   _____
   Par. 4

6. to question the truth of; to doubt

   _____
   Par. 5

7. spoken with a lack of respect; disdain

   _____
   Par. 10

8. Check the sentence in which *state* has the same meaning as it does in paragraph 3.

   _____ Naomi was eager to return to her home state after traveling for so long.

   _____ Please state your name after the beep.

9. Check the sentence in which *content* has the same meaning as it does in paragraph 4.

   _____ I think that the content of this book will interest you.

   _____ Tony was content with the gifts he had received.

Rewrite the phrases below in the possessive form.

10. the words of Rain _____

11. the quarrel of the colors _____

12. the rumbling of the thunder _____

Reading Skills

1. Why were the colors quarreling?

   _____
   _____

2. What reason did Yellow give for being the most important color?

   _____
   _____

3. Do you think that one of the colors makes a better argument than the others? Explain.

   _____
   _____

4. What did Rain ask the colors to do each time it rained?

   _____
   _____

5. What do you think the colors in this legend might symbolize, or stand for? Do you think there is a deeper meaning to the story? Explain.

   _____
   _____
   _____

6. Does this story take place in reality, or is it a fantasy? How can you tell?

   _____
   _____

7. In this legend, the colors are personified. How did the author accomplish this?

   _____
   _____
   _____

An Arc of Light

What causes rainbows?

1   Almost every culture has stories and legends about the large arcs of color that stretch across the sky when weather conditions are right. Irish folklore tells of leprechauns hiding pots of gold at the end of the rainbow. Chinese mythology explains rainbows as openings in the sky that have been sealed by a goddess using stones of seven different colors. In Hindu mythology, a rainbow is viewed as the bow of the god of thunder and lightning. Rainbows even appear in popular modern culture. Remember Dorothy singing "Somewhere Over the Rainbow" in *The Wizard of Oz*?

2   Rainbows enchant and mystify people because they are beautiful but fleeting. Conditions must be exactly right in order for rainbows to form. They are usually seen at the end of a rain shower, on the opposite side of the sky from the sun.

3   Although sunlight appears to be white, it is actually made up of all the colors in the spectrum. When sunlight enters a raindrop, it is bent, or refracted, and the light's individual strands of color become visible. The wavelengths of different colors vary, which is why each color bends slightly differently to produce the bands of color known as a rainbow.

4   Rainbows are usually described as comprising seven colors: red, orange, yellow, green, blue, indigo, and violet. An acronym for remembering the order of the colors is the name ROY G. BIV, in which each letter stands for a color in the spectrum.

5   Several people may see a rainbow at the same time, but they are not all seeing the same rainbow. Rainbows don't exist at an exact location in the sky, and the way they appear is dependent upon a specific point. Each of your eyes even perceives a rainbow slightly differently. This means that you'll never see the exact same rainbow as someone else, unless you are looking at a photograph!

6   Rainbows are always seen during the day because they require sunlight to form. However, it is possible to see a moonbow, or a nighttime rainbow, on nights when the moon shines particularly brightly. A moonbow is formed in the same way a rainbow is, but it is not nearly as bright. In fact, it appears to be whitish in color because the human eye cannot discern bright colors in dim light.

7   If weather conditions have not been right for you to spot a rainbow in the sky, you can make your own at home or at school. You'll just need a large, clear, circular glass or jar of water, a small mirror, and a flashlight. Place the mirror in the water and tilt it slightly upward. Go into a completely dark room that has white walls, and shine the flashlight on the mirror. You'll be able to see a colorful rainbow you created yourself.

Vocabulary Skills

1. The Latin root **spec** means *see*. Find a word in paragraph 3 with the root **spec**.

   _____

2. The Latin root **fract** means *break*. Find a word in paragraph 3 with the root **fract**.

   _____

3. The Greek root **photo** means *light*. Find a word in paragraph 5 with the root **photo**.

   _____

Find the compound words from the selection that contain the words below.

4. bow _____
   <small>Par. 1</small>

5. lore _____
   <small>Par. 1</small>

6. some _____
   <small>Par. 1</small>

7. light _____
   <small>Par. 3</small>

8. wave _____
   <small>Par. 3</small>

Reading Skills

1. Why do each of the colors in a rainbow bend slightly differently?

   _____

   _____

2. What is one way to remember the order of colors in a rainbow?

   _____

3. Why does a moonbow appear to be whitish in color?

   _____

   _____

4. What materials do you need to create your own rainbow?

   _____

5. What is the only way to see exactly the same rainbow someone else sees?

   _____

6. How are a rainbow and a moonbow different? How are they similar?

   _____

   _____

Write **T** before the sentences that are true. Write **F** before the sentences that are false.

7. _____ Leprechauns hide pots of gold at the end of the rainbow in Chinese mythology.

8. _____ Sunlight is made of all the colors in the spectrum.

9. _____ Most rainbows are seen on snowy days when the temperature dips below freezing.

10. _____ Everyone looking at a rainbow will see exactly the same image of a rainbow.

11. _____ Dorothy is a character in *The Wizard of Oz*.

Study Skills

Use a dictionary to help you divide these words into syllables.

1. m y t h o l o g y

2. d i f f e r e n t

3. b e a u t i f u l

4. a c r o n y m

5. s e v e r a l

Island Roots

Have you ever traced your family tree?

1 Calvin walked into the dining room carrying his backpack and several books. "This table is a disaster area," he told Will, pushing some papers and books aside to clear a small space.

2 "Be careful," Will cautioned his little brother. "Everything is in chronological order, and I don't want to have to reorganize it."

3 Calvin raised his eyebrows. As far as he could tell, there was no order at all to the papers on the table, but he decided not to mention it to his brother. "I'm going to ride my bike to the library," said Calvin. "I was going to ask you if you wanted to come along, but it looks like you have your hands full right now."

4 Will nodded. "I have a genealogy project due next week. I think I have most of the information I need, but I have to pull it all into some kind of cohesive story."

5 "What's genealogy?" asked Calvin, sliding his backpack onto his shoulders.

6 "It's the study of your family's history and roots," explained Will. "Haven't you noticed how busy I've been for the last couple of weeks? I've been researching this project for days. The Internet has been pretty helpful in finding names, birth records, and obituaries. I've also interviewed a lot of our older relatives over the phone. There are things that they remember that I wouldn't have been able to find anywhere else. That's part of the reason this project is so important," he said. "I don't want our family's history to get lost. If I record it, it will exist for our great-great-grandkids."

7 Calvin peered over his brother's shoulder and pointed to the family tree that Will had sketched on an oversized piece of paper. "Is this mom's side of the family?" he asked.

8 Will nodded. "I don't have as much information about her side as I do about Dad's. The interesting thing is that I can't read some of the letters I found."

9 Calvin looked confused. "Is the handwriting really bad, or are they written in another language?"

10 "Mom and I looked at them together, and as far as we can tell, they are written in Gullah. Mom's family was originally from Africa, but for the last 200 years, they have lived on the islands off the coast of South Carolina. Some people there still speak Gullah, which is a mix of English and different African languages. Mom even thinks that a couple of our distant relations might still live there."

11 "Wow," said Calvin, pulling up a chair next to his brother. "How are you going to find out what the letters say?"

12 "I don't think I'll have time to do it before this project is due," said Will, "but I've found a few online Gullah dictionaries that will help me translate them. Mom also said we might be able to take a family trip to South Carolina this summer."

13 "Genealogy is a lot more interesting than it sounds," said Calvin. "Can I help you with this?"

14 Will laughed. "I thought you'd never ask!"

Vocabulary Skills

Write the words from the story that have the meanings below.

1. warned

   _____
   Par. 2

2. the order in time in which something occurred

   _____
   Par. 2

3. notices appearing in newspapers that announce a person's death

   _____
   Par. 6

4. relatives

   _____
   Par. 10

Write the idiom from paragraph 3 on the line next to its meaning.

5. to be busy _____

Find the metaphor in paragraph 1, and write it on the line.

6. _____

Circle the homophone that correctly completes each sentence below.

7. For hours after Rosa heard the good news, she was in a _____. (days, daze)

8. Lex _____ when he read the headline on the newspaper's front page. (sighed, side)

Reading Skills

1. Where did Will get the information for his research?

   _____

2. Why does Will feel that researching his family's history is important?

   _____

   _____

3. How long has the boys' extended family lived on the South Carolina Sea Islands?

   _____

4. Do you think that Will and Calvin will continue to be interested in their family's history even after Will's project is complete? Explain.

   _____

   _____

Study Skills

Use the family tree below to answer the questions that follow.

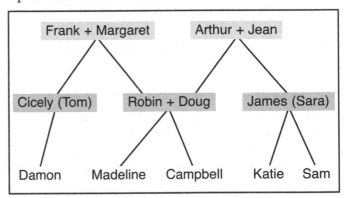

1. What are the names of Katie and Sam's parents?

   _____

2. What is Robin's sister's name?

   _____

3. What is Damon's grandfather's name?

   _____

A Slice of Sea Island Life

Have you ever heard of the Gullah people of the southeastern United States?

1   If you look at a map of the southeastern United States, you will see a string of islands that runs along the coast of South Carolina, Georgia, and northern Florida. These islands are often called the *Sea Islands*. On the map, they probably appear no different than anywhere else in the country. But if you were to visit the islands, you would discover a unique culture and way of life that have been preserved for more than a century.

2   The name *Gullah* refers to both a group of people and a language. Many Africans were brought to America against their will to work on southern plantations. They harvested cotton and rice, among many other crops, as well as cared for the families of the plantation owners.

3   When the Civil War ended in 1865, the slaves were freed or abandoned. Many stayed to live and work in the area. Because the islands were accessible only by boat, the people were isolated from mainstream culture. The customs and traditions they brought with them from Africa remained largely unchanged for many years.

4   The Gullah language evolved as a way for people who didn't speak the same language to communicate with one another. It is a combination of many West African languages mixed with English. An English speaker would be able to pick out familiar words here and there, but you probably would not understand most of what was being said.

5   For many years, it seemed as though the Gullah language was in danger of dying out, as the culture became more influenced by the culture of the rest of the United States. However, historical preservationists have been recently recording people speaking the language, as well as compiling dictionaries of various words and their meanings and pronunciation. They are doing their best to insure that the language is preserved for future generations.

6   The Gullah language isn't the only unique aspect of the native Sea Islanders. They have many traditions that are an important part of their culture. For example, the art of basket weaving has been passed down for many generations. A native grass that grows near the ocean, called *sweetgrass*, is used by the Gullah to create beautiful handmade baskets. The grass is coiled and then sewn together using a needle made from a spoon handle, bone, or nail.

7   Fish nets are also traditionally handmade in the Gullah culture. Fishing has been an essential part of life in the Sea Islands for many years. Fishermen knitted their own nets by hand using a needle made of palmetto wood, in a tradition carried over from West Africa. It is less common to see these handmade nets today, but some fishermen preserve the craft so that it remains a part of life on the islands.

8   Today, you can still see the influence of the past in the South Carolina Sea Islands. The beauty of the Gullah people's way of life still exists, and it brings a wonderful local flavor and color to the area. As interest and awareness in this historical culture grows, so does the chance that it will survive for future generations to appreciate.

Vocabulary Skills

Write the words from the passage that have the meanings below.

1. the power or ability to choose or make decisions for oneself

   _____
   Par. 2

2. able to be reached

   _____
   Par. 3

3. grew or developed from one thing into another

   _____
   Par. 4

4. people who work to preserve something for the future

   _____
   Par. 5

5. wound into a spiral or ring

   _____
   Par. 6

Use a dictionary to help you place the words below into the correct categories.

patio	origami
karate	czar
tornado	bronco
mammoth	

6. Japanese   7. Russian   8. Spanish

   _____   _____   _____

   _____   _____   _____

                         _____

Reading Skills

1. Where are the Sea Islands located?

   _____

   _____

2. Why did the Gullah language evolve?

   _____

   _____

3. Name two Gullah traditions that are still practiced today.

   _____

4. What is one reason the African customs of the Gullah people remained unchanged for so long?

   _____

   _____

5. Do you think it is important for the Gullah heritage and way of life to be preserved? Explain.

   _____

   _____

6. What do you think the author's purpose was for writing this selection?

   _____

   _____

Circle the word that best completes each sentence below.

7. Historically, the Gullah have been _____ craftspeople.

   cultural   talented   preserving

8. In today's world, the Gullah culture is a(n) _____ snapshot of the past.

   unreasonable   temporary   unique

The Art of the Islands

What inspires Gullah artist Jonathan Green?

1   If you have ever seen the art of Jonathan Green, it is not likely that you will soon forget it. His paintings are bold and colorful, lively and cheerful. Green depicts a way of life that is rapidly disappearing. It is a way of life that he remembers with fondness from his childhood in the South Carolina Sea Islands.

2   Jonathan Green was born in 1955 in Gardens Corner, South Carolina, a region of the state known as the Low Country. The second of seven children, Green was raised by his maternal grandmother, Eloise Stewart Johnson. As he grew up, he was immersed in Gullah culture—a culture that placed great value on tradition, family, and community. Although Green had to travel to other parts of the world before he could fully appreciate his rich heritage, the basic elements of his culture eventually found their way into his unique form of artistic expression.

3   After Green graduated from high school, he joined the military. It seemed like a good opportunity for him to see the world and to receive an education. When he completed his military service, Green attended the Art Institute of Chicago. While he was in school, he worked part-time as a security guard at an art museum. This allowed him to study the work of the masters. He imitated their work at first, learning what made them so well respected. Then, Green found his own style and direction and began painting South Carolina's Gullah Islands, the world he knew best.

4   Jonathan Green's artwork is filled with everyday images of Gullah life as he remembered it growing up. His paintings show people hanging laundry out to dry, picking oysters, telling stories, and attending weddings and funerals. Water is found in many of his paintings because it plays an important role in the lives of people who live along the coast and on the islands.

5   Human beings are also found in nearly all of Green's work, indicating the importance of family and community to the culture. The faces of the people in his paintings are usually without features. This can be interpreted as Green's way of showing how the everyday lives and experiences of people are universal.

6   The Gullah way of life is changing as children grow up and move away to larger towns and cities. The Gullah dialect is disappearing with the older generations. Even the landscape of the islands is changing, as condominiums, malls, and fast-food restaurants begin to take over. Jonathan Green knows that his artwork cannot change what is happening to the area where he grew up. But his paintings can raise awareness of what is in danger of being lost and preserve the memories of a rich and colorful way of life.

Vocabulary Skills

Write the words from the passage that have the meanings below.

1. surrounded by; deeply involved with

   _____
   Par. 2

2. something handed down through the generations

   _____
   Par. 2

3. the various parts of the face

   _____
   Par. 5

4. explained or understood in a certain way

   _____
   Par. 5

5. shared with everyone; common

   _____
   Par. 5

6. language that is used by a certain group or region of a country

   _____
   Par. 6

In each row, circle the two words that belong together.

7. opportunity respect tradition custom

8. region language memories area

9. landscape preserve indicate maintain

10. The Latin root **mater** means *mother*. Find a word in paragraph 2 with the root **mater**.

    _____

11. The Latin root **commun** means *common*. Find a word in paragraph 2 with the root **commun**.

    _____

12. The Greek root **gen** means *birth* or *race*. Find a word in paragraph 6 with the root **gen**.

    _____

Reading Skills

1. Check the words that best describe Jonathan Green.

   _____ athletic   _____ creative

   _____ artistic   _____ caring

   _____ talkative

2. Check the word that best describes what type of selection this is.

   _____ autobiography

   _____ fiction

   _____ biography

3. Do you think Jonathan Green will continue making paintings of his Gullah heritage?

   _____

   _____

4. Name two things that frequently appear in Green's paintings.

   _____

5. Which of the following would be the most likely subject of one of Green's paintings?

   _____ a realistic portrait of a mother and child

   _____ the skyline of a city at night

   _____ fishermen hauling in their nets

6. How many children were there in Green's family?

   _____

7. Why do you think that Green had to go away in order to be able to appreciate his culture and heritage?

   _____

   _____

Answer Key

Page 3

Vocabulary Skills

Write the words from the story that have the meanings below.

1. happening after some time
   eventually Par. 1

2. cone-shaped devices used for projecting sounds
   megaphones Par. 9

3. directing attention
   referring Par. 10

4. completely absorbed or occupied
   engrossed Par. 12

5. options; choices
   alternatives Par. 14

An **idiom** is a group of words that has a special meaning. For example, the idiom *hit the hay* means *to go to bed*. Write the idiom from paragraph 8 on the line next to its meaning.

6. something of interest; something a person enjoys **cup of tea**

A **prefix** is a group of letters added to the beginning of a word to change its meaning. The prefix **un-** means *not*. For example, *uninterested* means *not interested*. Add **un** to each word below. Then, write the meaning of the new word.

7. __un__ aware **not aware**

8. __un__ fortunate **not fortunate**

9. __un__ healthy **not healthy**

10. __un__ even **not even**

Reading Skills

1. Why were the Godfreys in Japan?
   to visit Mrs. Godfrey's college roommate

2. What do you think Emily meant when she said, "American baseball may never be quite as interesting again"?
   In comparison to American baseball, Japanese baseball seems more interesting and exciting to her.

3. What is one way American and Japanese baseball are similar? What is one way they are different?
   Possible answers: Some of the snacks served at the games are the same. Japanese baseball games have male cheerleaders.

4. Do you think that Alex and Emily will go to another JBall game if they have a chance? Why or why not?
   Answers will vary.

Circle the word that best completes each sentence.

5. Alex and Emily decide to try food that they would not be _____ to find at an American game.
   allowed (**likely**) impressed

6. The Godfreys are _____ to learn how American and Japanese baseball are different.
   (**curious**) refusing apprehensive

7. Noisemakers are a popular _____ at Japanese baseball games.
   explanation resource (**custom**)

3

Page 5

Vocabulary Skills

In each row, circle the word that does not belong.

1. popular famous (**encouraged**) legendary
2. recognize (**continue**) acknowledge notice
3. (**establish**) incredible amazing astounding

Read each word below. Then, write the letter of its abbreviation in the space beside it.

4. __b__ Major League Baseball **a.** LA
5. __d__ statistics **b.** MLB
6. __a__ Los Angeles **c.** NY
7. __c__ New York **d.** stats

Reading Skills

1. Check the sentence that best states the main idea of the passage.

   __✓__ Although baseball is thought of as an American sport, there are many fans and talented players of Japanese baseball, or *yakyu*.

   ____ American teams toured Japan in the early 1900s and played exhibition games against the local amateurs.

   ____ Horace Wilson brought baseball to Japan in the 1870s.

2. Number the events below to show the order in which they happened.

   __1__ Horace Wilson introduced baseball to his students.

   __3__ World War II interrupted Japanese baseball.

   __4__ The Giants won nine consecutive national championships.

   __2__ Babe Ruth and Lou Gehrig played baseball in Japan.

3. Check the phrase that best describes the author's purpose.

   __✓__ to inform

   ____ to entertain

   ____ to persuade

4. Why is Sadahara Oh's last name so appropriate?
   It means *king*, and he is the king of baseball in Japan.

5. Why did Japan's leaders like baseball?
   It contained elements that were already part of Japanese culture.

Study Skills

Use the table below to answer the questions that follow.

Japanese Baseball Teams	Stadiums
Yomiuri Giants	Tokyo Dome
Nippon Ham Fighters	Tokyo Dome
Yakult Swallows	Meiji-Jingu Stadium
Seibu Lions	Seibu Dome
Yokohama Baystars	Yokohama Stadium
Orix Blue Wave	Green Stadium
Chunichi Dragons	Nagoya Dome

1. Which stadium is the home of two teams?
   Tokyo Dome

2. What is the home team for the Nagoya Dome?
   Chunichi Dragons

3. Which stadium would the Godfreys and the Itos have visited in the previous story?
   Meiji-Jingu Stadium

5

Page 7

Vocabulary Skills

Write the words from the story that have the meanings below.

1. genuine; like the real thing
   authentic Par. 1

2. to have been without; to have been missing
   lacked Par. 2

3. quickly; without delay
   promptly Par. 3

Underline the compound word in each sentence. Then, write the two words that make up each compound.

4. Emily likes some types of **seafood**.
   sea **food**

5. The Itos showed the Godfreys how to pick up sushi with their **chopsticks**.
   chop **sticks**

6. Sometimes a piece of fish is placed on top of the rice-filled roll.
   some **times**

Reading Skills

A **fact** is something that is known to be true. An **opinion** is what a person believes. It may or may not be true. Write **F** before the sentences that are facts. Write **O** before the sentences that are opinions.

1. __O__ Sushi is delicious.

2. __F__ The chef spreads a layer of sticky rice over the sheet of seaweed.

3. __O__ Wasabi ruins the flavor of sushi.

4. __F__ Mrs. Ito makes some suggestions about what to order.

5. Check the line beside the word or words that best describe what type of passage this is.

   ____ informational text

   __✓__ fiction

   ____ tall tale

6. How are Alex and Emily different?
   Alex is more adventurous than Emily is about trying new foods.

7. Why isn't everyone surprised that Alex likes sushi?
   He was looking forward to trying authentic Japanese food.

8. What holds everything together in a roll of sushi?
   a thin sheet of seaweed

9. What is *wasabi*?
   a very spicy condiment

10. Why does Mr. Godfrey say, "Our kids are turning into some very well-seasoned eaters"?
    Alex and Emily both enjoy the sushi and want to find a restaurant at home that serves it.

Study Skills

The word you look up in a dictionary is called an **entry word**. An entry word is usually a base word. For example, if you want to find the meaning of *happier*, you would look up the base word *happy*. Write the entry word you would look for in a dictionary next to each word below.

1. excited **excite**

2. grinned **grin**

3. scanning **scan**

4. gesturing **gesture**

5. founded **found**

7

Page 9

Vocabulary Skills

Write the words from the passage that have the meanings below.

1. the process of growing and caring for something
   cultivation Par. 1

2. to trim away the unwanted parts of a tree or bush
   prune Par. 2

3. copied; made again
   reproduced Par. 4

The prefix **mis-** means *badly* or *wrongly*. For example, *misunderstand* means *understand wrongly*. Write a word to match each definition below. Then, write a sentence using each word.

4. to behave badly **misbehave**
   Answers will vary.

5. to spell wrongly **misspell**
   Answers will vary.

6. to match badly **mismatch**
   Answers will vary.

Reading Skills

Write **T** before the sentences that are true. Write **F** before the sentences that are false.

1. __F__ The tradition of raising bonsais was begun in Europe.

2. __T__ Japanese bonsais are usually grown in containers outdoors.

3. __T__ The owner of a bonsai must spend some time caring for the plant.

4. __F__ There are three basic styles of bonsai.

5. What do you think the phrase *time-honored tradition* means?
   something that is respected because it has existed for a long period of time

6. What are the three elements needed to create a successful bonsai?
   truth, goodness, and beauty

7. How are the cascade and semi-cascade styles of bonsai similar?
   In both styles the leaves and the branches cascade down toward the base of the plant.

8. What purpose would a reader have for reading this selection?

   ____ for pleasure or entertainment

   __✓__ for information

   ____ to form an opinion about bonsais

Study Skills

Read the dictionary entry below, and answer the questions that follow.

patient (pā′ shənt) *adj.* able to put up with things that are annoying without complaining
n. someone who is receiving medical treatment

1. What part of speech is *patient* when it is used to mean *able to put up with things that are annoying without complaining*?
   an adjective

2. What is the definition of *patient* when it is used as a noun?
   someone who is receiving medical treatment

3. Which syllable is stressed in *patient*?
   the first

9

Spectrum Reading Grade 6
152
Answer Key

Answer Key

Page 11

Vocabulary Skills

Write the words from the passage that have the meanings below.

1. the renewal and repair of a building
   renovation

2. determined the worth or condition of
   evaluated

3. viewed as appropriate for
   suited

4. to make richer or improve the quality of
   enrich

5. grown without the use of chemicals and pesticides
   organic

Read each word below. Then, write the letter of its abbreviation in the space beside it.

6. __b__ California   **a.** Jr.
7. __d__ United States   **b.** CA
8. __a__ Junior   **c.** yr.
9. __c__ year   **d.** U.S.

Write the idiom from paragraph 2 on the line next to its meaning.

10. goes together __hand in hand__

A word that sounds the same as another word but has a different spelling and meaning is a **homophone**. Circle the homophone that correctly completes each sentence below.

11. Neil Smith is a middle school _____. (principle, (principal))

12. I added a cup of chopped _____ to the vegetable soup. ((beets) beats)

Reading Skills

1. What is composting?
   a process in which leftover scraps of fruits and vegetables are used as fertilizer

2. Name four fruits or vegetables that are grown in the Edible Schoolyard.
   Answers will vary.

3. Do you think that other schools will create gardens based on Alice Waters's ideas?
   Answers will vary.

4. Check the sentence that best states the **main idea** of the selection, or tells what the passage is mostly about.
   ___ Alice Waters owns Chez Panisse Restaurant in California.
   ___ Students look forward to the time they spend gardening each week.
   _✓_ Alice Waters founded the Edible Schoolyard, a program in which students learn to grow and prepare their own foods.

5. Check the words that describe Alice Waters.
   _✓_ generous
   ___ unfriendly
   _✓_ talented
   _✓_ ambitious
   ___ stingy

11

Page 13

Vocabulary Skills

Write the words from the story that have the meanings below.

1. at first; originally
   initially

2. decided; fixed on an idea
   determined

3. money that is contributed to a good cause
   donations

4. money raised for a specific purpose
   funds

5. pledging or devoting oneself to an activity
   committing

An **antonym** is a word that means the opposite of another word. Find an antonym in the story for each of the words below.

6. departed __returned__
7. impossible __realistic__
8. destroy __create__
9. separate __combine__

Write the idiom from paragraph 6 on the line next to its meaning.

10. to start something __up and running__

Words that have two middle consonants are divided into syllables between the consonants. For example, pic/ture. Divide the words below into syllables using a slash (/).

11. g a r/d e n
12. b a s/k e t
13. p i c/n i c

Reading Skills

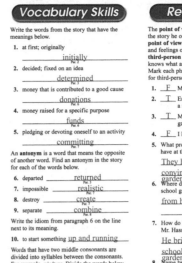

The **point of view** tells the reader whose view of the story he or she is reading. In **first-person point of view**, the reader knows the thoughts and feelings of the person telling the story. In **third-person point of view**, the reader only knows what an outsider knows about a character. Mark each phrase below **F** for first-person and **T** for third-person.

1. __F__ My cousin P.J. lives in Washington.
2. __T__ Emilio's aunt is the co-owner of a nursery.
3. __T__ Mr. Hasselbach has a vegetable garden.
4. __F__ I hope Ms. Milano likes our idea.
5. What problem do Drew, Emilio, and Michi have at the beginning of the story?
   They have to figure out how to convince Ms. Milano that the garden is a good idea.
6. Where did Drew get the idea to start a school garden at his middle school?
   from his cousin P. J.
7. How do Drew, Emilio, and Michi know that Mr. Hasselbach has a garden at home?
   He brings in vegetables to school that he grew in his garden at home.
8. Name two ideas that the students have that they think will make Ms. Milano more likely to approve their plan.
   Answers will vary.

13

Page 15

Vocabulary Skills

Write the words from the recipe that have the meanings below.

1. once in a while
   occasionally

2. letting some light through; somewhat clear
   translucent

3. chopped into small pieces
   diced

4. to set aside for later use
   reserve

5. parallel to the longest side
   lengthwise

Read each word below. Then, write the letter of its abbreviation on the line beside the word.

6. __b__ teaspoon   **a.** oz.
7. __a__ ounce   **b.** tsp.
8. __d__ inch   **c.** F
9. __c__ Fahrenheit   **d.** in.

Underline the compound word in each sentence. Then, write the two words that make up each compound.

10. Simmer the vegetables and tomato sauce in a large saucepan.
    sauce   pan

11. Freeze leftovers to enjoy on another day.
    left   overs

Reading Skills

1. Check the line beside the word or words that best describe what type of nonfiction passage this is.
   _✓_ how-to
   ___ biography
   ___ persuasive text

2. Number the tasks below to show the order in which they should be done.
   _4_ Combine the cheeses, eggs, and spices.
   _2_ Ask an adult to drain the lasagna noodles.
   _1_ Boil a pot of water.
   _3_ Simmer the vegetable mixture.
   _5_ Allow the lasagna to cool.

3. Why do you think you should wash your hands after handling the eggs?
   Possible answer: You could become sick.

4. For how long should you boil the lasagna noodles?
   8 to 10 minutes

5. What is the total amount of time the lasagna will bake?
   30 minutes

6. What five vegetables are used in this recipe?
   red bell pepper, green bell pepper, yellow onion, tomatoes, and zucchini

7. Check the phrase that best describes the author's purpose.
   ___ to tell a story about a family who makes a lasagna
   _✓_ to explain how to make lasagna
   ___ to persuade the reader to make lasagna for dinner

15

Page 17

Vocabulary Skills

Write the words from the story that have the meanings below.

1. changed from a gas into a liquid form
   condensed

2. very hungry
   famished

3. to change in a dramatic way
   transform

4. a strongly held belief
   conviction

5. questioning; not convinced
   skeptical

6. continuing to do something even when it gets difficult
   perseverance

A **synonym** is a word that has the same meaning as another word. Read each word below. Then, write the letter of its synonym on the line beside the word.

7. __c__ warned   **a.** imaginative
8. __a__ creative   **b.** under
9. __d__ absolutely   **c.** cautioned
10. __b__ beneath   **d.** totally

Fill in the blanks below with the possessive form of the word in parentheses.

11. __Drew's__ casserole was very hot. (Drew)
12. The stepping stones symbolized the __school's__ appreciation. (school)
13. __Ms. Milano's__ speech was brief. (Ms. Milano)

Reading Skills

Circle the word that best completes each sentence below.

1. The students put a great deal of _____ into the preparation of the meal.
   (effort) guidance transformation

2. Ms. Milano _____ Drew, Emilio, and Michi's contributions.
   regrets (appreciates) plans

3. The stepping stones are _____ with their names and the date.
   requested remembered (engraved)

4. Name two things the students did to transform the lunchroom.
   Answers will vary.

5. Why did Ms. Milano give Drew, Michi, and Emilio stepping stones?
   to thank them for their hard work and to help future students remember their contributions

6. Why do you think Ms. Milano was skeptical when the students first presented her with the idea of starting a school garden?
   She knew it would be a lot of work and was not sure if it would be successful.

7. About how much of the food the students served did they grow themselves?
   about three-quarters of the food

17

Answer Key

Page 19

Vocabulary Skills

Write the words from the story that have the meanings below.

1. causing fear
   bloodcurdling _{Par. 2}

2. held tightly together
   clenched _{Par. 2}

3. needing immediate attention
   urgently _{Par. 3}

4. well known for something unpleasant or unfavorable
   notorious _{Par. 4}

5. stretching the neck to see better
   craning _{Par. 8}

Circle the homophone that correctly completes each sentence below.

6. Lucy had three mosquito _____ on her arm. (bytes/**bites**)

7. The owl's _____ woke Savannah and her mom. (**wails**/whales)

8. Check the sentence in which *racket* has the same meaning as it does in paragraph 12.

   _____ Hasaan borrowed my tennis racket on Monday.

   ✓ There was a great deal of racket when Mattie dropped the box of toys down the stairs.

Find the compound words from the selection that contain the words below.

9. light **flashlight** _{Par. 1}

10. moon **moonlight** _{Par. 9}

11. stairs **downstairs** _{Par. 12}

Reading Skills

1. Number the events below to show the order in which they happened.

   1 Savannah switched off her flashlight.

   4 Savannah and her mom saw the owl's eyes gleaming in the moonlight.

   5 Savannah's dad poured himself a glass of orange juice.

   2 Savannah ran into her parents' bedroom.

   3 Savannah's mom looked for her slippers.

2. Find one sentence that shows Savannah was frightened by the screaming she heard.

   Possible answer: Savannah lay stiffly and silently in her bed waiting to see what would happen.

3. If Savannah hears a barn owl again someday, do you think she will be frightened? Why or why not?

   Answers will vary.

4. What problem did Savannah have in the story?

   She was frightened by a terrible screaming sound from the backyard.

5. Why weren't Savannah and her mom surprised when the owl's cries didn't wake up Savannah's dad?

   He was known for being able to sleep through almost anything.

6. How were Savannah and her mom able to identify the owl's call?

   They found a Web site that had audio clips of different bird calls.

19

Page 21

Vocabulary Skills

Write the words from the passage that have the meanings below.

1. different; unlike others
   diverse _{Par. 2}

2. a quality or characteristic
   attribute _{Par. 3}

3. sharp; sensitive
   keen _{Par. 3}

4. makes better or stronger
   enhances _{Par. 4}

5. dulls the sound
   muffles _{Par. 4}

6. connections made between things
   associations _{Par. 5}

In each row, circle the word that does not belong.

7. precise (**ability**) exact accurate

8. (**approach**) nocturnal darkness night

9. diverse different (**symbolize**) varying

The suffix **-ly** means *in a certain way*. For example, *gently* means *in a gentle way*. Write a word to match each definition below. Then, write a sentence using each word.

10. in a smooth way **smoothly**
    Answers will vary.

11. in a certain way **certainly**
    Answers will vary.

12. in a sudden way **suddenly**
    Answers will vary.

Reading Skills

1. How are barn owls different from common owls?

   Barn owls have a light-colored heart-shaped face.

2. Why is the owl's sense of hearing important to its survival?

   because they hunt at night

3. How do archaeologists know that ancient Egyptians respected owls?

   They found mummified owls in Egyptian tombs.

4. What is unusual about the owl's neck and eyes?

   The owl's eyes do not move, but its neck can turn about 270 degrees.

5. In what part of the world does the smallest owl live?

   Mexico and the southwestern United States

6. What is one reason that owls have been feared in some cultures?

   They are nocturnal creatures.

7. A **summary** is a short sentence that tells the most important facts about a topic. Check the sentence below that is the best summary for paragraph 3.

   ✓ Owls hunt at night.

   _____ Owls have a sharp sense of hearing, which helps them to be strong hunters.

   _____ Some owls' ear openings are positioned asymmetrically.

21

Page 23

Vocabulary Skills

Write the words from the passage that have the meanings below.

1. to stand for or represent
   symbolize _{Par. 1}

2. the quality or condition of being able to be seen
   visibility _{Par. 2}

3. attached in midair; hanging
   suspended _{Par. 5}

4. to bring together in order to make more powerful
   concentrate _{Par. 6}

Check the meaning of the underlined word in each sentence.

5. Uncle Jasper gave two <u>quarters</u> to each of his nephews.

   ✓ currency worth 25 cents

   _____ an area in which one sleeps or lives

6. The <u>beam</u> of the flashlight illuminated the hallway.

   ✓ a ray of light

   _____ a big, happy smile

Compound words are divided into syllables between the two words that make the compound. For example, *eye/sight*. Divide the words below into syllables using a slash (/).

7. l i g h t / h o u s e

8. s h o r e / l i n e

9. c o a s t / l i n e

Reading Skills

1. How do we know that lighthouses have existed for at least 3,000 years?

   In Homer's *Iliad*, which was written around 1200 B.C., he refers to lighthouses.

2. How far can the Fresnel lens project light?

   28 miles

3. Why aren't lighthouse keepers necessary for today's lighthouses?

   Almost all lighthouses are automated.

4. What are two ways in which lighthouses may be different from one another?

   Answers will vary.

5. Why do you think that historians think it is important to preserve lighthouses?

   Possible answer: They are an important piece of the past.

6. What did early versions of lighthouses look like?

   They were made of iron baskets that were suspended from long poles.

7. Check the phrase that best describes the author's purpose.

   ✓ to share the history of lighthouses

   _____ to persuade the reader to visit a lighthouse

   _____ to explain how lighthouses were built

23

Page 25

Vocabulary Skills

Write the words from the story that have the meaning below.

1. to put something off for a later time
   procrastinate _{Par. 1}

2. a new and improved version of something
   revision _{Par. 2}

3. shook or trembled with fear
   shuddered _{Par. 2}

Underline the compound word in each sentence. Then, write the two words that make up each compound.

4. Paloma looked for a rubber band in her <u>backpack</u>.
   back _____ pack

5. Paloma wore her hair in a <u>ponytail</u>.
   pony _____ tail

6. The <u>notebook</u> contained Mr. Molina's assignment.
   note _____ book

7. The heavy rain sounded like <u>footsteps</u>.
   foot _____ steps

A **simile** compares two things using the words *like* or *as*. Find the simile in paragraph 4 and write it on the line below.

8. The heavy rain beat against my lighthouse like a thousand footsteps racing up and down the walls.

Reading Skills

1. What kind of animal is Sadie? How can you tell?

   Sadie is a cat. She curls up on Paloma's lap and meows.

2. What problem does Paloma have at the beginning of the story?

   She is having a hard time thinking of a short story to write, and she is running out of time.

3. Find an example of a sentence or phrase Paloma uses to create tension in her story.

   Answers will vary.

4. The next time she has to write a story for school, do you think Paloma will put it off again? Why or why not?

   Answers will vary.

5. Where does Paloma get her story idea?

   from a trip her family took to the Outer Banks

Mark each sentence below **F** if it is in first-person point of view and **T** if it is in third-person point of view.

6. **F** I was relying on Sadie's calmness to get me through the hurricane.

7. **T** Paloma reread Mr. Molina's assignment.

8. **F** I looked up at the staircase and shuddered.

Study Skills

Use a dictionary to help you divide these words into syllables.

1. p r o / c r a s / t i / n a t e

2. f i g / u r / a / t i v e

3. d a n / g e r / o u s

4. h u r / r i / c a n e

5. t o r / n a / d o

25

Answer Key

Vocabulary Skills (27)

Write the words from the passage that have the meanings below.

1. unmoving
   stationary _Par. 1_
2. survived
   weathered _Par. 2_
3. the process of being worn away over time by natural forces
   erosion _Par. 3_
4. to show to be reasonable
   justify _Par. 4_
5. empty
   vacant _Par. 4_

Write the words from the story that match the abbreviations below.

6. NC — North Carolina _Par. 1_
7. wks. — weeks _Par. 2_
8. ft. — feet _Par. 2_
9. min. — minute _Par. 3_

Rewrite each phrase using a possessive. If the noun is plural and ends in s, add the apostrophe (') after the s to show possession. For example, *bags of the girls* would be written as the *girls' bags*.

10. the history of the lighthouse
    the lighthouse's history
11. the opinion of the protesters
    the protesters' opinion
12. the estimate of the planners
    the planners' estimate

Reading Skills (27)

1. Number the events below to show the order in which they happened.
   - 2 People were worried that the lighthouse would collapse.
   - 5 The relocation was a success.
   - 1 The Cape Hatteras Lighthouse was completed in 1870.
   - 3 The lighthouse was removed from its existing foundation.
   - 4 Onlookers watched the slow progress of the lighthouse's move.

2. Check the line beside the word or words that best describe what type of passage this is.
   - ___ biography
   - ✓ historical nonfiction
   - ___ fiction

3. Check the sentence that best states the main idea of the passage.
   - ___ The Cape Hatteras Lighthouse in Buxton, North Carolina, is the tallest lighthouse in the United States.
   - ___ The process used to move the Cape Hatteras Lighthouse was very slow.
   - ✓ In 1999, the Cape Hatteras Lighthouse was moved further inland to prevent its destruction due to erosion.

4. What are the Diamond Shoals?
   a dangerous, shallow area about 14 miles off the coast of Cape Hatteras

5. What is one reason that some people protested moving the lighthouse?
   Answers will vary.

27

Vocabulary Skills (29)

Write the words from the passage that have the meanings below.

1. remote; set apart
   isolated _Par. 1_
2. accepted; suitable or proper
   appropriate _Par. 4_
3. curious about; interested in
   intrigued _Par. 4_
4. the state or quality of being alone or far away from things
   solitude _Par. 5_
5. to praise
   commend _Par. 5_

Write a synonym from the story for each of the words below.

6. unusual — uncommon _Par. 2_
7. seldom — rarely _Par. 2_
8. responsibilities — duties _Par. 3_
9. talented — skilled _Par. 4_

Check the meaning of the underlined word.

10. The lenses had to be polished regularly.
    - ✓ in a regular way
    - ___ capable of being regular
    - ___ not regular

11. Captain Lewis was unable to perform his duties as lighthouse keeper.
    - ___ extra able
    - ✓ not able
    - ___ the act of being able

Reading Skills (29)

1. Check the words that best describe Ida Lewis.
   - ✓ hardworking
   - ✓ determined
   - ___ nosy
   - ✓ strong-willed
   - ___ unpredictable

Write T before the sentences that are true. Write F before the sentences that are false.

2. F It was more common for women than for men to be lighthouse keepers.
3. F After his stroke, Captain Lewis was able to resume his job as lighthouse keeper.
4. T Ida kept the light at Lime Rock for 39 years.
5. T President Ulysses S. Grant visited Ida in Rhode Island.
6. T Today, Lime Rock Lighthouse is called Ida Lewis Lighthouse.

7. Why did all the attention make Ida uncomfortable?
   Ida was used to the solitude and quiet of a lighthouse keeper's life.

8. Why do you think that we don't know for sure how many people Ida rescued?
   Answers will vary.

9. How old was Ida when she began tending the lighthouse?
   15

10. What were two jobs of lighthouse keepers before lighthouses became automated?
    cleaning and polishing the lamps and lenses, keeping the lamps filled with fuel

29

Vocabulary Skills (31)

Write the words from the story that have the meanings below.

1. a specific body position
   pose _Par. 1_
2. resembling things that are real or actual
   realistic _Par. 3_
3. a story or description
   narrative _Par. 5_
4. to put on display
   mount _Par. 7_
5. the order in which events happened
   chronological _Par. 7_

Circle the homophone that correctly completes each sentence below.

6. The pants were too large and sat well below Meghan's (waist) waste.
7. There is a small scratch on the right (lens) lends of my sunglasses.
8. Did you (based baste) the turkey yet?

Find an antonym in the story for each of the words below.

9. boring — interesting _Par. 4_
10. worthless — valuable _Par. 13_
11. unknown — famous _Par. 14_

Reading Skills (31)

Write F before the sentences that are facts. Write O before the sentences that are opinions.

1. O Keeping a photo diary is a difficult assignment.
2. F Dante's brother's name is Wesley.
3. O Dante's classmates will find it easy to create a narrative from his photos.
4. F Mrs. Carter spilled some orange juice.
5. O Mr. Carter has a good sense of humor.

6. The **protagonist** is the main character in a story, or the person the story is mostly about. Who is the protagonist in this story?
   Dante

7. Why doesn't Dante want to leave out any details of his day?
   He wants it to be a realistic narrative.

8. Why does Wesley joke that photos of him will be valuable one day?
   because he wants to be a famous basketball player

9. During what time of day does the story take place? How can you tell?
   morning; The Carters are having breakfast, and Mrs. Carter says that it is 7 o'clock in the morning.

31

Vocabulary Skills (33)

Write the words from the passage that have the meanings below.

1. make a copy of
   reproduce _Par. 1_
2. a piece of equipment used for a specific purpose
   device _Par. 2_
3. allowed to be reached by light
   exposed _Par. 3_
4. to make up for something
   compensate _Par. 4_

Read each word below. Then, write the letter of its synonym on the line beside the word.

5. d complicated — a. common
6. a typical — b. round
7. b circular — c. create
8. c produce — d. complex

Reading Skills (33)

1. How is a camera's aperture similar to the iris in a human eye?
   They are both circular openings that can be adjusted to let in more or less light.

2. What is one example of a time you might want to use a slow shutter speed?
   Possible answer: taking a picture in low light

3. What does the Latin term *camera obscura* mean?
   dark chamber

4. How are digital cameras different from traditional cameras?
   Instead of using chemical film, a digital camera uses a light-sensitive electrical device.

5. What are the two main devices that control light in a camera?
   the shutter and the aperture

6. Why do you think it is easier to use an automatic camera than a manual camera?
   Answers will vary.

7. Check the phrase that best describes the author's purpose.
   - ___ to persuade
   - ___ to entertain
   - ✓ to inform

Study Skills

Fill out the registration form for a photography class. Then, answer the questions about the form.

```
1. _____
   last name        first name    middle initial
2. _____
   street address
3. _____
   city          state       zip code
4. _____
   phone number    e-mail address (optional)
5. _____
   age                      grade
What experience, if any, have you had with photography?
(Use the reverse side of the form if you need additional
space.)
```

1. What is the one piece of information that is optional?
   e-mail address

2. If you need more space to answer the question, what should you do?
   use the reverse side of the form

3. On which line should you write your age and grade in school?
   line five

33

Spectrum Reading Grade 6

Answer Key

Page 35

Vocabulary Skills

Write the words from the story that have the meanings below.

1. having attention drawn away
   distracted
2. to make a written copy of
   transcribe
3. people who act as guides or teachers
   mentors
4. having the power to change or effect
   influential
5. making a record of
   documenting

Words that have two middle consonants are divided into syllables between the consonants. For example, pic/ture. Divide the words below into syllables using a slash.

6. c a p/t u r e
7. c e n/t e r
8. a d/m i r e

The suffix **-able** means capable of or tending to. For example, reasonable means capable of reason. Write a word to match each definition below. Then, write a sentence using each word.

9. tending to honor **honorable**
   Answers will vary.
10. capable of being washed **washable**
    Answers will vary.
11. capable of breaking **breakable**
    Answers will vary.

Reading Skills

1. Why does Dante want to record his interview with Mr. Salinas?
   He does not want to be distracted by having to take notes.
2. What job did Mr. Salinas have before he became a photographer?
   high school English teacher
3. Name two people who have influenced Mr. Salinas's work.
   Possible answers: Elizabeth Chu, Walker Evans, Alfred Stieglitz
4. What does Mr. Salinas like about his job?
   Possible answer: It does not feel like a job.

Circle the word that best completes each sentence below.

5. Mr. Salinas was _____ with the work of Alfred Stieglitz and Walker Evans.
   uninterested (impressed) disappointed
6. Dante's questions for Mr. Salinas were _____
   irritating encouraging (thoughtful)
7. Mr. Salinas _____ that his work can be frustrating at times.
   (mentioned) aspired demanded
8. After his interview with Mr. Salinas, do you think that Dante will still want to become a photographer? Explain your answer.
   Answers will vary.

35

Page 37

Vocabulary Skills

Write the words from the passage that have the meanings below.

1. looked at with wonder; captivated
   mesmerized
2. potential; a reason for expecting future excellence
   promise
3. satisfying
   fulfilling
4. represent
   depict
5. unique; uncommon
   distinctive
6. eager and enthusiastic
   avid
7. Check the sentence in which trip has the same meaning as it does in paragraph 2.
   _____ Don't trip over that cord!
   _✓_ Kelly and Amy are planning a trip to Paris in the fall.
8. Check the sentence in which tone has the same meaning as it does in paragraph 5.
   _____ Maria was able to tone her muscles through frequent swimming.
   _✓_ I could see a yellowish tone in the stormy sky.

Write the idiom from paragraph 1 on the line next to its meaning.

9. to sound familiar **ring a bell**

Reading Skills

1. Check the line beside the word or words that best describe what type of passage this is.
   _____ historical fiction
   _✓_ biography
   _____ persuasive
2. Check the sentence below that is the best summary for paragraph 7.
   _✓_ Adams was an environmentalist who was able to help the cause he believed in through his photographs of natural places.
   _____ Adams visited Sequoia, Mount Rainier, and Glacier National Parks.
   _____ The Sierra Club is a conservation group.
3. Check the words that best describe Ansel Adams.
   _✓_ talented
   _____ anxious
   _✓_ enthusiastic
   _✓_ creative
   _____ suspicious

Write **T** before the sentences that are true. Write **F** before the sentences that are false.

4. _F_ Adams was born on the East Coast.
5. _F_ Adams received his first camera from a teacher.
6. _T_ Adams was also a talented musician.
7. _T_ The majority of Adams's photographs are black and white.
8. _F_ Adams is still alive and lives California today.

37

Page 39

Vocabulary Skills

Write the words from the passage that have the meanings below.

1. very important
   monumental
2. widespread
   prevalent
3. common; usual
   customary
4. freed
   liberated

Write the words from the selection that match the abbreviations below.

5. WWII **World War II**
6. OH **Ohio**
7. MT **Montana**
8. cent. **century**

Reading Skills

1. Check the sentence that best states the main idea of the selection.
   _____ Margaret Bourke-White photographed Cleveland's steel mills in the 1920s.
   _✓_ Margaret Bourke-White was a talented photojournalist who traveled the world and broke new ground for women.
   _____ Margaret Bourke-White was one of LIFE magazine's first four photographers.

2. Is this selection a fantasy, or does it take place in reality? How can you tell?
   reality; Answers will vary.
3. Why was Bourke-White's job unusual for a woman?
   At that time, it was still customary for women to work mostly in the home, taking care of a family and a household.
4. What did Bourke-White plan to be before she discovered photography?
   a herpetologist
5. What was unusual about Bourke-White's industrial pictures?
   Bourke-White managed to make the photographs of machinery and factories both artistic and beautiful.
6. Number the events below to show the order in which they happened.
   _4_ Bourke-White photographed the liberation of the concentration camps.
   _3_ Bourke-White began working for LIFE magazine.
   _2_ Henry Luce hired Bourke-White to work at Fortune.
   _1_ Bourke-White graduated from college.

Study Skills

A pronunciation key is a list of sound symbols and key words. They show how to pronounce words. Use the pronunciation key on the inside back cover of this book to write the words that match these pronunciations.

1. /sir vī′ ver/ **survivor**
2. /ma shē′ ner ē/ **machinery**
3. /fāst/ **faced**
4. /grōth/ **growth**

39

Page 41

Vocabulary Skills

Write the words from the story that have the meanings below.

1. young animals such as bears, foxes, or tigers
   cubs
2. to tame or train something wild for human use
   domesticate
3. bringing something into a country from another country
   importing
4. responsible; like an adult
   mature

Words that end in **le** are usually divided into syllables before the consonant that precedes it. For example, ta/ble. Divide the words below into syllables using a slash (/).

5. h a n/d l e
6. p e o/p l e
7. g e n/t l e
8. d i m/p l e

In each row, circle the word that does not belong.

9. small miniature (enormous) tiny
10. mature (innocent) trustworthy responsible
11. (argue) research inquire question
12. hedgehog (exotic) tiger dog

Reading Skills

1. What kinds of exotic animals did Ari and his mom see when they were online?
   Answers will vary.

2. Why did Ari decide to write a letter to the television show he watched?
   Ari thought the show was irresponsible for not explaining both sides of the story.
3. Why did Mrs. Stein say that Ari was mature and responsible?
   because he made a mature and thoughtful decision about owning an exotic pet
4. Do you think that Ari will be a good pet owner? Why or why not?
   Answers will vary.

Mark each sentence below **F** if it is in first-person point of view and **T** if it is in third-person point of view.

5. _F_ I can't believe we're going to get a dog or cat!
6. _T_ Mrs. Stein put down her knitting.
7. _T_ Ari turned on the computer.
8. _F_ I think that writing a letter is an excellent idea.

Study Skills

A library's reference system can help you find a book. Use the information below to answer the questions that follow.

Call No:	441.86 WO
Author:	Wolfowitz, Eliza
Title:	Everything You Need to Know About Adopting a Pet
Publisher:	Leesburg Lane Publishing, 2004

1. What is the author's last name?
   Wolfowitz
2. Who is the book's publisher?
   Leesburg Lane Publishing

41

Answer Key

Page 43

Vocabulary Skills

Write the words from the passage that have the meanings below.

1. meetings
   encounters (Par. 1)

2. unusual; from another part of the world
   exotic (Par. 2)

3. left or deserted
   abandoned (Par. 3)

4. quick to attack; forceful
   aggressive (Par. 6)

5. as a whole; in general
   overall (Par. 6)

Circle the homophone that correctly completes each sentence below.

6. Can you _____ this dress for me by Friday? (alter, altar)

7. Raj's _____ at the performance gave me confidence. (presents, presence)

8. How much does that bag _____? (weigh, way)

Write **S** if the possessive word is singular. Write **P** if it is plural.

9. _S_ the python's cage
10. _P_ the creatures' habitats
11. _S_ Florida's natural areas
12. _P_ the animals' environment

Reading Skills

1. Check the phrase that best describes the author's purpose.
   ___ to entertain
   _✓_ to inform
   ___ to instruct

2. An **analogy** is a comparison between two things that may seem to be unalike but that have at least one similarity. An analogy is used to compare two things in paragraph 7. What are they?
   dominoes and the environment

3. Name two animals that are nonnative species in southern Florida.
   Answers will vary.

4. Why is it hard to care for a full-grown Burmese python?
   because it is so large

5. Why are exotic pets more likely to survive in the wild in a state like Florida than they are in a state like Ohio or Montana?
   because Florida's climate is warmer, wetter, and more tropical

6. Do you think that abandoned exotic animals will continue to be a problem in Florida? Explain your answer.
   Answers will vary.

7. How would you define the term *invasive species*?
   Possible answer: nonnative species that have a negative effect on the local environment

43

Page 45

Vocabulary Skills

Write the words from the passage that have the meanings below.

1. described by
   characterized (Par. 1)

2. more than enough; plentiful
   abundant (Par. 3)

3. covered with thick, green plant growth
   lush (Par. 3)

4. the plants and animals that make up an environment and affect one another
   ecosystem (Par. 4)

5. to eat, drink, or use up
   consume (Par. 6)

6. native
   indigenous (Par. 6)

Find the compound words from the selection that contain the words below.

7. grass   **grasslands** (Par. 2)
8. fall   **rainfall** (Par. 3)
9. planes   **airplanes** (Par. 6)
10. farm   **farmland** (Par. 6)

Read each pair of words listed below. If the words are synonyms, write **S** on the line. If the words are antonyms, write **A** on the line.

11. _A_ expanded   shrank
12. _S_ suitable   appropriate
13. _S_ influence   affect
14. _A_ lowered   raised

Reading Skills

Write **F** before the sentences that are facts. Write **O** before the sentences that are opinions.

1. _F_ The Everglades National Park covers about 1.5 million acres.
2. _F_ Melaleuca trees consume a great deal of water.
3. _O_ Everyone should visit the Everglades at least once.
4. _O_ The Everglades are most beautiful in the summer.
5. _F_ The Everglades are the only place in the world where crocodiles and alligators coexist.

6. What is the author trying to persuade the reader of in this passage?
   that the Everglades are worth protecting

7. Think about what you know about rain forests. Name two ways in which rain forests and the Everglades are similar.
   Answers will vary.

8. About how many species of birds are there in Everglades National Park?
   350

9. Why were melaleuca trees planted in the Everglades?
   to consume water

Circle the word that best completes each sentence.

10. Many people believe it is important to _____ our nation's wild places.
    destroy   investigate   preserve

11. It can be difficult to _____ the balance of an ecosystem.
    explain   maintain   cancel

45

Page 47

Vocabulary Skills

Write the words from the passage that have the meanings below.

1. the places where plants and animals live
   habitats (Par. 1)

2. a scientist who studies birds
   ornithologist (Par. 1)

3. to reach a decision
   conclude (Par. 2)

4. to list and describe items of a particular type
   catalog (Par. 2)

5. proceeding, even in dangerous circumstances
   venturing (Par. 3)

6. short trips or journeys
   excursions (Par. 4)

Circle the homophone that correctly completes each sentence below.

7. Audubon _____ a piece of yarn to the legs of the birds. (tied, tide)

8. Have you ever _____ the call of a chickadee? (heard, herd)

Check the meaning of the underlined word in each sentence.

9. Audubon conducted the first bird-banding experiments in the United States.
   ___ behaved in a certain way
   _✓_ directed

10. Birds were usually the subject of Audubon's paintings.
    _✓_ things being studied
    ___ the word or group of words in a sentence that performs the action

Reading Skills

1. Check the line beside the word or words that best describe what type of passage this is.
   _✓_ biography
   ___ myth
   ___ historical fiction

2. Check the sentence that best states the main idea of the selection.
   ___ Audubon was born in Haiti but moved to the United States as a teenager.
   ___ The National Audubon Society was founded to honor John James Audubon.
   _✓_ Audubon was a painter and ornithologist who created one of the most comprehensive catalogs of birds in America.

3. Check the words that best describe John James Audubon.
   _✓_ intelligent
   ___ cheerful
   ___ unfriendly
   _✓_ artistic
   _✓_ adventurous

4. Explain how Audubon's bird-banding experiment worked.
   By tying yarn to the birds' legs, he was able to see that they came back to the same nesting places each year.

5. Why do you think that today's conservation groups would not approve of Audubon's methods?
   because he killed so many birds

47

Page 49

Vocabulary Skills

Write the words from the story that have the meanings below.

1. careful thought or discussion
   deliberation (Par. 7)

2. dependable
   reliable (Par. 11)

3. unchanging
   constant (Par. 12)

4. arrangement or place
   formation (Par. 13)

5. Check the sentence in which *rose* has the same meaning as it does in paragraph 7.
   ___ Annabelle chose a beautiful red rose for the bouquet.
   _✓_ The plane rose higher and higher into the air.

6. Check the sentence in which *check* has the same meaning as it does in paragraph 10.
   ___ David wrote a check to pay for the groceries.
   _✓_ Did you check the oil level in the car this morning?

7. Check the sentence in which *bill* has the same meaning as it does in paragraph 13.
   _✓_ The woodpecker's bill is long and thin.
   ___ Please ask the waiter for our bill.

Fill in the blanks below with the possessive form of the word in parentheses.

8. **Olivia's** mom gave her dad a birdfeeder for his birthday. (Olivia)

9. **Birds'** colorings are not always a reliable way to identify them. (Birds)

10. Jaya, Olivia, and Mr. Vasquez crossed the street to get to the **park's** entrance. (park)

Reading Skills

1. **Hyperbole** is an exaggerated statement that is used to make a point. For example, the sentence *I am so hungry I could eat a horse* means that the speaker is extremely hungry, not that she could actually eat a horse. Find the hyperbole in paragraph 3, and write it on the line below. Then, explain what you think it means.
   We don't want to be eaten alive out there. Answers will vary.

2. Why do you think Mr. Vasquez says they should look for a trail that isn't too wooded and that has open areas and some water?
   Answers will vary.

3. Find one sentence that shows that Mr. Vasquez is knowledgeable about birding.
   Answers will vary.

4. Name two birds that Jaya and the Vasquezes saw on their walk.
   Answers will vary.

5. Why is a bird's shape often a better clue to identifying it than its color?
   because a bird's coloring can appear different depending on the light

6. Do you think that Olivia and Jaya will want to go birding again? Why or why not?
   Answers will vary.

49

Answer Key

Page 51

Vocabulary Skills

Write the words from the story that have the meanings below.

1. distributed; set aside
   allotted
2. filled with surprise or astonishment
   marveled
3. to change from a solid to a liquid
   dissolve
4. attraction
   appeal
5. staying in one place in the air
   hovering
6. to refill
   replenish

Find the compound words from the selection that contain the words below.

7. bird **hummingbirds**
8. heart **heartbeat**
9. back **paperback**

The prefix **ir-** means *not*. Write the meaning of each word below. Then, use it in a sentence.

10. irregular **not regular**
    Answers will vary.
11. irresponsible **not responsible**
    Answers will vary.
12. irresistible **not resistible**
    Answers will vary.

Reading Skills

1. Check the phrase that best describes the author's purpose.
   ✓ to entertain
   ___ to instruct
   ___ to persuade

2. Number the events below to show the order in which they happened.
   5 Jaya says they'll have to learn the rest from experience.
   4 Olivia began to gather up the books on the table.
   1 Jaya's gym class took their heart rates.
   2 Olivia tells Jaya that there are more than 300 species of hummingbird.
   3 Olivia said she would start a list of plants that hummingbirds like.

3. How did hummingbirds get their name?
   The beating of their wings makes a humming noise.
4. Why were Jaya and Olivia researching hummingbirds?
   They wanted to have plants in their garden that would attract hummingbirds.
5. Why are hummingbird feeders usually red?
   because hummingbirds are attracted to red flowers
6. If you added one-quarter cup of sugar to a hummingbird feeder, how much water would you need to add?
   one cup
7. How often do hummingbirds need to eat?
   every ten minutes

Page 53

Vocabulary Skills

Write the words from the passage that have the meanings below.

1. occurring once each year
   annual
2. observe
   witness
3. unusual; setting something apart from others
   distinctive
4. to search for food
   forage
5. dry
   arid
6. perfect
   ideal

Read each pair of words listed below. If the words are synonyms, write **S** on the line. If the words are antonyms, write **A** on the line.

7. **A** graceful   clumsy
8. **S** important   significant
9. **A** shallow   deep
10. **S** unique   unusual

Reading Skills

1. Why are sandhill cranes classified as omnivorous?
   because they eat both plants and animals
2. The selection says that Rowe Sanctuary provides blinds for visitors. What do you think this means?
   Answers will vary.

3. Where do sandhill cranes live during the winter?
   Texas, New Mexico, and northern Mexico
4. What attracts the cranes to Platte River?
   Possible answer: The Platte River is a wide, shallow body of water in a typically dry area.
5. Check the sentence that best states the main idea of the passage.
   ✓ Every spring, thousands of sandhill cranes stop at Nebraska's Platte River during their northern migration.
   ___ The most distinctive features of sandhill cranes are their long necks and legs.
   ___ Rowe Sanctuary in Gibbon, Nebraska, is one of the best places for viewing sandhill cranes.

Write **F** before the sentences that are facts. Write **O** before the sentences that are opinions.

6. **F** The summer homes of sandhill cranes are in places like Canada and Alaska.
7. **O** There is nothing as beautiful as a sandhill crane taking flight.
8. **F** Sandhill cranes like the environment of marshes and bogs.
9. **O** The best place to view sandhill cranes is Rowe Sanctuary.
10. **F** Large numbers of people come to watch the cranes migrate every spring.

Page 55

Vocabulary Skills

Write **S** if the possessive word is singular. Write **P** if it is plural.

1. **P** students' suggestions
2. **S** Ms. DeJohn's list
3. **P** spiders' webs
4. **S** the exhibit's location
5. **P** the pandas' cage

In each row, circle the word that does not belong.

6. rare   unusual   (typical)   uncommon
7. portion   fraction   part   (whole)
8. emigrate   (visit)   move   relocate

Reading Skills

1. Check the line beside the word or words that best describe what type of selection this is.
   ✓ fiction
   ___ autobiography
   ___ biography

2. How can you tell that Ms. DeJohn's class is excited about their trip to the Smithsonian?
   Answers will vary.

3. Why can't the class visit all of the Smithsonian's museums during their trip to Washington, D.C.?
   There are too many different museums.

4. What does Chris want to see at the National Museum of American History?
   an exhibit on the Information Age

5. What problem does Ms. DeJohn's class have at the beginning of the story? How do they resolve it?
   deciding which museums to visit; Each student tells what he or she would like to see, and then as a class they decide which four museums sound the best.

6. Who are Anita and Arabella?
   space spiders

7. Why do you think it might be interesting to visit a "hands on history" exhibit?
   Answers will vary.

Study Skills

Write the name of the reference source you could use to answer each question below.

dictionary	thesaurus
atlas	encyclopedia

1. Where is Indonesia?
   atlas
2. How does the telegraph work?
   encyclopedia
3. What does the root *tele* mean?
   dictionary
4. What is another word for *additional*?
   thesaurus

Page 57

Vocabulary Skills

Write the words from the passage that have the meanings below.

1. objects that are worth remembering
   memorabilia
2. enormous; wide-reaching
   vast
3. financially supported
   funded
4. the act of scattering or spreading out
   diffusion
5. moved to action
   inspired

Circle the homophone that correctly completes each sentence below.

6. Henry Hungerford did not have an ___ to whom he could leave his wealth. ((heir,) air)
7. James Smithson ___ on his fortune to his nephew. (past, (passed))
8. The Smithsonian is located in our nation's ___. ((capital,) capitol)

Divide the words below into syllables using a slash (/).

9. a m/p l e
10. n o/b le
11. g e n/t l e
12. s i m/p l e

Reading Skills

1. Approximately how many items are there in the Smithsonian's collection?
   143 million

2. Do you think that the Smithsonian Institution will continue to accumulate more artifacts? Why or why not?
   Answers will vary.

3. How is the Smithsonian's National Zoological Park different from its other museums?
   Possible answer: The exhibits are living animals.

4. What body of government decided how Smithson's money would be used?
   Congress

5. Name two items you could find displayed in the National Museum of American History.
   Answers will vary.

6. Does this selection take place in reality, or is it a fantasy? How can you tell?
   reality; Answers will vary.

7. Check the word or words that best describe what type of passage this is.
   ___ how-to
   ✓ informative
   ___ biography

Answer Key

Page 59

Vocabulary Skills

Write the words from the passage that match the abbreviations below.

1. mg. _milligrams_
2. Nat'l _National_
3. UV _ultraviolet_

The prefix **re-** means *again*. For example, *restart* means *to start again*. Underline the word with a prefix in each sentence, and then write the word's meaning on the line.

4. The diamond Tavernier bought was <u>recut</u>.
   cut again
5. Mrs. McLean wanted her diamond to be <u>reset</u>.
   set again
6. Throughout history, the Hope diamond has been <u>resold</u> many times.
   sold again

Reading Skills

1. On the lines below, write a summary for paragraph 5.
   Answers will vary.
2. What happens when the Hope diamond is exposed to ultraviolet light?
   It will glow red for a few seconds.
3. According to legend, what happens to owners of the Hope diamond?
   They will have great misfortune.
4. How did Harry Winston send the Hope diamond to the Smithsonian Institution?
   through the U.S. Postal Service

5. Who owned the Hope diamond before Harry Winston?
   Evalyn Walsh McLean
6. Number the events below to show the order in which they happened.
   _4_ Mrs. McLean had the Hope diamond reset.
   _3_ Lord Francis Hope sold the Hope diamond.
   _5_ Harry Winston donated the Hope diamond to the Smithsonian Institution.
   _1_ Jean-Baptiste Tavernier traveled to India.
   _2_ The French Blue diamond was stolen in a robbery of the French crown jewels.

Study Skills

Look at the following dictionary entry. Then, answer the questions that follow.

record (rek′ urd) (*noun*) 1. a disk on which music is recorded 2. a written history of something
(rē kôrd′) (*verb*) to store sound or pictures for later use

1. Which syllable is stressed when the word *record* is used as a noun?
   first
2. What part of speech is *record* when it is used to mean *a disk on which music is recorded*?
   noun

59

Page 61

Vocabulary Skills

Write the words from the passage that have the meanings below.

1. agencies of mass communication, such as news organizations
   media
2. tried to achieve; worked toward
   pursued
3. attraction
   allure
4. of or in the air
   aerial
5. built to meet specific needs or according to specific guidelines
   customized

Find the states in the passage that match the abbreviations below.

6. MI _Michigan_
7. MN _Minnesota_
8. NE _Nebraska_
9. MO _Missouri_

Read each word below. Then, write the letter of its antonym on the line beside the word.

10. _c_ generous   a. minor
11. _d_ wealthy   b. everywhere
12. _a_ major   c. stingy
13. _b_ nowhere   d. poor

Reading Skills

1. Check the word or words that best describe what type of passage this is.
   _____ historical fiction
   _✓_ historical nonfiction
   _____ legend
2. Check the words that best describe Charles Lindbergh.
   _✓_ adventurous
   _____ quiet
   _✓_ determined
   _____ kind
   _✓_ daring
3. What did Lindbergh have to do in order to win the Orteig prize?
   fly nonstop from New York City to Paris
4. Why was Lindbergh's plane named *The Spirit of St. Louis*?
   because the city of St. Louis helped fund his flight
5. Why do you think Lindbergh was one of America's first celebrities?
   Answers will vary.
6. Where is *The Spirit of St. Louis* kept today?
   the Smithsonian Institute's National Air & Space Museum
7. Check the sentence that best states the main idea of the passage.
   _____ The dance called the Lindy Hop was named for Charles Lindbergh.
   _____ Lindbergh graduated first in his military pilot class.
   _✓_ Lindbergh, one of America's first celebrities, flew nonstop from New York City to Paris.

61

Page 63

Vocabulary Skills

Write the words from the story that have the meanings below.

1. gloomily; in a depressed way
   dejectedly
2. certain to happen
   imminent
3. without wasting time or energy
   efficient
4. producing the desired effect
   effective
5. extra
   spare

Write the idiom from paragraph 6 on the line next to its meaning.

6. trying not to cry _fighting back tears_

Write **S** if the possessive word is singular. Write **P** if it is plural.

7. _P_ the Mahaulus' house
8. _S_ the family's memories
9. _P_ the girls' expressions
10. _S_ the volcano's eruption
11. _S_ the government's system

Find a synonym in the story for each of the words below.

12. option _alternatives_
13. protected _safe_
14. attempting _trying_

Reading Skills

1. Why do Mr. and Mrs. Mahaulu think that the family needs to move?
   The danger of living next to an active volcano is too great.
2. Mr. Mahaulu says that volcanoes are a fact of life in Hawaii. What does he mean?
   Answers will vary.
3. What problem do the Mahaulus have in the story?
   Possible answer: accepting that they have to move
4. Find a sentence in the story showing that one or both of the girls are not enthusiastic about moving.
   Possible answer: "There are so many things I'll miss here," said Kala quietly.
5. What arguments to Leilani and Kala use to try to persuade their parents not to move?
   The volcano has not erupted yet; the government has warning systems in place.
6. Check the phrase that best describes the author's purpose.
   _____ to instruct
   _✓_ to persuade
   _____ to entertain

63

Page 65

Vocabulary Skills

Circle the word that best completes each sentence below.

1. Jack Thompson has become _____ to living in the path of an active volcano.
   related (accustomed) furious
2. Thompson enjoys living in a beautiful and _____ area.
   terrifying common (remote)
3. Thompson uses several _____ energy sources.
   (alternative) expensive unrealistic

The suffix **-ous** means *full of*. For example, *joyous* means *full of joy*. Write the definition of the underlined word in each sentence.

4. Thompson must always be <u>cautious</u> of where he steps.
   full of caution
5. Thompson's story has become <u>famous</u> because it is so unusual.
   full of fame
6. Most people would feel <u>nervous</u> living in Jack Thompson's home.
   full of nerves

Reading Skills

1. How is Royal Gardens different than other subdivisions?
   Answers will vary.
2. What does it mean to live "in close quarters" with the volcano?
   It means living close to, or side-by-side, with the volcano.

3. Why do you think that Thompson refused to move when everyone else sought shelter in safer places?
   Answers will vary.
4. Check the sentence below that is the best summary for paragraph 3.
   _____ The lava that flows near Thompson's home averages about 2,000 degrees.
   _✓_ Thompson respects the power of the volcano but has become used to living so close to it.
   _____ The lava consumed many homes in Thompson's neighborhood.

Write **T** before the sentences that are true. Write **F** before the sentences that are false.

5. _F_ Kilauea stopped erupting about ten years ago.
6. _T_ Thompson collects and stores rainwater.

Study Skills

A library's reference system can help you find a book. Use the information below to answer the questions that follow.

Call No:	866. 94 GI
Author:	Gilchrist, Alexander
Title:	Unusual Homes: People Who Live in Extreme Places
Publisher:	Hayberry Press, 2005

1. What is the author's last name?
   Gilchrist
2. In what year was the book published?
   _2005_

65

Answer Key

Page 67

Vocabulary Skills

Write the words from the passage that have the meanings below.

1. fiction in which an element of science plays an important role; it often takes place in the future

   science fiction

2. without stopping; all the time

   constantly

3. to crash or strike together

   collide

4. the place where two things come together

   juncture

5. the rubbing together of two objects or surfaces

   friction

6. heavy; having the parts packed tightly together

   dense

Read each pair of words listed below. If the words are synonyms, write **S** on the line. If the words are antonyms, write **A** on the line.

7. __A__ frequent   uncommon
8. __S__ huge   enormous
9. __S__ strong   powerful
10. __A__ rise   fall

Words that have a single middle consonant are usually divided into syllables before the consonant. For example, *e/vil* or *o/pen*. Divide the words below into syllables using a slash (/).

11. e/rupt
12. a/long
13. o/ver

Reading Skills

1. What is one difference between the way that scientists view volcanoes and most other people view them?

   Possible answer: People see volcanoes as erupting mountains, but scientists see them as temporary structures.

2. For what reason is the San Andreas Fault well known?

   Possible answer: because earthquakes are common there

3. The author compares the rate at which Earth's plates move with something that is more familiar. What is the other element in the comparison?

   human fingernails

4. Name two continents that border the Ring of Fire.

   Possible answers: Asia, North America, South America

5. What percentage of the world's volcanoes are located in the Ring of Fire?

   75 percent

6. Why does magma rise to the surface?

   because it is lighter, or less dense, than the rocky material that surrounds it

7. What purpose would a reader have for reading this passage?

   ____ for pleasure or entertainment

   __✓__ for information

   ____ to learn how to solve a problem

67

Page 69

Vocabulary Skills

Write the words from the passage that have the meanings below.

1. to ruin or destroy

   devastate

2. something that interrupts or alters events

   disturbance

3. moves back; moves away from

   recedes

4. periods of time in between events

   intervals

5. watch; closely observe

   monitor

Read each word below. Then, write the letter of its abbreviation in the space beside it.

6. __d__ hour   a. m.p.h.
7. __c__ Alaska   b. HI
8. __a__ miles per hour c. AK
9. __b__ Hawaii   d. hr.

Reading Skills

1. Check the line beside the word that best describes what type of passage this is.

   ____ biography

   __✓__ informational

   ____ fiction

2. What does the word *tsunami* mean in Japanese?

   harbor wave

3. What are two possible causes of tsunamis?

   earthquake or underwater volcanic eruption

4. What is one way in which tsunamis are different than other waves?

   Answers will vary.

5. What is one positive effect of the 1946 tsunamis?

   creation of the Pacific Tsunami Warning System

6. Name two countries that were affected by the tsunami of 2004.

   Thailand, India, Indonesia

7. Why didn't the Pacific Tsunami Warning System alert people of the 2004 tsunami?

   There was no warning system for the Indian Ocean.

Circle the word that best completes each sentence below.

8. Tsunamis can cause great _____.

   accuracy (destruction) earthquakes

9. Scientists are looking for ways to be able to better _____ the arrival of tsunamis.

   explain control (predict)

10. Tsunamis are not _____ caused by meteorites.

   (frequently) oddly powerfully

Study Skills

Use a dictionary to help you divide the words below into syllables.

1. t s u/n a/m i
2. g o/v e r n/m e n t
3. d e v/a s/t a/t i o n
4. t e c h/n o l/o/g y
5. e/n o r/m o u s
6. m e/t e/o r/i t e

69

Page 71

Vocabulary Skills

Write the words from the story that have the meanings below.

1. a group of animals that lives or travels together

   flock

2. the touching of two people or objects

   contact

3. with amazement and disbelief

   incredulously

Write the idiom from paragraph 10 on the line next to its meaning.

4. watched or observed   kept an eye on

Find the compound words from the selection that contain the words below.

5. fire   firewood
6. dish   dishtowel
7. mate   classmate

Check the meaning of the underlined word.

8. Mrs. Rosen looked <u>calmly</u> at the bats flying overhead.

   ____ not calm

   __✓__ in a calm way

   ____ capable of being calm

9. Charley and Mattie were <u>unaware</u> of their mother's experiences with bats.

   __✓__ not aware

   ____ aware again

   ____ wrongly aware

Reading Skills

Mark each sentence below **F** if it is in first-person point of view and **T** if it is in third-person point of view.

1. __F__ I love making s'mores!
2. __T__ Charley rinsed the dishes in a tub of clean water.
3. __F__ I went to San Antonio to visit a friend from college.
4. __T__ Mr. Rosen said that vampire bats don't live in North America.

Write **F** before the sentences that are facts. Write **O** before the sentences that are opinions.

5. __F__ Mattie gathered wood for the fire.
6. __O__ Everything is more enjoyable when you are camping.
7. __F__ Mexican free-tailed bats come to Bracken Cave to give birth and raise their young.
8. __O__ The sky is most beautiful at dusk.

9. How do you think Mattie and Charley will feel the next time they see a bat? Why?

   Answers will vary.

10. What ingredients are used to make s'mores?

    graham crackers, chocolate, and marshmallows

11. Find one sentence that shows that Mattie enjoys camping. Write it on the lines below.

    Answers will vary.

12. Where is Bracken Cave located?

    Texas

71

Page 73

Vocabulary Skills

Write the words from the passage that have the meanings below.

1. the ways others judge the worth or quality of something

   reputations

2. amounts

   quantities

3. active at night

   nocturnal

4. sound, light, or heat that is sent back from a surface

   reflected

5. having the quality of being different, or unlike others

   diversity

6. a place where one lives

   residence

Find a synonym in the story for each of the words below.

7. trustworthy   reliable
8. incredible   amazing
9. eat   consume
10. areas   regions
11. total   complete

Write **S** if the possessive word is singular. Write **P** if it is plural.

12. __P__ animals' reputations
13. __P__ trees' growth
14. __S__ the plant's pollen
15. __S__ the bat's wings

Reading Skills

1. Explain how *echolocation* works.

   Possible answer: Bats make a noise and then listen for its echo, forming a mental picture of their surroundings based on the way the echo sounds.

2. What is the author trying to persuade the reader of in this selection?

   that bats are good creatures to have around

3. How can you encourage bats to live near your home?

   by building a bat house

4. Why do you think some people are afraid of bats?

   Answers will vary.

5. Write two ways in which species of bats may differ from one another.

   Possible answers: size, coloring, eating habits

Write **T** before the sentences that are true. Write **F** before the sentences that are false.

6. __T__ Some bats pollinate plants and flowers.
7. __F__ More than 3,000 species of bats exist.
8. __T__ Bats are nocturnal creatures.
9. __T__ The smallest bat in the world weighs less than a penny.
10. __F__ Bats feed only on insects.

11. Check the phrase that best describes the author's purpose.

    ____ to instruct

    __✓__ to inform

    ____ to entertain

73

Answer Key

Page 75

Vocabulary Skills

Underline the compound word in each sentence. Then, write the two words that make up each compound.

1. It was a good day for spotting wildlife.
   wild / life

2. Dragonflies flew along the trail ahead of the Rosens.
   dragon / flies

3. The Rosens put fresh blueberries on their granola.
   blue / berries

Circle the homophone that correctly completes each sentence below.

4. Mr. Rosen _____ a snack for the family. (pact, packed)

5. Three quails wandered into _____. (sight, site)

6. Mrs. Rosen dangled her _____ in the water. (feat, feet)

Reading Skills

1. Number the events below to show the order in which they happened.
   2 The Rosens drove to the trailhead.
   4 Mrs. Rosen lowered her feet into the water.
   5 Charley and Mattie looked for their bathing suits.
   1 The Rosens made scrambled eggs.
   3 Charley took a picture of the quails.

2. Find the example of hyperbole in paragraph 14, and write it on the line below. Then, explain what you think it means.
   I never would have guessed in a million years; Answers will vary.

3. Dialogue is what a character says. The words in dialogue are always in quotation marks. On the line below, write the words that are dialogue in paragraph 13.
   Your bathing suits are in my backpack.

4. Why do you think "Charley's and Mattie's eyes grew wide" in paragraph 8?
   Answers will vary.

Study Skills

Use the table below to answer the questions that follow.

Spring	Temp (°F)	Area	State
Healing Spring	86	Roanoke	Virginia
Scenic Hot Springs	122	Seattle	Washington
Baker Hot Spring	108	Concrete	Washington
Caddo Gap Springs	95	Little Rock	Arkansas
Morning Mist Springs	205	Ashton	Wyoming

1. Which hot spring has the hottest water?
   Morning Mist Springs

2. What is the name of the spring located near Seattle, Washington?
   Scenic Hot Springs

3. Where is Caddo Gap Springs located?
   Little Rock, AR

75

Page 77

Vocabulary Skills

Write the words from the passage that have the meanings below.

1. area
   vicinity

2. relating to a treatment or cure
   therapeutic

3. illnesses
   ailments

4. beautiful and decorative
   ornate

5. a large amount of something in one place
   concentration

6. free of germs
   sterile

The suffix -less means to be without. For example, fearless means to be without fear. Write a word to match each definition below. Then, write a sentence using each word.

7. to be without odor odorless
   Answers will vary.

8. to be without use useless
   Answers will vary.

9. to be without a point pointless
   Answers will vary.

Reading Skills

1. What benefit do people expect to gain from drinking or bathing in the hot springs?
   They believe it could heal their ailments and improve their health.

2. When were most of the bathhouses on Bathhouse Row constructed?
   during the 1920s

3. What is the average temperature of the water?
   143 degrees Fahrenheit

4. How did NASA scientists use water from the hot springs?
   to store samples of moon rock

5. Do you think the hot springs at Hot Springs National Park will ever run out of water? Explain your answer.
   Possible answer: No, because the hot springs have existed for thousands of years.

6. Number the events below to show the order in which they happened.
   5 Many bathhouses were built in Hot Springs, Arkansas.
   4 Hot Spring Reservation was renamed Hot Springs National Park.
   1 Native Americans used the hot springs for many years before Europeans discovered them.
   3 Hot Spring Reservation was established.
   2 The U.S. purchased the Louisiana Territory.

Study Skills

Write the entry word you would look for in a dictionary next to each word below.

1. established establish
2. healing heal

77

Page 79

Vocabulary Skills

Write the words from the passage that have the meanings below.

1. sensible; having good judgment
   levelheaded

2. changed the order of
   reversed

3. meant to be
   destined

4. gives up a career, usually at a certain age
   retires

5. not speaking too highly about one's abilities or accomplishments
   humble

Write the words from the story that match the abbreviations below.

6. NBA National Basketball Association
7. TX Texas
8. Sept. September
9. pts. points

Find the compound words from the selection that contain the words below.

10. land homeland
11. ground background
12. mean meantime
13. light spotlight

Reading Skills

1. Check the word that best describes what type of passage this is.
   ___ autobiography
   ✓ biography
   ___ fantasy

2. Check the words that best describe Yao Ming.
   ✓ sensible
   ___ creative
   ✓ athletic
   ___ rude
   ✓ hardworking

3. Why weren't Yao's parents surprised when he grew to be 7 feet 6 inches tall?
   His parents are both much taller than average.

4. What do you think Yao will do when he retires from his career in basketball? Explain your answer.
   Answers will vary.

5. What persuaded Yao's parents to allow him to attend the junior sports school?
   They thought it would give him a better chance of attending a good college.

6. Why do you think Yao Ming gained fame and popularity so quickly?
   Answers will vary.

79

Page 81

Vocabulary Skills

Write the words from the passage that have the meanings below.

1. ability to move
   mobility

2. happening earlier in time
   former

3. not active or busy
   idle

4. the condition of restoring to health
   rehabilitation

5. qualified; fit to be chosen
   eligible

Write the words from the story that match the abbreviations below.

6. WWII World War II
7. VA Veteran's Association
8. PVA Paralyzed Veterans of America
9. IL Illinois

10. The Latin root mob means move. Find a word in paragraph 1 with the root mob.
    mobility

11. The Latin root act means do. Find a word in paragraph 1 with the root act.
    activity

12. The Latin root form means shape. Find a word in paragraph 2 with the root form.
    formed/forming

Reading Skills

Write T before the sentences that are true. Write F before the sentences that are false.

1. F The first military wheelchair basketball team was called the Kansas City Wheelchair Bulldozers.

2. T Today, there are more than 160 NWBA teams.

3. F The first NWBA tournament was not held until the 1990s.

4. T All participants in wheelchair basketball games must have a physical disability.

5. How does the physical advantage foul rule help keep the game fair?
   All players must remain fully seated, so they remain equally matched in terms of physical ability.

6. Why was wheelchair basketball first invented?
   as an outlet for the energy and athleticism of WWII vets who were in wheelchairs

7. What was the name of the original California wheelchair basketball team?
   Birmingham Flying Wheels

8. Why are points awarded to each player depending on the severity of his or her disability?
   to make sure the teams are fairly matched

9. Check the phrase that best describes the author's purpose.
   ___ to persuade the reader to attend a wheelchair basketball game
   ✓ to explain the origins and rules of wheelchair basketball
   ___ to instruct the reader on how to join a wheelchair basketball league

81

Answer Key

Page 83

Vocabulary Skills

Write the words from the story that have the meanings below.

1. moving carefully and skillfully
   maneuvering (Par. 2)

3. something that motivates a person to behave in a certain way
   incentive (Par. 5)

4. highly admired and respected
   prestigious (Par. 7)

5. a minimum level to be reached before acceptance
   qualifying (Par. 6)

Find an antonym in the story for each of the words below.

6. few _____ **plenty** (Par. 9)
7. mild _____ **spicy** (Par. 10)
8. farther _____ **closer** (Par. 12)

Compound words are divided into syllables between the two words that make the compound. For example, *eye/sight*. Divide the words below into syllables using a slash (/).

9. w h e e l / c h a i r
10. h o m e / m a d e
11. m i d / d a y
12. d o o r / w a y

Reading Skills

1. What analogy does Uncle Jorge make when he is talking about his everyday tires as compared to his racing tires?
   The difference between wearing running shoes and loafers.

2. How is a racing wheelchair different from a regular wheelchair? How are they similar?
   Possible answer: They both have two large wheels, but the racing wheelchair has an additional small third wheel in front.

Write F before the sentences that are facts.
Write O before the sentences that are opinions.

3. **F** Uncle Jorge has completed a marathon before.
4. **O** Uncle Jorge will probably complete the marathon in less time than his friend.
5. **F** Tasha and Julio ate the pretzels Uncle Jorge baked.
6. **F** The package contained Uncle Jorge's racing gloves.
7. **O** Uncle Jorge makes the best soft pretzels.

8. Check the words that best describe Uncle Jorge.
   _____ impatient
   ✓ competitive
   ✓ determined
   _____ lonely
   ✓ enthusiastic

Study Skills

Use the pronunciation key on the inside back cover of this book to write the words that match these pronunciations.

1. /thôt′ fəl lē/ **thoughtfully**
2. /lō′ fərz/ **loafers**
3. /trā′ ning/ **training**
4. /mâr′ ə thon′/ **marathon**
5. /pär tis′ i pāt′/ **participate**

83

Page 85

Vocabulary Skills

Write the words from the story that have the meanings below.

1. admitted
   confessed (Par. 2)

2. not looking forward to
   dreading (Par. 4)

3. a feeling of sureness in one's abilities
   confidence (Par. 8)

4. open to ideas or suggestions
   receptive (Par. 8)

5. raced at a high speed for a short distance
   sprinted (Par. 9)

6. Check the sentence in which *spoke* has the same meaning as it does in paragraph 1.
   ✓ The writer spoke about her career during the school assembly.
   _____ One spoke on my bicycle wheel is broken.

7. Check the sentence in which *cause* has the same meaning as it does in paragraph 5.
   ✓ My sister is selling magazines to raise money for a good cause.
   _____ I think that eating too much candy is the cause of my stomachache.

Write the idiom from paragraph 7 on the line next to its meaning.

8. easy; simple to do **a piece of cake**

Reading Skills

1. What problem does Tasha have in the story?
   She is nervous about asking people to sponsor her for the race.

2. How does Julio help her resolve her problem?
   He gives her a pep talk and gives her suggestions of people to ask.

3. Name one way in which Tasha and Julio are similar.
   Answers will vary.

4. Name one way in which Tasha and Julio are different.
   Answers will vary.

5. What charitable organization will Julio and Tasha help by running the race?
   The Leukemia Society

6. Why does Julio think that it would be a good idea to ask their neighbors to pledge money during the block party?
   He thinks that everyone will be in a good mood.

7. The **theme** of a story is its subject. It tells what idea the story is mostly about. Check the word below that best describes the theme of "A Reason to Run."
   _____ fitness
   ✓ friendship
   _____ loyalty

Circle the word that best completes each sentence below.

8. Tasha feels that she can _____ **succeed** with Julio's support.
   win (**succeed**) apply

9. Julio **encourages** Tasha to have more confidence in herself.
   (**encourages**) discourages requests

85

Page 87

Vocabulary Skills

Write the words from the passage that have the meanings below.

1. supplied with water
   hydrated (Bullet 3)

2. to keep in a certain condition
   maintain (Bullet 4)

Circle the homophone that correctly completes each sentence below.

3. The lengths of ribbon _____ by about four inches. (**vary**) very
4. Can you pack another _____ of fruit in my lunch? (**piece**) peace
5. The seafood chowder contained fish, lobster, clams, and _____. (muscles) (**mussels**)

Use a dictionary to help you place the words below into the correct category of origin.

spaghetti	bouquet
debris	coyote
rodeo	piano
fiancé	

6. French | 7. Italian | 8. Spanish
debris | **spaghetti** | **rodeo**
fiancé | **piano** | **coyote**
bouquet | |

Reading Skills

1. What are some types of fitness activities mentioned in the selection besides running?
   hiking, ice skating, jumping rope, and playing basketball

2. What do you think cross-training is?
   exercising by participating in different types of activities that work different muscles

3. Why shouldn't children under the age of 14 regularly run more than three miles at a time?
   Their bones are still growing, and the soft cartilage at the ends of the bones can be injured.

4. What purpose would a reader have for reading this selection?
   _____ for pleasure or entertainment
   _____ to form an opinion about running
   ✓ to learn how to become a runner

5. Write a summary sentence for paragraph 5.
   Possible answer: It is a good idea to vary your activities and to rest at least one day a week.

6. What kind of information could you record in a runner's log?
   the weather, your route, the distance you ran, and how you felt

7. Do you think the author is trying to persuade the reader of anything in this selection? Explain.
   Answers will vary.

87

Page 89

Vocabulary Skills

Write the idiom from paragraph 1 on the line next to its meaning.

1. felt refreshed **caught their second wind**

A **metaphor** is a comparison of two things without using the word *like* or *as*. For example, *Her fingers were icicles.* Find the metaphor in paragraph 1, and write it on the line.

2. **the sun was a ball of fire**

The suffix **-est** means *most*. For example, *highest* means *most high*. Write a word to match each definition below. Then, write a sentence using each word.

3. most bright **brightest**
   Answers will vary.

4. most young **youngest**
   Answers will vary.

5. most happy **happiest**
   Answers will vary.

Reading Skills

1. Write one sentence from the story that indicates how the Taylors felt about discovering the bioluminescence.
   Possible answer: This is incredible.

2. What happened when Sophie kicked the water?
   There was an explosion of a milky-green light.

3. What explanation does Mrs. Taylor have for why the water is glowing?
   She says there is a high concentration of tiny organisms in the water that create light.

4. Why do you think the Taylors didn't notice the glowing water right away?
   They were looking at the stars in the sky.

5. Do you think that Sophie and Miles will try to learn more about bioluminescence when they get home? Why or why not?
   Answers will vary.

Read the sentences below. Write **B** next to the sentence if it tells about something that happened before Miles and Sophie noticed the water was glowing. Write **A** if it describes something that happened after.

6. **A** Mrs. Taylor swirled her hands in the water.
7. **B** Mr. Taylor collected the game pieces from the coffee table.
8. **B** Miles and Sophie picked out constellations in the night sky.
9. **B** Miles and Sophie took off their flip-flops.
10. **A** Mrs. Taylor knelt beside Sophie.

Study Skills

Guide words are printed at the top of each page in a dictionary. The guide word at the left is the first word on the page. The guide word at the right is the last word on the page. Check each word that could be found on a page having the guide words shown in dark print.

1. error—estimate
   ✓ essence   **✓** escalator
   _____ eucalyptus

2. acute—administer
   _____ activist   _____ acre
   ✓ adhesive

3. rugged—rupture
   ✓ ruin   **✓** rumor   _____ rustle

89

162

Answer Key

Answer Key

Page 91

Vocabulary Skills

Write the words from the passage that have the meanings below.

1. to hide by blending into one's surroundings
   __camouflage__ Par. 3

2. an animal that hunts other animals
   __predator__ Par. 3

3. something that attracts
   __lure__ Par. 6

4. a body part that extends out from the body
   __appendage__ Par. 6

5. to move forward in spite of risk
   __venture__ Par. 6

6. odd or mysterious; causing an uneasy feeling
   __eerie__ Par. 7

7. The Latin root **mar** means *sea*. Find a word in paragraph 1 with the root **mar**.
   __marine__

8. The Latin root **fic** means *make* or *do*. Find a word in paragraph 2 with the root **fic**.
   __efficient__

9. The Latin root **tract** means *pull* or *drag*. Find a word in paragraph 4 with the root **tract**.
   __attract__

Read each pair of words listed below. If the words are synonyms, write **S** on the line. If the words are antonyms, write **A** on the line.

10. __A__ attract   repel
11. __S__ helping   assisting
12. __S__ investigate   explore
13. __A__ create   destroy

Reading Skills

1. Write a sentence that tells the main idea of the passage.
   __Answers will vary.__

2. Explain one way in which an animal can use bioluminescence to lure prey.
   __Possible answer: Patterns of__ __bioluminescence on a shark's belly__ __may resemble small fish to predators__ __like tuna or mackerel.__

3. What kind of creature produces much of the visible bioluminescence near the ocean's surface?
   __dinoflagellates__

4. How does bioluminescence help camouflage the bobtail squid?
   __It spews a cloud of bioluminescent__ __chemicals at its predator, which confuses__ __the predator and allows the squid to escape.__

5. How is bioluminescence different from the light produced by a lightbulb?
   __Most of its energy is used to__ __create light instead of heat.__

6. What can cause dinoflagellates to glow?
   __any disturbance, including the__ __motion of waves, a boat, a__ __porpoise, or a hand__

7. Check the line beside the word or words that best describe what type of selection this is.
   ____ science fiction
   _✓_ informative
   ____ fantasy

91

Page 93

Vocabulary Skills

Write the words from the story that have the meanings below.

1. something that is felt or sensed
   __sensation__ Par. 5

2. making a face to indicate pain or discomfort
   __wincing__ Par. 5

3. make something feel better or less painful
   __soothe__ Par. 14

Find the simile in paragraph 1, and write it on the line below.
   __The late afternoon sun reflected off__
4. __the water and made it sparkle like a__ __sea of diamonds.__

Fill in the blanks below with the possessive form of the word in parentheses.

5. __Miles's__ foot swelled and turned red when he was stung. (Miles)

6. The __lifeguard's__ tower was located nearby. (lifeguard)

7. The __seashells'__ colors and sizes were quite diverse. (seashells)

8. The Latin root **flect** means *bend*. Find a word in paragraph 1 with the root **flect**.
   __reflected__

9. The Latin root **claim** means *shout*. Find a word in paragraph 2 with the root **claim**.
   __exclaimed__

10. The Latin root **doc** means *teach*. Find a word in paragraph 14 with the root **doc**.
    __doctor__

Reading Skills

1. Number the events below to show the order in which they happened.
   _5_ Mr. Taylor shook the lifeguard's hand.
   _1_ The Taylors watched a seagull catch a fish.
   _3_ The lifeguard cleaned the sting with alcohol.
   _2_ Sophie pointed to the sand-covered jellyfish.
   _4_ The lifeguard smeared meat tenderizer on Miles's foot.

2. If you don't have alcohol and meat tenderizer at home, what else can you use to treat a jellyfish sting?
   __vinegar, baking soda, and water__

3. Under what circumstances does the lifeguard recommend that Miles see a doctor?
   __if the area becomes any more__ __irritated in the next couple of hours__

4. Why does meat tenderizer soothe a jellyfish sting?
   __It is an enzyme which breaks down__ __the protein of jellyfish poison.__

5. What were the Taylors looking at when Miles was stung?
   __They were watching a seagull__ __catch a fish.__

6. How did the Taylors determine what Miles had stepped on?
   __Sophie saw a sand-covered__ __jellyfish on the beach.__

7. The climax of a story is the point of highest excitement. What is the climax in "A Stinging Surprise"?
   __when Miles gets stung by a__ __jellyfish__

93

Page 95

Vocabulary Skills

Check the meaning of each underlined word.

1. Many jellyfish are <u>colorless</u> because their bodies are made mostly of water.
   ____ in a colorful way
   _✓_ without color
   ____ capable of color

2. <u>Typically</u>, jellyfish are not dangerous to people.
   _✓_ in a typical way
   ____ not typical
   ____ typical again

Underline the compound word in each sentence. Then, write the two words that make up each compound.

3. Most of these creatures are found in <u>saltwater</u>.
   __salt__   __water__

4. Invertebrates do not have <u>backbones</u>.
   __back__   __bones__

5. There are about 2,000 species of <u>jellyfish</u>.
   __jelly__   __fish__

Reading Skills

1. Why does the author say that the description of a jellyfish might sound like a riddle?
   __The description is worded like a__ __riddle. The question sounds as though__ __it does not have a real answer.__

2. How much of a jellyfish's body is composed of water?
   __95%–99%__

3. What are nematocysts?
   __stinging cells__

4. Check the phrase that best describes the author's purpose.
   ____ to entertain
   _✓_ to inform
   ____ to persuade

Write **T** before the sentences that are true. Write **F** before the sentences that are false.

5. _F_ All species of jellyfish are totally harmless to humans.

6. _T_ Jellyfish do not have most of the organs that are common in other animals.

7. _F_ Jellyfish can move only where the wind and the tides take them.

8. _F_ Only about one-third of a jellyfish's body is water.

9. _T_ A few freshwater species of jellyfish do exist.

Study Skills

Write the name of the reference source you could use to answer each question below.

| encyclopedia | phone directory |
| dictionary | thesaurus |

1. How do you pronounce the word *nematocysts*?
   __dictionary__

2. Where do coral and sea anemones live?
   __encyclopedia__

3. What is another word for *potential*?
   __thesaurus__

4. How can you reach the information line at the National Oceanic Institute?
   __phone directory__

95

Page 97

Vocabulary Skills

Write the words from the story that have the meanings below.

1. pressed tightly against
   __plastered__ Par. 2

2. looked up to; respected
   __admired__ Par. 4

3. basic principles or skills
   __fundamentals__ Par. 6

4. restrictions; the act or quality of being limited
   __limitations__ Par. 6

5. sturdy; firm
   __stable__ Par. 10

Read each word below. Then, write the letter of its synonym on the line beside the word.

6. _c_ worried   a. middle
7. _d_ anticipated   b. novice
8. _b_ beginner   c. concerned
9. _a_ center   d. expected

10. Find the simile in paragraph 2, and write it on the line below.
    __her dark hair, which was as sleek__ __and glossy as an otter's fur__

11. What two things were compared to one another in question 10?
    __dark hair__   __otter's fur__

12. Choose one of the answers to number 11, and use it to create your own simile on the lines below.
    __Answers will vary.__

Reading Skills

1. Why does Kerry think that Sophie and Miles should start out using longboards?
   __They are easier to paddle, and__ __they catch waves more easily.__

2. What do you think Kerry means when she refers to the "sweet spot" on a surfboard?
   __the center of the board__

3. What is one way in which Miles and Sophie are different?
   __Sophie is more eager to try new__ __things than Miles is.__

4. What does Miles think surfing will feel like?
   __He thinks it will feel like flying through__ __the water or riding a bike down a steep__ __hill without using the brakes.__

5. What are the surfing terms for the front and back ends of a surfboard?
   __nose and tail__

6. Check the line beside the word or words that best describe what type of selection this is.
   ____ poetry
   _✓_ fiction
   ____ science fiction

Mark each sentence below **F** if it is in first-person point of view and **T** if it is in third-person point of view.

7. _F_ I wish I was as adventurous as my sister.

8. _T_ Sophie waved to her parents.

9. _F_ I've been surfing since I was only five years old.

10. _T_ Dylan shook himself off when he got out of the water.

97

Answer Key

Page 99

Vocabulary Skills

Write the words from the passage that have the meanings below.

1. pushed or moved forward
   propelled Par. 1
2. a search
   quest Par. 2
3. attracts; interests
   appeals Par. 3
4. a basic part of one's character or nature
   inherent Par. 4
5. a hormone that causes a rush of energy and feeling of excitement
   adrenaline Par. 4
6. relating to a subject about which there are opposing views
   controversial Par. 4

Find the compound words from the selection that contain the words below.

7. style **lifestyle** Par. 1
8. boards **surfboards** Par. 2
9. down **downhill** Par. 4

Circle the homophone that correctly completes each sentence below.

10. Many surfers prefer one type of _____ over another.
    ((board) bored)
11. Let's go to the _____ and watch the storm roll in. ((beach) beech)
12. I will _____ the turkey again in about an hour. ((baste) based)

Reading Skills

Write F before the sentences that are facts. Write O before the sentences that are opinions.

1. **O** Laird Hamilton is the most talented surfer alive today.
2. **F** Surfing became very popular in the 1950s and 1960s.
3. **F** The surfing spot Teahupoo is located near Tahiti.
4. **O** No one can appreciate the power of the ocean the way a surfer does.
5. **F** Laird Hamilton has surfed at speeds of up to 50 miles per hour.
6. Why did the new fiberglass and foam surfboards cause a rise in surfing's popularity?
   They were less expensive and easier to use.
7. What draws people to high-speed activities?
   the adrenaline rush they feel
8. What is tow-in surfing?
   the use of jet skis to tow surfers to areas that are farther from shore
9. What do you think the surfing term wipeout means?
   a wreck
10. Write a summary sentence for paragraph 4.
    Possible answer: Surfers enjoy surfing because they love the ocean and the adrenaline rush they get from riding big waves.

99

Page 101

Vocabulary Skills

1. The Latin root **nat** means *born*. Find a word in paragraph 2 with the root **nat**.
   native
2. The Latin root **duc** means *lead*. Find a word in paragraph 6 with the root **duc**.
   inducted

In each row, circle the word that best completes each sentence below.

3. People who listened to Kahanamoku speak found his enthusiasm for the ocean and for surfing to be _____.
   common ((contagious) annoying
4. Celebrity did not seem to _____ Kahanamoku's personality.
   display create (alter)

Reading Skills

1. What are two jobs that Kahanamoku held that were unrelated to swimming or surfing?
   actor and mayor
2. Do you think that surfing would have spread to other areas of the world without Duke Kahanamoku's encouragement and enthusiasm? Why or why not?
   Answers will vary.
3. Find a sentence in the selection showing that Kahanamoku was a talented and successful swimmer, and write it on the lines below.
   Answers will vary.

4. Check the sentence that best states the main idea of the selection.
   _____ Duke Kahanamoku's full name was Duke Paoa Kahinu Makoe Hulikohoa Kahanamoku.
   _____ Duke Kahanamoku was the first person to be inducted into both the Swimming Hall of Fame and the Surfing Hall of Fame.
   ✓ Duke Kahanamoku was known as the "father of modern surfing" because he helped bring the sport to areas of the world outside of Hawaii.

Study Skills

Use the timeline of Duke Kahanamoku's life to answer the questions that follow.

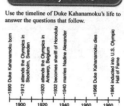

1. In what year were the Olympics held in Antwerp, Belgium?
   1920
2. Was Kahanamoku inducted into the U.S. Olympic Hall of Fame before or after his death?
   after
3. In what year did Kahanamoku marry?
   1940

101

Page 103

Vocabulary Skills

Write the words from the story that have the meanings below.

1. very strong; thorough
   intensive Par. 2
2. an agreement or pledge to a certain event or activity
   commitment Par. 4
3. present or put forward
   pose Par. 4
4. freedom from worry; a feeling of comfort
   ease Par. 3
5. put together
   compile Par. 4

Use a dictionary to help you place the words below into the correct category of origin.

mosquito	confetti
ballet	gourmet
cello	bizarre
avocado	tortilla

6. French 7. Spanish 8. Italian
   ballet   mosquito   cello
   gourmet   avocado   confetti
   bizarre   tortilla

Reading Skills

1. What prize will the team that wins the championship receive?
   Each member will receive a $1,000 college savings bond. The winning school will receive two computers.

2. Do you think that Mr. Ishikawa is a good coach? Why or why not?
   Answers will vary.
3. In paragraph 5, the author describes Ms. Cane as having "an infectious laugh." What do you think this means?
   Possible answer: Her laugh makes other people want to laugh too.
4. What are three words you could use to describe Ms. Cane's personality?
   Possible answers: friendly, helpful, knowledgeable
5. What purpose would a reader have for reading this selection?
   ✓ for pleasure or entertainment
   _____ for information
   _____ to learn how to be on an academic game show

Study Skills

Read the television studio's rules and regulations, and answer the questions that follow.
• Student must currently be enrolled in classes at the school he/she is representing.
• Student must be between the ages of 11 and 14 at the time of taping.
• No cameras or videotaping devices are allowed in the studio at time of taping.
• Students' names may be used for promotional purposes before the airing of the show.

1. How old must a student be at the time of taping in order to be a contestant?
   11-14
2. Can students or their families record the show as it is being taped?
   no

103

Page 105

Vocabulary Skills

Write the words from the passage that have the meanings below.

1. sent from one place to another
   transmitted Par. 1
2. identify with certainty
   pinpoint Par. 2
3. an original model
   prototype Par. 2
4. important; the thing on which something else depends
   pivotal Par. 3
5. very important; essential
   crucial Par. 3
6. of or relating to the country or country living
   rural Par. 1

Read each word below. Then, write the letter of its antonym on the line beside the word.

7. **c** separate   a. cheap
8. **a** expensive   b. national
9. **d** weak   c. together
10. **b** local   d. strong

Divide the words below into syllables using a slash (/).

11. per/fect
12. worth/while
13. sig/nal
14. ca/ble
15. e/qual

Reading Skills

1. What was the first TV show to be regularly shown in color?
   Bonanza
2. Who are the two people that are often given credit for inventing television?
   Philo Taylor Farnsworth and Vladimir Zworykin
3. What Latin and Greek roots are found in the word *television*? What do they mean?
   tele and **vis**; *far* and *sight*
4. About how much would a 1930s television have cost in today's dollars?
   $7,000
5. Check the phrase that best describes the author's purpose.
   _____ to entertain
   ✓ to inform
   _____ to persuade

Circle the word that best completes each sentence below.

6. Televisions became _____ priced after World War II.
   significantly ((reasonably) highly
7. John Watson's _____ thinking led to the invention of cable TV.
   ((creative) unimaginative selfish
8. Farnsworth and Zworykin both _____ to the invention of the modern television.
   developed requested ((contributed)

105

Answer Key

Page 107

Vocabulary Skills

Write the words from the passage that have the meanings below.

1. the way in which one is viewed or perceived
   perception

2. changed for the better; reformed
   redeemed

3. estimated as being less in size or importance
   underestimated

4. to mourn; to feel very sad about a loss
   grieve

5. felt comforted and less anxious
   reassured

6. wildly excited
   frenzied

Check the meaning of the underlined word in each sentence.

7. Today, television is a major source of news.
   ✓ important; significant
   ___ a military rank

8. The family was glued to the television as the story unfolded.
   ✓ watched closely
   ___ attached with a sticky substance

Circle the homophone that correctly completes each sentence below.

9. Will you be ___ to stay up late to see the end of the movie? (allowed, aloud)

10. Television has played an important ___ in American history. (roll, role)

Reading Skills

Write T before the sentences that are true. Write F before the sentences that are false.

1. F Nixon stated that he did not receive any questionable gifts.

2. F About 75 percent of Americans who owned televisions watched Armstrong and Aldrin walk on the moon.

3. T The Beatles appeared on the Ed Sullivan Show in 1964.

4. T Lyndon Johnson became president after Kennedy's assassination.

5. Do you think that television as a source of news will be as important in the future as it has been in the past? Explain.
   Answers will vary.

6. How did the "Checker's Speech" change the way people thought of Richard Nixon?
   People liked Nixon better. They saw a side of him they had not seen before.

7. Do you think it is fair for people to base their opinions on what they see as well as what they hear? Explain.
   Answers will vary.

8. What kind of effect did television have on the popularity of the Beatles?
   It caused a sharp rise in their popularity.

9. How did Kennedy and Nixon appear to be different from one another during their televised debate?
   Nixon was scowling and uncomfortable, and Kennedy was smiling and looked confident.

107

Page 109

Vocabulary Skills

Write the words from the story that have the meanings below.

1. taking place without warning
   abrupt

2. made sure of
   confirmed

3. quickly and skillfully
   deftly

4. with affection
   fondly

Add a prefix or suffix from the below to each word to form a new word.

| -ly | -est | re- |
| mis- | -able | |

5. patient patiently
6. comfort comfortable
7. arrange rearrange
8. funny funniest
9. gradual gradually
10. step misstep

Reading Skills

1. What do you think Grandma means when she says she learned to survive in the woods, "at least in theory"?
   Possible answer: that she knows how to survive in the woods, but she has never actually put her knowledge to use

2. Who do you think is older, Becca or Meghan? Why?
   Meghan. Possible answer: because she has been canoeing before and she helps Grandma paddle.

3. How did Grandma learn to canoe?
   She learned when she was a summer camp counselor.

4. What advice does Grandma give Becca when she is climbing into the canoe?
   to not stand up all the way and not make any abrupt movements

5. What is one difference between a natural lake and a reservoir?
   Possible answer: Reservoirs are created by humans.

6. Why does Grandma think that Grandpa wanted canoeing lessons?
   so he could get to know her better

7. What is the setting for this story?
   a reservoir

Study Skills

Check each word that could be found on a page having the guide words shown in dark print.

1. grudge—guitar
   ✓ guardian   ___ groundhog
   ✓ grumpy

2. decipher—deer
   ___ defend   ✓ dedicate
   ___ decorate

3. sherbet—shipyard
   ___ shelter   ___ shear
   ✓ shingle

109

Page 111

Vocabulary Skills

Write the words from the passage that have the meanings below.

1. allowed; made possible
   enabled

2. to supply with water using artificial means
   irrigate

3. not enough to meet a demand
   scarce

4. to direct the course or path of something
   navigate

5. to bring under control and put to use
   harness

6. took the place of
   displaced

Write the abbreviation for each state in the space beside it.

7. Nevada NV
8. Arizona AZ
9. Pennsylvania PA
10. Colorado CO

Check the meaning of the underlined word.

11. The earliest dams may date back 5,000 years.
   ___ in an early way
   ✓ most early
   ___ not early

12. Parts of the Ma'rib Dam have been rebuilt.
   ✓ built again
   ___ not yet built
   ___ capable of being built

Reading Skills

1. What is one benefit to beavers of having the entrance to a lodge located underwater?
   The pond serves as a natural defense against predators.

2. How old is the Ma'rib Dam?
   about 2,700 years old

3. Why do dams cause problems for migrating fish?
   The fish are kept from moving up and down stream for feeding and reproduction.

4. Why do canals often contain locks?
   so that boats can travel on rivers that are blocked by dams

5. What are two reasons the Three Gorges Dam is being constructed in China?
   to control flooding and to fill some of China's electrical needs

6. What purpose would a reader have for reading this selection?
   ___ for pleasure or entertainment
   ✓ for information
   ___ to learn how to build a dam

7. On the lines below, write a summary for paragraph 2.
   Possible Answer: Humans have been building dams since the beginning of civilization.

111

Page 113

Vocabulary Skills

Check the meaning of the underlined word in each sentence.

1. Salmon were a staple of life for the Colville tribe of the Pacific Northwest.
   ___ a small piece of metal used for attaching sheets of paper to one another
   ✓ something basic and necessary

2. The dam can produce an enormous amount of hydroelectric power.
   ✓ create
   ___ fresh fruits and vegetables

Read each word below. Then, write the letter of its synonym on the line beside the word.

3. c essential   a. disturb
4. a disrupt   b. regarded
5. d variety   c. necessary
6. b considered   d. assortment

Reading Skills

1. On the lines below, write a sentence that describes the main idea of the selection.
   Answers will vary.

2. Why does the author say that the money the government paid could not buy back what the Colville tribe had lost?
   The Colville tribe could never regain the land that they lost, and money could not make up for their loss.

3. How long did it take to complete construction on the Grand Coulee Dam?
   nine years

4. Is Franklin Delano Roosevelt Lake a natural or human-made lake? How do you know?
   It was made by humans. It is a reservoir that was produced by the creation of the dam.

5. In paragraph 7, the author compares the height of the dam to the height of two well-known landmarks. What are they?
   the Statue of Liberty and Niagara Falls

6. Check the phrase that best describes the author's purpose.
   ✓ to share information about the Grand Coulee Dam
   ___ to entertain
   ___ to persuade the reader to visit the Grand Coulee Dam

Study Skills

Use the schedule below to answer the questions that follow.

Grand Coulee Dam Visitors' Center Schedule
September 7–November 30
9 A.M.–5 P.M. (every day)
December and January
CLOSED
February 1–Memorial Day Weekend
9 A.M.–5 P.M. (every day)
Memorial Day Weekend–July 31
8:30 A.M.–11 P.M. (every day)

1. What will the visitors' center hours be on March 8?
   They will be open from 9 A.M.–5 P.M.

2. During which two months will the center be closed?
   December and January

3. When will the center extend its daily hours?
   from Memorial Day Weekend to July 31

113

Answer Key

Page 115

Vocabulary Skills

1. The Latin root **ann** means *year*. Find a word in paragraph 2 with the root **ann**.
   annual

2. The Greek root **graph** means *write*. Find a word in paragraph 9 with the root **graph**.
   autographed

3. The Latin root **loc** means *place*. Find a word in paragraph 11 with the root **loc**.
   local

4. Check the sentence in which *fair* has the same meaning as it does in paragraph 2.
   ✓ All the booths for the fair have been set up.
   ___ Few people thought that the referee's call was fair.

5. Check the sentence in which *dull* has the same meaning as it does in paragraph 5.
   ___ Remind me to have this dull knife sharpened.
   ✓ I expected the movie to be dull, so I was surprised to find it so interesting.

Reading Skills

Write **F** before the sentences that are facts. Write **O** before the sentences that are opinions.

1. O Tanika worries too much.
2. O This year's book fair will be better than previous fairs.
3. F Rachael Weinstock's mom is the author of a picture book.
4. F Caleb's class has a turtle and some fish.

Mark each sentence below **F** if it is in first-person point of view and **T** if it is in third-person point of view.

5. F I think this book fair will be a success.
6. T Caleb looked through the list books the librarians ordered.
7. F My sister might have some sports equipment we could use.
8. What are two ideas that Tanika and Caleb have to make this year's book fair more exciting?
   They want to set up areas with different themes and have authors come to sign their books.
9. Why does Caleb think that Mr. Davies might be able to help?
   He used to be an editor for a children's book publisher.

Read the descriptions below. Write **C** next to the phrase if it describes Caleb. Write **T** if it describes Tanika.

10. C feels calm and confident about the success of the book fair
11. T suggests setting up areas with different themes
12. T offers to bring in ice skates and mittens for the winter display

115

Page 117

Vocabulary Skills

Write the words from the story that have the meanings below.

1. amazement
   awe

2. distributing; dividing up
   allocating

3. money marked for a specific purpose
   funds

4. items that are needed or necessary
   necessities

5. gratitude
   appreciation

6. the skill and knowledge of someone experienced
   expertise

Circle the homophone that correctly completes each sentence below.

7. Do you know what the taxicab ___ will be? (fair (fare))
8. The winning ___ will receive a trophy. (teem (team))
9. The building on the corner will be ___ to make room for the new mall. (raised (razed))
10. Which word in paragraph 1 has a prefix and a suffix? uncertainly
11. Write the prefix, suffix, and word's meaning on the lines below.
    un, ly; in a not certain way

Reading Skills

1. Why do Caleb and Tanika think that the students should be able to vote on the books that will be added to the library?
   The fair was a team effort. Students from every class contributed.

2. Do you think that Caleb and Tanika work well together as a team? Why or why not?
   Answers will vary.

3. Why did Mr. Rutledge and Mrs. Angley decide to ask for Caleb and Tanika's help?
   The book fair was the most successful fair the school had held. Mrs. Angley and Mr. Rutledge thought that Tanika and Caleb deserved a lot of the credit.

4. What is the setting for this story?
   the school library

5. Do you think that Caleb and Tanika will choose to work together on future projects? Explain.
   Answers will vary.

6. Check the line beside the word or words that best describe what type of selection this is.
   ___ a tall tale
   ✓ realistic fiction
   ___ historical fiction

117

Page 119

Vocabulary Skills

Write the words from the passage that have the meanings below.

1. the field of study dealing with the development and use of money, goods, and services
   economics

2. something that moves one to action
   inspiration

3. to give one's time or attention completely
   devote

4. made up; imaginary
   fictional

Rewrite the phrases below in the possessive form.

5. the novels of Louis Sachar
   Louis Sachar's novels

6. the aide of the teacher
   the teacher's aide

7. the habits of the writers
   the writers' habits

8. the characteristics of the person
   the person's characteristics

Reading Skills

1. Check the words that best describe Louis Sachar.
   ✓ creative
   ✓ humorous
   ___ unpredictable
   ✓ intelligent
   ___ nosy

2. What purpose would a reader have for reading this selection?
   ✓ for information about the life and work of Louis Sachar
   ___ to learn how to solve a problem
   ___ to form an opinion about the work of Louis Sachar

3. Check the line beside the word or words that best describe what type of selection this is.
   ___ autobiography
   ___ historical nonfiction
   ✓ biography

4. Name two series of books that Louis Sachar has written.
   Marvin Redpost and Wayside School

5. Why didn't Sachar become a full-time writer as soon as his first book was published?
   He didn't feel confident he could make a living as a writer.

6. What happens after Sachar has completed the first draft of a book?
   He rewrites it five or six times before he sends it to his publisher.

7. Name two sources of ideas for Sachar's stories and characters.
   Possible answers: his memories of childhood; his experiences teaching; his daughter's life

119

Page 121

Vocabulary Skills

Write the words from the passage that have the meanings below.

1. very eager; having a large appetite
   voracious

2. the words to a song
   lyrics

3. to put forward or turn in for consideration
   submit

4. to follow a set of rules
   conform

5. refusals of acceptance
   rejections

6. the quality of continuing to do something in spite of hardship or difficulties
   perseverance

Reading Skills

1. Check the phrase that best describes the author's purpose.
   ✓ to instruct
   ___ to entertain
   ___ to inform

2. Name three things you might record in a writer's notebook.
   Possible answers: dreams, song lyrics, everyday thoughts and observations

3. What does the author mean by "Do your homework"?
   Carefully research publishers and magazines, and follow their guidelines.

4. Why is perseverance an important quality for a writer to have?
   You may receive many rejections before you are published.

5. Why do you think that most writers like to read?
   Answers will vary.

6. On the lines below, write a summary of Step 3.
   It is important that you write every day so that you get into the habit and so that you can clear your mind, of things that are less important or uninteresting.

Study Skills

Use the submission guidelines below to answer the questions that follow.

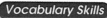

> **Willow Lake Press**
> **Guidelines for Submission**
>
> Currently accepting: fiction picture books; nonfiction early readers (especially about sports, animals, and science); young adult fiction
>
> Format: Submission must be typed and printed on plain white 8 1/2 x 11 paper. Your name should appear on the top right corner of each page.
>
> Send your manuscript and a self-addressed stamped envelope (SASE) to—Submissions Editor, Willow Lake Press, 445 Rockbridge Way, Daleville, WI 28556.

1. What is a SASE?
   a self-addressed stamped envelope

2. What nonfiction early reader topics is Willow Lake Press interested in?
   sports, animals, and science

3. Where should your name appear on your manuscript?
   on the top right corner of each page

121

Answer Key

Page 123

Vocabulary Skills

Write the words from the story that have the meanings below.

1. overturned
   capsized Par. 2

2. a boat or ship
   vessel Par. 3

3. spread or scattered around
   strewn Par. 4

4. something that is used as a temporary substitute
   makeshift Par. 4

5. went back to something that was already begun
   resumed Par. 7

Circle the homophone that correctly completes each sentence below.

6. My back was _____ for a week after I helped Aliya move. (soar/(sore))

7. We planted a row of _____ trees beside the driveway. (beach/(beech))

8. Do _____ ride your bicycle without wearing a helmet! ((not)/knot)

Underline the word with a prefix or a suffix in each sentence. Then, write the meaning of the word on the line.

9. The sand felt <u>unpleasant</u> in my mouth.
   not pleasant

10. The day was warm, and the sky was <u>cloudless</u>.
    without clouds

Find the metaphor in paragraph 3, and write it on the line.

11. My stomach was an animal.

Reading Skills

1. Why didn't the narrator escape from the sinking ship on one of the lifeboats?
   He believed that a captain
   should go down with his ship.

2. Name three items the narrator found in the canvas bag.
   Possible answers: a knife, a
   blanket, a bottle of water, four
   cans of food, and a box of matches

3. **Personification** is a literary device in which human characteristics are given to inanimate objects. In the sentence *Sam's bed beckoned to him invitingly*, Sam's bed is personified. Find an example of personification in the story, and write it on the line below.
   the sun was glaring angrily at me

4. What do you think the book Tyler was reading when he fell asleep was about?
   a shipwreck; a castaway

5. From what point of view are the first seven paragraphs of the story told?
   first-person point of view

6. From what point of view is the last paragraph told?
   third-person point of view

7. What purpose would a reader have for reading this selection?
   _____ for information
   ✓ for entertainment
   _____ to answer a specific question

123

Page 125

Vocabulary Skills

Check the correct meaning of the underlined word.

1. *Robinson Crusoe* appeals to people <u>regardless</u> of age or nationality.
   _____ full of regard
   ✓ without regard for
   _____ capable of regarding

2. Selkirk could <u>easily</u> control the rat population by feeding the island's cats.
   _____ most easy
   _____ not easy
   ✓ in an easy way

In each row, circle the word that does not belong.

3. construct (break) build assemble

4. imaginative creative inventive (precise)

5. difficult (lonely) challenging hard

Reading Skills

1. What nationality was Selkirk?
   Scottish

2. Why do you think Selkirk called out to the *Cinque Ports* as it sailed away from the island?
   He was having second thoughts
   about his decision.

3. How do we know so many details about Selkirk's experiences on the island?
   Woodes Rogers, the captain of
   the Duke, wrote a book that
   included Selkirk's experiences.

5. What is one difference between Robinson Crusoe and Alexander Selkirk?
   Possible answer: Selkirk asked
   to be left on his island, and
   Crusoe was shipwrecked.

6. Is *Robinson Crusoe* fantasy, or does it take place in reality?
   fantasy

7. Is *A Cruising Voyage Round the World* fantasy, or does it take place in reality?
   It takes place in reality.

Circle the word that best completes each sentence below.

8. Selkirk's use of _____ thinking allowed him to survive on the island.
   optimistic (creative) frequent

9. It was difficult for Selkirk to _____ to life in society.
   (readjust) communicate accustom

10. Woodes Rogers's book _____ Selkirk's experiences.
    neglected ridiculed (detailed)

Study Skills

Use the pronunciation key on the inside back cover of this book to write the words that match these pronunciations.

1. /sŭr vīv'/ survive
2. /ad ven' chür/ adventure
3. /pŏp' yə lā' shən/ population
4. /ri mān'/ remain
5. /lōn' lē nes/ loneliness

125

Page 127

Vocabulary Skills

Write the words from the story that have the meanings below.

1. the edge or outer limits of a city or town
   outskirts Par. 1

2. breathing in
   inhaling Par. 6

3. for the most part
   primarily Par. 7

4. to grow successfully; flourish
   thrive Par. 9

Find the compound words from the selection that contain the words below.

5. board _____ cardboard
6. land _____ landscape
7. green _____ greenhouse
8. brush _____ paintbrush

Reading Skills

1. Number the events below to show the order in which they happened.

   5 Joseph showed Chiara and her mom several of his favorite desert plants.

   4 Chiara ate her breakfast in the car.

   1 The Giardinis moved to Arizona from Massachusetts.

   3 Mrs. Giardini said she missed the greenery in her old backyard.

   2 Chiara found her mother sitting on the deck sipping coffee.

2. What problem do Chiara and her mom have at the beginning of the story?
   They miss the garden and the greenery
   at their old home in Massachusetts.

3. Do you think that planting a garden will help the Giardinis feel more at home in Arizona? Why or why not?
   Answers will vary.

4. What is one way in which Massachusetts and Arizona are different?
   Possible answers: the temperature; the
   landscape; the region of the country

5. What does Mrs. Giardini mean when she says, "Arizona and Massachusetts could be different planets"?
   The two states seem very
   different to her.

6. Name the two different settings in this story.
   the Giardini's house; the nursery

Study Skills

Write the name of the reference source you could use to answer each question below.

| atlas | dictionary |
| newspaper | encyclopedia |

1. What will the weather be like in Phoenix on Saturday?
   newspaper

2. Which five states surround Massachusetts?
   atlas

3. What are the characteristics of a desert?
   encyclopedia

4. What is the origin of the word *cactus*?
   dictionary

127

Page 129

Vocabulary Skills

Write the words from the passage that have the meanings below.

1. the process by which liquid changes into vapor or gas
   evaporation Par. 1

2. water that falls to Earth in the form of rain or snow
   precipitation Par. 1

3. hills of sand that are pushed into shape by the wind
   dunes Par. 4

4. dry; having little rainfall
   arid Par. 6

5. an area of flat land that is higher than the surrounding land
   plateau Par. 7

Reading Skills

1. How much of Earth's land surface do deserts cover?
   about one-third

2. Who was Marco Polo?
   a Venetian traveler and explorer

3. Why do some people compare sand dunes to ocean waves?
   They resemble giant, frozen waves.

4. What is an oasis? What is the plural form of oasis?
   an area of moisture and plant
   life in the desert; oases

Write **T** before the sentences that are true. Write **F** before the sentences that are false.

5. F Most of Earth's deserts are made of sand.

6. T The Sahara receives almost no rainfall.

7. T The Mojave Desert is the largest American desert.

8. F The Gobi is located in northern Africa.

Study Skills

A **bibliography** is a list of articles or books that an author referred to when writing his or her own work. Use the bibliographic entries below to answer the questions that follow.

Chin, Cynthia. *Deserts of the World*. New York: McNaughton Publishers, Inc., 2001.
Gordon, Oliver. "The Effects of Global Warming on Desert Temperatures." *EnviroWorld*. (January, 2005): 45–52.

1. Who is the author of the magazine article?
   Oliver Gordon

2. In what year was *Deserts of the World* published?
   2001

3. On which pages of the January 2005 issue of *EnviroWorld* would you find the article referenced above?
   45–52

129

Spectrum Reading Grade 6

Answer Key

167

Answer Key

Page 131

Vocabulary Skills

Write the words from the passage that have the meanings below.

1. put in position for use
   installed

2. from time to time
   periodically

3. supposed
   assumed

4. faraway; isolated
   remote

5. far removed
   secluded

Use a dictionary to help you place the words below into the correct categories.

finale	fiasco
bouquet	suite
tornado	pasta
chef	fiesta

6. Spanish 7. Italian 8. French

tornado **finale** **bouquet**

fiesta **fiasco** **chef**

pasta **suite**

Write **S** if the possessive word is singular. Write **P** if it is plural.

9. **S** the phone booth's location
10. **P** the callers' nationalities
11. **S** Godfrey Daniels's interest
12. **P** the tourists' visits

Reading Skills

1. How did Godfrey Daniels publicize the Mojave Desert phone booth?
   He wrote about it on the Internet and posted its number there.

2. Do you think the National Parks Service and Pacific-Bell made the right decision to remove the phone booth? Explain.
   Answers will vary.

3. What happens if someone calls the phone booth today?
   The phone will ring only on the caller's end.

4. Why was the phone booth originally installed?
   for use by miners and their families

5. On the lines below, write the main idea of paragraph 6.
   People liked making a connection with strangers because it made the world seem smaller.

Write **T** before the sentences that are true. Write **F** before the sentences that are false.

6. **T** The phone booth was originally intended to be used by miners.
7. **F** The phone booth is still in working order today.
8. **T** Godfrey Daniels posted the number of the booth on the Internet.
9. **F** The phone booth was located in Arizona.
10. **T** People seemed to like the idea of connecting with others in faraway places.

131

Page 133

Vocabulary Skills

Write the words from the story that have the meanings below.

1. getting used to; becoming accustomed to
   adjusting

2. to focus one's thoughts or think deeply about
   concentrate

3. a dent
   indentation

4. placed one's hands in the shape of a cup
   cupped

Circle the homophone that correctly completes each sentence below.

5. When Emi pulled the bird's _____ it flapped its wings. (**tail**, tale)

6. Please _____ down the following information. (right, **write**)

7. The _____ family will be attending the reunion. (**whole**, hole)

Underline the compound word in each sentence. Then, write the two words that make up each compound.

8. Aunt Suki discovered some origami papers in her suitcase.
   suit **case**

9. She was looking for a crossword puzzle to work on because she couldn't sleep.
   cross **word**

10. Oatmeal with cinnamon and bananas is my favorite way to start the day.
    oat **meal**

Reading Skills

Mark each sentence below **F** if it is in first-person point of view and **T** if it is in third-person point of view.

1. **F** Can we rent a movie tonight?
2. **F** I moved to the United States when I was 19 years old.
3. **T** Ken examined the origami frog.
4. **F** I find origami to be a relaxing hobby.
5. **T** Emi and Ken liked hearing stories about their mother as a little girl.

6. How is Aunt Suki related to Emi and Ken's mother?
   She is their mother's sister.

7. Where did Aunt Suki grow up?
   in Japan

8. What does Emi mean when she says they'll pass the tradition "up instead of down"?
   She is making a joke because traditions are usually passed "down" to the next generation.

9. What does Aunt Suki do when she can't sleep?
   She does origami.

10. What feature do Aunt Suki and her sister share?
    They each have a dimple.

11. What purpose would a reader have for reading this selection?
    _____ to learn
    _____ to form an opinion
    ✓ for entertainment

133

Page 135

Vocabulary Skills

Write the words from the passage that have the meanings below.

1. made of many parts
   complex

2. like a custom that has been passed down
   traditionally

3. things that are forbidden and should be avoided
   taboos

4. detailed; fancy
   elaborate

5. copy
   duplicate

6. The Greek root **saur** means *lizard*. Find a word in paragraph 1 with the root **saur**.
   stegosaurus

7. The Latin root **var** means *different*. Find a word in paragraph 1 with the root **var**.
   variety

8. The Latin root **form** means *shape*. Find a word in paragraph 3 with the root **form**.
   transformed

9. The Latin root **lab** means *work*. Find a word in paragraph 5 with the root **lab**.
   elaborate

Find an antonym in the story for each of the words below.

10. novice **expert**
11. complicated **simple**
12. boring **fascinating**

Reading Skills

1. What does the word *origami* mean in Japanese?
   paper folding

2. Name two materials other than origami paper that have been used in modern origami.
   Possible answers: tissue paper, silk, foil, bubblegum wrappers

3. Why do you think that serious origamists do not use scissors or glue?
   because it would alter the types of things they could make

4. How many diagrams would you have to follow to create an origami model of the *Starship Enterprise*?
   72

Write **T** before the sentences that are true. Write **F** before the sentences that are false.

5. **F** Origami paper tends to be thicker than regular paper.
6. **T** People have experimented with using materials other than paper to create origami figures.
7. **F** Akira Yoshizawa was the first person to practice origami in Japan.
8. **T** The kite, fish, bird, and frog are four origami bases.
9. **T** Some historians believe origami has its origins in China.
10. Check the sentence below that is the best summary for paragraph 6.
    _____ Yoshizawa published origami books during the 1950s.
    ✓ Origami diagrams are important because they allow people to share their designs for particular figures.
    _____ Diagrams show the folds needed to make origami figures.

135

Page 137

Vocabulary Skills

Write the words from the story that have the meanings below.

1. an amount or serving of something taken at one time
   dose

2. dedicated to a particular purpose
   committed

3. a saying or expression that is overused
   cliché

Write the idiom from paragraph 1 on the line next to its meaning.

4. declining; getting worse **going downhill**

In each row, circle the word that does not belong.

5. hear audio **explain** listen
6. memory **believe** remember reminisce
7. marvelous **interesting** great fantastic

Divide the words below into syllables using a slash (/).

8. a f/t e r
9. b r e a k/f a s t
10. a/c r o s s
11. s i n/g l e
12. e y e/s i g h t

Reading Skills

1. Why does Pablo make a face after he tries his grandpa's omelet?
   He thinks it is too spicy.

2. How are the Braille contractions that Grandpa talks about different from the contractions you are familiar with?
   They are single letters that represent a word instead of one word that is a combination of two words.

3. How can Grandpa type without seeing the keyboard?
   He has been typing for a long time and has the position of the keys memorized.

4. Name two reasons that Grandpa prefers audio books to Braille books.
   Braille books can be large and awkward. He likes the different voices that the readers use on audio books.

5. Number the events below to show the order in which they happened.
   3 Grandpa explained Grade 2 Braille to Pablo.
   4 Pablo hugged his grandpa.
   1 Pablo sat down at the breakfast table.
   2 Grandpa turned on the computer.

Study Skills

Use the letters of the Braille alphabet to decode the words below.

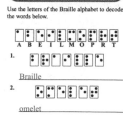

A B E I L M O P R T

1. Braille

2. omelet

137

Answer Key

Page 139

Vocabulary Skills

Write the words from the passage that have the meanings below.

1. to notice or discover something
   detect (Par. 2)
2. delicate; easy to break or harm
   fragile (Par. 2)
3. faulty; not working properly
   defective (Par. 2)
4. an impressive group
   array (Par. 4)
5. not obvious
   subtle (Par. 5)

Find the compound words from the selection that contain the words below.

6. light **lightbulb** (Par. 2)
7. ball **eyeball** (Par. 5)
8. in **indoors** (Par. 3)

9. Check the sentence in which *glasses* has the same meaning as it does in paragraph 2.
   ✓ Do you like my new glasses?
   ___ I need four coffee mugs and four juice glasses.

10. Check the sentence in which *pupil* has the same meaning as it does in paragraph 3.
    ✓ The pupil determines how much light is allowed into the eye.
    ___ The best pupil in the class received a perfect grade on her spelling test.

11. Check the sentence in which *cells* has the same meaning as it does in paragraph 6.
    ___ Bees' honeycomb contains hundreds of cells.
    ✓ The cells reproduced at a rapid rate.

Reading Skills

1. What do pupils control?
   the amount of light entering the eye
2. What is the colored part of the eye called?
   the iris
3. If you walked from a dark room into a brightly-lit room, how would the size of your pupils change?
   They would become smaller.
4. What colors do the cone-shaped cells in your eyes detect?
   yellow, green, and blue
5. What kind of cells are missing from the eyes of a person who is colorblind?
   one or more types of cone-shaped cells
6. Name two ways in which cone-shaped cells and rod-shaped cells are different from one another.
   Possible answers: Rods are more sensitive to light than cones. Cones allow you to see color images, and rods produce only black and white images.
7. What is the purpose of the cornea?
   to protect the more fragile parts of the eyeball
8. What purpose would a reader have for reading this selection?
   ___ to form an opinion
   ✓ to learn
   ___ for entertainment

139

Page 141

Vocabulary Skills

Write the words from the passage that have the meanings below.

1. seriously; extremely
   severely (Par. 3)
2. created; invented
   devised (Par. 3)
3. changed; altered
   modified (Par. 6)
4. long and boring; time-consuming
   tedious (Par. 6)
5. automatic; working without human assistance
   automated (Par. 8)

Read each pair of words listed below. If the words are synonyms, write **S** on the line. If the words are antonyms, write **A** on the line.

6. **S** surround   encompass
7. **A** presence   absence
8. **A** specific   general
9. **S** available   accessible

10. The Latin root **commun** means *common*. Find a word in paragraph 4 with the root **commun**.
    communication
11. The Latin root **vis** can mean *see*. Find a word in paragraph 4 with the root **vis**.
    vision
12. The Latin root **ver** can mean *truth*. Find a word in paragraph 6 with the root **ver**.
    universal

Reading Skills

1. What was the problem with materials intended for blind people before the creation of the Braille system?
   They were carved in wood, cut in cardboard, or made from lead, so there was a limited amount of materials available. Also, blind students had no way of writing.
2. How was Braille's system different from Barbier's?
   It used a system of 6 dots instead of 12.
3. How old was Braille when he invented his dot-reading system?
   15
4. How are Braille books produced today?
   Computer programs translate written words into Braille code, which is sent to machines that electronically make the printing plates.
5. Check the line beside the word or words that best describe what type of selection this is.
   ✓ historical fiction
   ___ historical nonfiction
   ___ fiction
6. Check the words that best describe Louis Braille.
   ___ cheerful   ___ outgoing
   ✓ inventive   ✓ determined
   ✓ original
7. Check the word below that best describes the theme of "Eyes on the Ends of Your Fingers."
   ___ disability   ✓ creative thinking
   ___ friendship   ___ honor

141

Page 143

Vocabulary Skills

Write the words from the story that have the meanings below.

1. better than others
   superior (Par. 1)
2. the state of having lost or been beaten
   defeat (Par. 1)
3. declared
   proclaimed (Par. 2)
4. treated as unimportant
   dismissed (Par. 4)
5. a foolish idea
   folly (Par. 4)
6. to question the truth of; to doubt
   dispute (Par. 5)
7. spoken with a lack of respect; disdain
   scoffed (Par. 10)

8. Check the sentence in which *state* has the same meaning as it does in paragraph 3.
   ___ Naomi was eager to return to her home state after traveling for so long.
   ✓ Please state your name after the beep.

9. Check the sentence in which *content* has the same meaning as it does in paragraph 4.
   ___ I think that the content of this book will interest you.
   ✓ Tony was content with the gifts he had received.

Rewrite the phrases below in the possessive form.

10. the words of Rain **Rain's words**
11. the quarrel of the colors **the colors' quarrel**
12. the rumbling of the thunder **the thunder's rumbling**

Reading Skills

1. Why were the colors quarreling?
   Each thought that he or she was superior to all other colors.
2. What reason did Yellow give for being the most important color?
   Yellow is the color of the sun.
3. Do you think that one of the colors makes a better argument than the others? Explain.
   Answers will vary.
4. What did Rain ask the colors to do each time it rained?
   join together and stretch across the sky in a giant bow of color
5. What do you think the colors in this legend might symbolize, or stand for? Do you think there is a deeper meaning to the story? Explain.
   Answers will vary. Possible answer: They might symbolize the different people of the world. The story could mean that everyone is unique and valuable in his or her own way.
6. Does this story take place in reality, or is it a fantasy? How can you tell?
   fantasy; Answers will vary. Possible answers: Colors can't talk. Rain can't talk. There is a scientific explanation for how rainbows are created.
7. In this legend, the colors are personified. How did the author accomplish this?
   Possible answers: The colors can talk; They have personalities, feelings, and ideas.

143

Page 145

Vocabulary Skills

1. The Latin root **spec** means *see*. Find a word in paragraph 3 with the root **spec**.
   spectrum
2. The Latin root **fract** means *break*. Find a word in paragraph 3 with the root **fract**.
   refracted
3. The Greek root **photo** means *light*. Find a word in paragraph 5 with the root **photo**.
   photograph

Find the compound words from the selection that contain the words below.

4. bow **rainbows** (Par. 1)
5. lore **folklore** (Par. 2)
6. some **somewhere** (Par. 4)
7. light **sunlight** (Par. 5)
8. wave **wavelengths** (Par. 3)

Reading Skills

1. Why do each of the colors in a rainbow bend slightly differently?
   They have different wavelengths.
2. What is one way to remember the order of colors in a rainbow?
   by using the acronym ROY G. BIV
3. Why does a moonbow appear to be whitish in color?
   because the human eye cannot discern bright colors in dim light
4. What materials do you need to create your own rainbow?
   a glass or jar of water, a small mirror, and a flashlight
5. What is the only way to see exactly the same rainbow someone else sees?
   look at a photograph
6. How are a rainbow and a moonbow different? How are they similar?
   Both are the result of light entering drops of water, but the light in a rainbow comes from the sun, while the light in a moonbow comes from the moon.

Write **T** before the sentences that are true. Write **F** before the sentences that are false.

7. **F** Leprechauns hide pots of gold at the end of the rainbow in Chinese mythology.
8. **T** Sunlight is made of all the colors in the spectrum.
9. **F** Most rainbows are seen on snowy days when the temperature dips below freezing.
10. **F** Everyone looking at a rainbow will see exactly the same image of a rainbow.
11. **T** Dorothy is a character in *The Wizard of Oz*.

Study Skills

Use a dictionary to help you divide these words into syllables.

1. m y/th o l/ó/g y
2. d i f/f e r/e n t
3. b e a u/t i/f u l
4. a/c r o/n y m
5. s e v/e/r a l

145

Spectrum Reading Grade 6

169

Answer Key

Page 147

Vocabulary Skills

Write the words from the story that have the meanings below.

1. warned
   cautioned

2. the order in time in which something occurred
   chronological

3. notices appearing in newspapers that announce a person's death
   obituaries
   Par. 6

4. relatives
   relations
   Par. 10

Write the idiom from paragraph 3 on the line next to its meaning.

5. to be busy   it looks like you have
   your hands full

Find the metaphor in paragraph 1, and write it on the line.

6. This table is a disaster area.

Circle the homophone that correctly completes each sentence below.

7. For hours after Rosa heard the good news, she was in a _____. (days (daze))

8. Lex _____ when he read the headline on the newspaper's front page. ((sighed)/side)

Reading Skills

1. Where did Will get the information for his research?
   from the Internet and from phone
   interviews with older relatives

2. Why does Will feel that researching his family's history is important?
   He doesn't want his family's
   history to be lost.

3. How long has the boys' extended family lived on the South Carolina Sea Islands?
   for the past 200 years

4. Do you think that Will and Calvin will continue to be interested in their family's history even after Will's project is complete? Explain.
   Answers will vary.

Study Skills

Use the family tree below to answer the questions that follow.

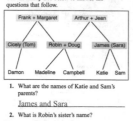

Frank + Margaret   Arthur + Jean

Cicely (Tom)   Robin + Doug   James (Sara)

Damon   Madeline   Campbell   Katie   Sam

1. What are the names of Katie and Sam's parents?
   James and Sara

2. What is Robin's sister's name?
   Cicely

3. What is Damon's grandfather's name?
   Frank

147

Page 149

Vocabulary Skills

Write the words from the passage that have the meanings below.

1. the power or ability to choose or make decisions for oneself
   will
   Par. 2

2. able to be reached
   accessible
   Par. 2

3. grew or developed from one thing into another
   evolved
   Par. 4

4. people who work to preserve something for the future
   preservationists
   Par. 5

5. wound into a spiral or ring
   coiled

Use a dictionary to help you place the words below into the correct categories.

patio	origami
karate	czar
tornado	bronco
mammoth	

6. Japanese   7. Russian   8. Spanish
   karate   mammoth   patio
   origami   czar   tornado
                              bronco

Reading Skills

1. Where are the Sea Islands located?
   off the southeastern coast of the
   United States

2. Why did the Gullah language evolve?
   so that people who didn't speak
   the same language could
   communicate with one another

3. Name two Gullah traditions that are still practiced today.
   basket weaving and fish net
   knitting

4. What is one reason the African customs of the Gullah people remained unchanged for so long?
   The islands were isolated from
   the mainland for many years.

5. Do you think it is important for the Gullah heritage and way of life to be preserved? Explain.
   Answers will vary.

6. What do you think the author's purpose was for writing this selection?
   Answers will vary.

Circle the word that best completes each sentence below.

7. Historically, the Gullah have been _____ craftspeople.
   cultural   (talented)   preserving

8. In today's world, the Gullah culture is a(n) _____ snapshot of the past.
   unreasonable   temporary   (unique)

149

Page 151

Vocabulary Skills

Write the words from the passage that have the meanings below.

1. surrounded by; deeply involved with
   immersed
   Par. 2

2. something handed down through the generations
   heritage
   Par. 2

3. the various parts of the face
   features
   Par. 5

4. explained or understood in a certain way
   interpreted
   Par. 5

5. shared with everyone; common
   universal
   Par. 5

6. language that is used by a certain group or region of a country
   dialect
   Par. 6

In each row, circle the two words that belong together.

7. opportunity   respect   (tradition)   (custom)

8. (region)   language   memories   (area)

9. landscape   (preserve)   indicate   (maintain)

10. The Latin root **mater** means *mother*. Find a word in paragraph 2 with the root **mater**.
    maternal

11. The Latin root **commun** means *common*. Find a word in paragraph 2 with the root **commun**.
    community

12. The Greek root **gen** means *birth* or *race*. Find a word in paragraph 6 with the root **gen**.
    generations

Reading Skills

1. Check the words that best describe Jonathan Green.
   ____ athletic   ✓ creative
   ✓ artistic   ✓ caring
   ____ talkative

2. Check the word that best describe what type of selection this is.
   ____ autobiography
   ____ fiction
   ✓ biography

3. Do you think Jonathan Green will continue making paintings of his Gullah heritage?
   Answers will vary.

4. Name two things that frequently appear in Green's paintings.
   human figures and water

5. Which of the following would be the most likely subject of one of Green's paintings?
   ____ a realistic portrait of a mother and child
   ____ the skyline of a city at night
   ✓ fishermen hauling in their nets

6. How many children were there in Green's family?
   7

7. Why do you think that Green had to go away in order to be able to appreciate his culture and heritage?
   Answers will vary.

151

Notes

Notes

Notes